The
the I
field
Ja
acco
subje
of m

Ia
Sa
A

Ta
book
time
cont

Jago
Chic

CK

Contemporary Fiction

Jago Morrison

Routledge
Taylor & Francis Group

LONDON AND NEW YORK

First published 2003
by Routledge
11 New Fetter Lane, London EC4P 4EE

Simultaneously published in the USA and Canada
by Routledge
29 West 35th Street, New York, NY 10001

Routledge is an imprint of the Taylor & Francis Group

Typeset in Goudy by
Keystroke, Jacaranda Lodge, Wolverhampton
Printed and bound in Great Britain by
TJ International Ltd, Padstow, Cornwall

British Library Cataloguing in Publication Data
A catalogue record for this book is available from the British Library

Library of Congress Cataloging in Publication Data
A catalog record for this book has been requested

ISBN 0–415–19455–5 (hbk)
ISBN 0–415–19456–3 (pbk)

To Alison

Contents

Acknowledgements

Thanks are due to Nick Cox, Mary Eagleton, Max Farrar, John Lynch, Alison Morrison and Susan Watkins for commenting on drafts of the manuscript. Their suggestions and ideas were invaluable. I am grateful also to the following people for their advice, encouragement and support: Ross Abbinnett, Kamal Al-Solaylee, Pieter Bekker, Chris Bousfield, Claire Chambers, Mac Daly, Gabriele Griffin, Simon Gunn, Tom Herron, Mary McNally, Surya Shaffi, Simon Shepherd and Sue Vice. Thanks to my family, Howard, Patsy and Louise Morrison, for their love and lively interventions, and to my postgraduate students at Leeds Metropolitan University for many thought-provoking discussions of contemporary fiction. Finally, I am indebted to Talia Rodgers and Liz Thompson at Routledge for their patience and professionalism from start to finish.

Part I
Frameworks

Introduction
After the end of the novel

For several decades after the end of the Second World War, the novel appeared to be dead. As a vehicle for literary experimentation, on the one hand, it had been taken to the limits by modernists like Joyce, Woolf and Beckett. And, on the other hand, beset by the mass media of film, television and computers, book fiction could not hope to survive as a form of entertainment. For many commentators in the 1960s, fiction's fate seemed sealed. In 1962 the American theorist Marshall McLuhan caught the mood of many with his study *The Gutenberg Galaxy*, arguing that new electronic media were the future for human communication. The printed book itself, with its conformity, linearity and traditions of elitism, was about to be made obsolete by the technologies of a new, postliterate age.

Perhaps understandably, throughout this period the defensiveness of fiction writers is palpable. It is with a brittle irony that the postmodernist John Barth describes himself in 1967 as a 'print-oriented bastard', referring to the attacks of McLuhanites on the novel and novelists in general. In his famous essay 'The Literature of Exhaustion' Barth admits to a suspicion that the time of the novel may be up. In the same way that, in earlier eras, great forms such as classical tragedy, grand opera or the sonnet sequence had eventually succumbed to exhaustion, perhaps the novel had reached the end of its useful life.

In a book that reads like an obituary, a similar assessment is offered by Leslie Fiedler in *Waiting for the End: The American Literary Scene* (1965). According to Fiedler, the deaths of Hemingway and Faulkner at the beginning of the 1960s marked the end of the great age of US fiction. Little remained for contemporary writers but to fiddle amongst the ruins:

> There are various ways to declare the death of the novel: to mock it while seeming to emulate it, like Nabokov, or John Barth; to reify it into a collection of objects like Robbe-Grillet; or to *explode* it, like

William Burroughs; to leave only twisted fragments of experience and the miasma of death. The latter seems, alas, the American Way.

(p. 170)

Contemporary fiction, it seemed, had been overcome with 'the nausea of the end' (p. 171). Its readership was in terminal decline. Writers had become 'shrill and unconvincing . . . obvious and dull' (p. 177). 'Perhaps narrative will not continue much longer to be entrusted to print and bound between hard covers,' Fiedler speculates. 'There is always the screen, if the page proves no longer viable' (p. 177).

In Britain in the early 1970s, we see a similar scene of decline. From the most influential critics, such as Bernard Bergonzi (1970), David Lodge (1971) and Malcolm Bradbury (1973), there is little sense of vibrancy or fresh development. Instead, the concern of academics is to protect what is left of the 'English novel' from the threat of corruption and dissolution. As late as 1980, commentators like Chris Bigsby reflect a prevalent view of the novel in Britain as 'a cosily provincial, deeply conservative, anti-experimental enterprise, resistant to innovation' (p. 137). Frederick Bowers' essay of the same period, symptomatically entitled 'An Irrelevant Parochialism' (1980), corroborates this impression. All that is striking about the contemporary British novel is 'its conformity, its traditional sameness, and its realistically rendered provincialism. Shaped only by its contents, the British novel is the product of group mentality: local, quaint, and self-consciously xenophobic' (p. 150).

Looking back with the benefit of hindsight, therefore, it seems extraordinary just how misguided this 'death of the novel' thesis turned out to be. In fact, contemporary fiction was to undergo a renaissance over the next twenty years, re-establishing itself as the pre-eminent literary form by the turn of the twenty-first century. In terms of popularity, film and television did not deprive new fiction of its audience. Indeed, as Richard Todd (1996) shows from extensive publishing data, there is little evidence that any of the newer information and communication technologies have eroded fiction's reputation or readership. The repeated claims of a crisis in publishing are similarly difficult to sustain. As Todd shows, during the 1990s between 4,500 and 7,000 Booker-eligible or 'literary' fiction titles were being published annually in Britain and Commonwealth countries. If we add to their number the extensive range of fiction published in the United States, we can estimate that over 10,000 works are now published as 'literary' fiction in English every year. As far as the novel is concerned, therefore, on aesthetic and intellectual levels, as well as on the level of pure production and consumption, McLuhan's prediction of the death of the book has been comprehensively debunked.

One of the main reasons for fiction's resurgence as a literary form has been the range of new developments in the forms and concerns of the novel, many of which are explored in this book. It is these which provide the definitive refutation of the 'death of the novel' thesis. The period I discuss is one in which black and Asian American women writers like Toni Morrison, Alice Walker and Maxine Hong Kingston have transformed the literary main-stream in the United States. Formerly colonised nations such as Nigeria have comprehensively asserted themselves on the global literary scene. On the level of technique, South American postmodernists like Jorge Luis Borges have provided a generation of experimental writers with a whole new toolbox to work with. Post-feminist writers such as Angela Carter and Jeanette Winterson have pushed the narrative representation of gender to conclusions inconceivable in the work of Iris Murdoch or even Doris Lessing. Writers like Salman Rushdie, working from self-consciously postcolonial and migrant positions, have challenged the novel's traditional relation to nationhood and identity.

In view of these developments, it is particularly ironic that Bigsby's and Bowers' essays on the redundancy and exhaustion of contemporary fiction, quoted above, were published in the very same issue of the literary periodical *Granta* that carried the first draft of Rushdie's groundbreaking *Midnight's Children*. Indeed, this coincidence gives a useful clue as to how to read the 'death of the novel' thesis of the 1960s and 1970s. In retrospect, the perception of fiction as exhausted and provincial in that period often reflects little more than the critical assumptions and reading habits which underpinned dominant critical opinion. In well-regarded studies such as Bernard Bergonzi's *The Situation of the Novel* (1970), for example, there is no recognition of the importance of new African American fictions emerging in the United States, fictions which were to change and enervate the American literary scene profoundly. Instead, disparaging reference is made to a descent into 'genre fiction' such as 'the Negro novel'. In the established view which Bergonzi reflects, such developments seemed to offer little to our assumed task – understanding the 'Englishness' of English fiction. Similarly, it is symptomatic that contemporary works by such figures as Chinua Achebe, one of the most innovatory and important voices in West African fiction in English, warrant no mention here at all.

Speaking of his experience at Cambridge in the 1970s, the theorist and critic Henry Louis Gates Jr confirms the same impression. For him, a narrowness of reading habits at the heart of the literary establishment at that time was the major barrier to the recognition of new developments in the novel. Even at postgraduate level, as Gates says in his study *Figures in Black* (1987), an interest in new literatures was unwelcome in all of the dominant schools of literary criticism.

Even in the literature departments of universities in formerly colonised countries, a culture of disdain for new Asian, African and South American writing in particular survived well into the 1970s and beyond. As the Kenyan writer Ngugi wa Thiong'o (1993) comments, 'the English department at Makerere, where I went for my undergraduate studies, was probably typical of all English departments in Europe or Africa at that time. It studied English writing of the British Isles' (p. 7).

In the United States, there is a similar picture of conservatism and ethnocentrism, even in universities where black scholars had gained a significant number of faculty positions. As Houston A. Baker Jr and Patricia Redmond (1989) argue, in this period it was necessary for black scholars and critics to collaborate strenuously simply to combat 'the academy's indifference or hostility to their work' (p. 3). Indeed, as late as the early 1990s, when the study of 'new literatures' had begun to successfully entrench itself in the curricula of British universities, and when leading publishers such as Heinemann had begun to market postcolonial writing with vigour, Toni Morrison (1992) still refers to the habitual 'silence and evasion' characterising the treatment of black writing by the American literary establishment:

> Like thousands of avid nonacademic readers, some powerful literary critics in the United States have never read, and are proud to say so, *any* African American text . . . It is interesting, not surprising, that the arbiters of critical power in American literature seem to take pleasure in, indeed relish, their ignorance of African American texts.
>
> (Morrison, 1992, p. 13)

At the same moment that leading white critics were bemoaning the exhaustion and parochialism of the novel, then, it is clear that much of the most interrogative contemporary writing in English was being ignored or bypassed unrecognised.

If, on both sides of the Atlantic, writers and scholars encountered a generalised resistance to much of the most interrogative literature of the period, moreover, this was not merely coincidental. Rather, it undoubtedly reflected a reluctance to revise traditional notions of what might constitute 'English Literature', and what the goals of studying it might be. In their study *The Empire Writes Back* (1989), Bill Ashcroft, Gareth Griffiths and Helen Tiffin bear witness to this tendency. As they suggest, the emergence of a whole range of new literatures in English in the post-war period represents a challenge to any notion of literary studies based on a parochial and traditional canon. Against the perception of the novel as an ailing, threatened form, the general posture of the literary establishment for several decades after the Second World War was one of defensiveness. In Britain particularly, laments for the death of the novel reflected, above all, a misapprehension about where new developments in fiction were likely to come from, and what kinds of rebirths for the novel might be possible.

Over the past two and a half decades, that scene has changed profoundly. Post-war literary studies has split in a number of directions, each pursuing distinct developments. Post-colonial studies has brought a new set of conceptual frameworks with which to address the contemporary renaissance in anglophone writing. Questions of ethnicity, gender and sexuality have become central to academic literary debate in Britain and the United States. The theoretical movements of structuralism and poststructuralism in the 1970s and 1980s have fed through into a range of critical perspectives and techniques.

Contemporary fictions are anything but homogeneous. On the contrary, they are interesting precisely for their ability to locate themselves in the interstices – the spaces between national cultures, genders and histories. In contemporary criticism this diversity of strategy is well reflected. Accordingly, in contrast to older studies which attempt to provide a summative account of 'the state of the novel', the assumption of this book is that the range and variety of contemporary writing demands similar variation in critical approach. In the four chapters that comprise Part I, I outline four contextual frameworks through which it is useful to read contemporary fiction, with changing emphases across different texts. In chapter 1, the representation of history is explored, with reference to the multi-dimensional transitions of the post-war period and claims in the late twentieth century of the 'End of History' itself. Chapter 2 moves on to the connected question of time, and the variety of responses in contemporary fiction to the radical rethinking of time in the New Physics, in philosophy and elsewhere. Chapter 3 is concerned with the disciplining of the flesh, exploring the provocative ways in which genders and bodies are re-imagined in recent writing. Chapter 4 turns then to the problem of 'race', examining the roots of race-thinking, its train of atrocities, and the ways in which writers have dealt with the legacy of both.

What is necessarily true of all contemporary fiction, like all literature, is that it needs to be read as a product of the cultural conditions from which it emerges. The past half century has been a period of massive, multi-dimensional cultural change. Major shifts and dislocations have occurred to older notions of racial and sexual identity. The fabric of history, collective memory and social time within which, a century ago, fiction could comfortably locate itself, has been subject to profound interrogation and transformation. As I have suggested, the purpose of the first part of this book is to outline some of the key frameworks within which contemporary fiction can be related to these processes of change. In Part II, individual writers are addressed using a range of (often hybrid) critical strategies. For reasons of usefulness and accessibility, much of my discussion is geared towards those texts in a writer's *œuvre* which have been most widely read and studied. Frequently, though, I do introduce less well-known texts for discussion and comparison. None of these discussions purports to be exhaustive. In many of the areas I touch on, there is already a substantial body of critical and theoretical writing. In others, a huge amount of work remains to be done. In each case, the readers' guide at the end of the book suggests directions for further exploration of the writers and issues raised.

1   History and post-histories

In an important way, the 'death of the novel' thesis of the 1950s, 1960s and 1970s reflects an anxiety in that period about the possibility of adequately addressing contemporary historical concerns in fiction. The scale of violence in the Second World War, the Nazi genocide, the atom bombing of Japan and, after them, the paranoiac politics of the Cold War – with a global nuclear conflagration held in suspense only by the promise of 'mutually assured destruction' – all of this seemed to have rendered fiction too flimsy a medium for history. Indeed, as early in the post-war period as 1946, in his essay 'The Future of Fiction', the British writer V. S. Pritchett was already warning that the capacities of the novel had been overcome by the events of recent times. Writers, by their very disorientation, had 'become the historian(s) of the crisis in civilization'. In subsequent decades, concerns have turned to the resurgence of nationalisms and racisms in multiple forms around the globe, and the apocalyptic stand-offs of the Cold War superpowers have already faded from the surface of collective memory. What has not faded from the minds of writers, however, is the problem of framing contemporary history in fiction.

In texts which deal with the most difficult themes of recent times, especially the Nazi Holocaust, the problem of writing history asserts itself particularly severely. As we will see, Holocaust fiction reflects the strategies of much contemporary fiction in this respect, frequently abandoning realistic representation in favour of sometimes tortuous techniques of deferral and disjunction. Memory, the most crucial resource of the novelist, becomes a difficult and painful process, counterpointed by thematics of amnesia.

In D. M. Thomas' controversial *The White Hotel* (1981), for example, the Nazi massacre at the Babi Yar gorge in Kiev is approached in a circling, gradual way. Genocide is figured not through memories but through pre-monitions, those of a psychiatric patient in Vienna twenty years before the war. As Thomas recognises, with material of this extreme kind, direct narration often becomes inadequate or impossible. As a result, the text diverges immediately from traditional novelistic forms, presenting itself instead as a disjointed collection of documents – an exchange of letters; a patient's journal; a series of obsessive, erotic and violent verses; a written-up psychoanalytic case study.

As *The White Hotel* moves towards the moment when the brute matter of genocide will have to be addressed, Thomas finds that he must defer to eye-witness testimony. In describing the atrocity itself, he uses the account of the survivor Dina Pronicheva in Anatoly Kuznetsov's *Babi Yar* (1970). In so doing, Thomas solves the problem of historical responsibility only to re-invoke it in different ways. His use of Kuznetsov's text in particular raises a whole set of fresh questions about narrative 'authenticity', and about who has the right to speak.

In a close reading, as Sue Vice (2000) has shown, we can see that in fact Thomas modifies Pronicheva's experiences in order to heighten the theme of violence/sexuality in his novel, as if her narrative of the massacre were somehow not abject enough. Readers and critics have disagreed violently in their impressions of this narrative strategy. In the final chapter of *The White Hotel*, these same problems emerge in a different way, as the author struggles to find some kind of fitting conclusion. After the horror of Babi Yar, his depiction of happy reunions in a 'promised land' which tries to be both Palestine and the Afterlife is, I think, seriously problematic. But having said that, one is left wondering what kind of conclusion could possibly give 'narrative closure' to historical contents of this kind.

Discussing the film-maker Claude Lanzmann and the cartoonist Art Spiegelman in her book *Voicing the Void: Muteness and Memory in Holocaust Fiction* (1997), Sara Horowitz shows how experiments in the form of contemporary narrative often represent an attempt to de-sanitise the historical, to disallow it from becoming background noise. Discussing Lanzmann's and Spiegelman's Holocaust texts, she says:

> the point is not so much to learn the facts directly from the mouths of survivors as it is to break down the cognitive and emotional barriers that keep the past safely in the past . . . so that the reader or viewer becomes not so much a listener to a story, a memory, but a witness to ongoing acts of remembering, of reliving.
>
> (p. 7)

As Horowitz shows, the problem of dealing adequately and responsibly with the legacy of the Nazi Holocaust has been one of the most difficult historical problems faced by writers in the post-war period. In attempting to address the seemingly unrepresentable we see the capacities of narrative stretched to the limit. Often in contemporary fiction, the Holocaust is invoked as the absent contents which can only be dealt with by allusion. Ian McEwan's *Black Dogs* (1992) is one such example. In this text, a succession of narrative strands weave between disjointed biographies, histories and memories in an attempt to cope with the legacies of the post-war period and to render them graspable and meaningful. Though there is a short scene in a concentration camp, the Holocaust is never directly narrativised. Instead it is alluded to through a recurring nightmare of rapacious dogs, which becomes the linking motif of the novel.

Amongst other texts which do attempt direct representation of genocide, such as Binjamin Wilkomirski's *Fragments* (1995), comparable strategies are still required. Wilkomirski's novel, which was originally published under the guise of an authentic survivor testimony, again deploys techniques of narrative breakdown, with nightmarish vignettes of memory offset by a constant invocation of amnesia. These kinds of self-conscious departures from the linear dynamics of older biographical and historical fiction are characteristic of many contemporary texts which return to the apparently unrepresentable.

Clearly, texts like Thomas's and Wilkomirski's attempt to encapsulate the horror of atrocity, and each makes a play for historical 'authenticity' by invoking the language of survivor testimony. In Thomas' case, this is borrowed and adapted to the novelist's purposes, leading to charges of plagiarism when *The White Hotel* first emerged. In Wilkomirski's case, the narrative form and thematic concerns of previous survivor testimonies are closely studied and simulated. Only after extensive journalistic investigation was the author 'Wilkomirski' identified as a fictional creation of a Swiss writer, Bruno Grosjean (see Maechler 2000). Each of these writers has attracted considerable controversy, because of the irreducible sense in their work of something for which 'inappropriateness' is not strong enough a word, a sense, then, of the 'dishonesty' of such clever novelistic technique when compared with the weight and mass of events. In an age in which conventional realistic narration has come to seem somehow naïve, unworthy of the serious novelist, we are still confronted with a demand for moral responsibility in relation to the past. As we will see in this book as a whole, across the range of contemporary fiction we can see a wide variety of attempts to respond anew to the paradoxical demands of history.

In the earlier realist traditions of the novel, to some at least, historical engagement appeared nothing like so problematic as it has come to seem in contemporary writing. For the historical materialist Georg Lukács in the 1930s, for example, fiction's whole justification was its ability to offer a true representation of its moment, a complete, objective vision of historical realities. Faced with the uncertainties, contradictions and confusions of everyday life, the novel's purpose was to cut through the surface of appearance, showing the relations of power that underlay it. Following on from Marx and Lenin, in his famous essay 'Realism in the Balance' (1938) Lukács stressed the importance of 'all-round knowledge' for understanding history and society. This was a knowledge that great literature was privileged to impart.

According to Lukács and his contemporary Ernst Bloch, by the 1930s modernist writers had already abandoned the responsibilities of their craft, in favour of empty experimentation. Targeting one of the most influential texts of the century, Lukács took James Joyce's *Ulysses* (1922) to task for its abandonment of realist representation. As a result, for Lukács *Ulysses* had been swallowed up by the very cultural breakdown it should be seeking to dissect:

> An empty shell and the most fantastic sellout; a random collection of notes on crumpled scraps of paper, gobbledygook, a tangle of slippery eels, fragments of nonsense, and at the same time the attempt to found a scholastic system on chaos; . . . confidence tricks in all shapes and sizes, the jokes of a man who has lost his roots; blind alleys but paths everywhere – no aims but destinations everywhere.
>
> (p. 34)

Contrasting Joyce's work with that of Thomas Mann, Lukács argues that it is the proper task of the novel to place contemporary cultural disintegration and disorientation in context, showing how it emerges as an *effect* of the historical moment. For Lukács, the power and subtlety of Mann's fiction is that, in examining aesthetic, psychological and social processes, it allows the reader an overall historical understanding:

> he knows how thoughts and feelings grow out of the life of society and how experiences and emotions are parts of the total complex of reality. As a realist he assigns these parts to their rightful place within the total life context. He shows what area of society they arise from and where they are going to.
>
> (Lukács, 1938, p. 36)

In the wake of the Holocaust only a few years later, it is difficult to imagine what kind of literary text could, any more, provide the kind of orderly overview and representative historical vision Lukács requires. In the wake of such events – and under the shadow too of the always imminent, nuclear holocaust that hung over the heads of everyone for the majority of the post-war period – it seemed to many writers that a new set of aesthetics was required, whether based on disjunction, allusion, dis-memory or something else, to deal with subject matter that is essentially overwhelming.

Transformations and migrations

As if the historic legacies of the Second World War did not provide enough of a challenge for writers, the period that followed has been one of repeated sea changes across the anglophone world. Amongst the most important of these has been the wholesale repulsion of European colonialism, beginning with India/Pakistan in the immediate post-war years, and spreading across the entire globe over the next three decades. Particularly in those parts of Africa, Asia and the Caribbean formerly colonised by Britain, the English language is intimately imbricated in these transitions. Hence the heterogeneous processes of decolonisation, reformation and migration are profoundly reflected in the development of anglophone writing in the contemporary period.

In the work of writers working from a range of cultural locations we can see attempts to frame this vast process of change in graspable form. As John Springhall (2001) points out, at the beginning of the Second World War one in every three people in the world was forced to live under colonial or imperial rule. By the turn of the millennium that figure was less than one in a thousand. In the United States, the struggle for black civil rights interlocks in complex ways with the narratives of postcolonial liberation. Vast processes of population migration across various axes around the globe have complicated parochial conceptions of ethnic and national identity, and accelerating economic globalisation has sprouted multiple new lines of communication and exchange. As Steven Connor argues in his study *The English Novel in History 1950–1995* (1996), therefore, the transitions of the post-war period have affected the nature and possibility of historical consciousness in profound ways:

> The conditions of extreme cultural interfusion, with the meetings and conflicts of cultural traditions brought about by large-scale migrations as a result of war and postcolonial resettlements, have combined with the growth of an ever-more inter-dependent global economy to create a splintering of history in the post-war world, a loss of the vision of history as one and continuous. But these very same conditions of mutual impingement have acted to make it impossible to maintain any form of local or individual history in isolation from all the other histories, and in doing so have enlarged the scope of the conversation and the collective memory that is constructed in the narration of histories.
>
> (p. 135)

Connor points to two distinct movements which need to be identified in historical consciousness, as it is reflected in post-war anglophone writing.

Firstly, we can see a growing scepticism towards imperious, imperialist 'grand narratives', and the proliferation of local and regional historical knowledges in their place. Secondly, in a kind of counter-movement, the transformations and migrations of post-war culture have led to a whole range of cultural exchanges and hybridisations, in a way which renders the idea of self-contained, nationally and ethnically defined historical consciousness somehow outdated and inadequate.

Amongst writers working from Britain or the United States, such as Salman Rushdie, Buchi Emecheta or Alice Walker, we can see the development of a variety of migrant and oppositional positions. Certainly, when set against their work, it is difficult to see how a fictional tradition based in provincial notions of, for example, essential 'Englishness' could have responded adequately to the kinds of global transitions I have outlined. Thus shifts in the forms and means of the contemporary novel have been an essential part of its interventions in the shifting narratives of contemporary world history.

To assume that, any more, it is credible for serious novelists to survey the historical landscape with the imperious authority attributed to nineteenth-century realists is not sustainable. Indeed, one of the characteristics of much contemporary writing is the way in which writers self-consciously acknowledge their *lack* of mastery of the historical, and of their own practices of narration. Salman Rushdie's novels *Midnight's Children* (1981) and *Shame* (1983), which are discussed in chapter 9, are particularly notable in this regard. For all the wrong reasons, though, it is Rushdie's 1988 novel *The Satanic Verses* which has become most obviously illustrative of the demise of 'authority' in contemporary fiction.

The Satanic Verses addresses the experience of postcolonial migration, dividing its focus between a number of characters, and weaving variously between India, England and the Middle East. Most controversially, it explores the crisis of faith experienced by a rich Indian movie star who falls to earth in the West. Throughout, the novel deploys techniques of historical pastiche, fantasy and hallucination, in what is undoubtedly a distinctive and important contribution to contemporary anglophone writing. The controversy over *The Satanic Verses*, which resulted in the issue of a death sentence or *fatwa* against Rushdie himself by the Iranian Islamic leader Ayatollah Khomeini, however, had little to do with the novel's specific literary engagements.

As Gayatri Spivak (1990) suggests, what it had a great deal more to do with were the parleys of Indian politicians seeking re-election, the columns of Western journalists keen to play the race card, and the postures of the British government and, not least, of Khomeini himself. Amid the hubbub of imperious proclamations, each striving to appropriate the author for divergent political agendas, Rushdie's authorial voice came to sound very small. As Spivak suggests, from an early stage Rushdie ceased to be the effective author of his text. In a very real sense, he became caught up in the process of history-making, in which far more powerful voices than his were shouting for dominance.

According to the postcolonial theorist Homi Bhabha (1994), what we have seen in recent times is the displacement of authoritarian histories rooted in the assumptions of imperialism, and in their place the eruption of 'a range of other dissonant, even dissident histories and voices' (p. 5), some of them local, many of them self-consciously hybrid and cross-cultural. What perhaps needs to be stressed more clearly than Bhabha does, though, is the relations of power that are involved in history-making. Certainly, grand narratives of nation and empire have been rigorously contested in contemporary writing, as have the grand narratives of faith enshrined by Christianity and Islam. As Bhabha argues, in our times 'the very concepts of homogenous national cultures, the consensual or contiguous transmission of historical traditions, or "organic" ethnic communities . . . are in a profound process of redefinition' (p. 5). Ironically, *The Satanic Verses* has much to say on these themes. As we can see from its reception, however, writing against the grain of these historically entrenched orthodoxies is not without dangers and difficulties.

Taking the different case of Toni Morrison, Homi Bhabha sees it as the responsibility of thinkers to contest History's authoritarian tendencies, laying bare the means by which it is produced, exhuming the silenced, problematic and unrepresented pasts which it works to cover over. In Morrison's novel *Beloved* (1988), certainly, we see an address to the past of African American slavery not as a past composed of assimilable facts, but as something much more difficult than that. Chapter 8 of this book explores Morrison's work in more detail. Like some of the other writers I have mentioned, she addresses historical questions from the starting point of amnesia, rather than from the assumption of knowledge. Rather than offering a grand historical sweep, her writing directs us to the stories of the 'disremembered', who by definition do not feature in the historian's reconstructed scheme.

Certainly, what I have described here as a crisis in historical representation is not recognised in all quarters. Amongst academic historians committed to the empirical documentation of 'events', particularly, there has understandably been a reluctance to acknowledge the changed perspectives on historical discourse and historical authority which have gained ground in literary studies. Within the discipline of History, theorists such as Hayden White have encountered what might best be described as a 'disabling disinterest' amongst historians, towards their critical analyses of historiography.

The focus of White's work is to illustrate the relationship between the construction of historical narratives and fictional ones. Looking at historical writing, he foregrounds the elements of selection, invention and emplotment which have always been part and parcel of the writing processes of historians. As long ago as the late 1970s, White and his contemporaries were urging a *rapprochement* between thinkers on the literary and historical sides of that traditional academic divide, and a revision of the methodologies deployed in both disciplines. In the field of contemporary fiction, critics such as Linda Hutcheon (1988b) have responded, drawing from a common palette of assumptions. Both stress the commonalities of fictional and historical narratives as modalities through which our public 'past' is produced as something knowable. Amongst fiction writers, as we can see in the texts of Morrison, Rushdie and others, the development of the 'post-historical novel' – the novel 'about' history, the novel written against history's grain – has also continued apace.

In order to respond to these developments in the contemporary novel, it has been necessary for criticism to develop a vocabulary to describe the changed conceptions of narration and collective memory they involve. In recent decades, a varied lexicon has emerged to illustrate the changed approach to historical representation in fiction. In Hutcheon's work, the term 'historiographic metafiction' is usefully coined to point to the self-reflexive commentary on the means and possibility of historical representation that we see in many contemporary texts. The term 'postmodernism', meanwhile, has also been used by influential theorists such as Fredric Jameson (1991) partly to illuminate the unstable relationships between contemporary culture and its histories. More recently, as we will see, the notion of 'spectrality' has been used to describe the ghostliness of history, the way the past seems continually to haunt contemporary culture, demanding exorcism.

Between the disciplines of history and literary studies, however, one particular term above all helps to illustrate the move away from traditional historical assumptions in recent decades. That is the notion of 'genealogy', used by the philosopher Friedrich Nietzsche in the 1870s and 1880s, and reworked by the French historian Michel Foucault and his followers a hundred years later. Because of the usefulness of 'genealogy' as a framework for understanding the strategies of contemporary fiction, I want to take a little space here to outline its key implications.

Genealogy

For Nietzsche, in *On the Genealogy of Morals* (1887), the meanings of 'history' are always reflections of power. As transformations of power relations take place, 'whatever exists, having somehow come into being, is again and again interpreted to new ends, taken over, transformed, and redirected by some power superior to it' (McGowan, pp. 77–8). Because the 'truths' of history are expressions of power, they are always being overtaken by 'a fresh interpretation, an adaptation through which any previous "meaning" and "purpose" are necessarily obscured or even obliterated'. Thus, for Nietzsche, 'the entire history of a "thing," an organ, a custom can in this way be a continuous sign-chain of ever new interpretations and adaptations'. Thus, as the theorist John McGowan (1991) usefully puts it, genealogy is concerned with tracing 'the history of meaning's production' (p. 78).

In Michel Foucault's work, genealogy is taken up again. For him, it offers a way of working with the idea of the past that is quite different from traditional historical study. Perhaps unsurprisingly, in Britain and America particularly there has been a huge amount of resistance to his methods within the academic discipline of History, and only in the past ten years or so have we begun to see Foucauldian assumptions beginning to percolate into the mainstream of the subject. But across a wide range of other areas, Foucault's methods have been very fruitfully applied and developed. In the writing of such figures as Salman Rushdie and Angela Carter, moreover, it is possible to see how a quasi-Foucauldian approach informs many of the most experimental strategies of contemporary fiction.

For Foucault, genealogy concerns the investigation of what he calls 'power/knowledge'. According to Foucauldian theory, the most important way in which power operates in modern societies is not through the practice of direct authoritarian rule, but through the operation of 'knowledges' and the institutionalised 'discourses' that produce them. Power and knowledge are thus seen as intimately interconnected. A good example of this is provided by the law. The way the law has come to operate is not by having armed police expensively stationed on every street corner but, rather, by securing mass assent to the *discourse* of legality and illegality. Thus, the law institutes itself as a knowledge of right and wrong, correct and incorrect behaviour. Clearly, the threat of penalties like imprisonment remains an important resource for discouraging resistance and 'illegal' behaviour in society. But far more important is the way the subject is conditioned to *regulate him/herself* within the defined and learnt codes of 'legal' conduct. Not punishment, but self-policing and surveillance have become the major tools of disciplinary control.

Gender and sexual identity can be thought of in a similar way. Here, Foucault looks at the way certain loaded oppositions – not just legal/illegal but also normal/deviant, healthy/unhealthy and so on – have been set in place by powerful discourses and institutions like medicine, psychiatry and criminology. Studies like *The History of Sexuality* (1976–84) explore the mechanisms whereby individuals have been encouraged to 'normalise' their desires and behaviours within the framework of 'legal/healthy/normal' inscribed by those discourses. In the collection *Power/Knowledge* (1980) Foucault describes this conception of power and its institutionalisation in quite a clear way:

> What I mean is this: in a society such as ours, but basically in any society, there are manifold relations of power which permeate, characterise and constitute the social body, and these relations of power cannot themselves be established, consolidated nor implemented without the production, accumulation, circulation and functioning of a discourse. There can be no possible exercise of power without a certain economy of discourses . . .
>
> (p. 93)

Similarly, in many contemporary fictions we can see how, in representing the past, conventional ideas of 'historical progress' are replaced by a sense of struggles between languages and knowledges. The author Ngugi wa Thiong'o provides a good example of this in his writings about Kenya and British imperialism. Under colonial rule, as Ngugi says in *Decolonising the Mind* (1981), language as much as bullets was the tool of subjugation. In his book, Ngugi's own experience of the colonial school system illustrates this well. There, the English language was imposed as the language of instruction and exchange, and used to enshrine a privileged discourse of education and intelligence. At the same time, local traditions of Orature (oral literature) were discouraged and marginalised as signs of 'stupidity' and 'under-development'.

In his own fiction, Ngugi plays on this relation of power/knowledge, by privileging the language of Gikuyu, and offering his texts in English only as translation. Here he differs significantly from other influential African writers such as Chinua Achebe, who adopt English on the grounds of its power as the international lingua franca. When the Western reader approaches a text like Ngugi's *Devil on the Cross* (1980, English translation 1982) he or she is consciously located outside the main orbit of the text, no longer in a position of automatic 'possession' of the privileged discourse.

Within the narrative, too, the struggle of disparate historical voices is foregrounded as a major theme. In this text, Ngugi's many narrative strands are likened to the entwined voices of an oratorio, composed as a wedding gift to his wife by the character Gatuiria. Sounds of pre-colonial Africa are gradually overlaid by the more strident tunes of imperialism, shifting and slippery voices of hypocrisy and collaboration, voices of struggle, of slavery and oppression, and finally of rebirth and revolution. Gatuiria wants to describe Kenyan history using the sounds of the European orchestra, overlaid with the rhythms and tones of Kenyan music. But the historical contents of his music keep overflowing the bounds of European musical notation. In the novel, this struggle between musical discourses becomes the index of a struggle of power between the residual culture of imperialism and the radical resistance of his companions. Caught between them, at the end of the text Gatuiria is left paralysed by ambivalence: 'he just stood in the courtyard, hearing his mind music that led him nowhere' (p. 254).

Although Ngugi is far from being Foucauldian in ideological terms, struggles over discourse are, for him, still synonymous with struggles of power. And of course the discourses of 'history' are entwined in those struggles. For the white British coloniser in nineteenth-century Africa, 'history' may well have consisted of the gratifying story of his progress, his enrichment and the expansion of his 'civilising mission'. For the activist and writer in colonialism's aftermath, that same 'history' becomes part of the ideological mess that must be cleared away, to allow for the regrowth of self-determination. Such processes are far from unproblematic: even the constitution of a unified Kenya in the form of a 'nation state' is a direct colonial legacy, because that very notion is a product of European political philosophy in the age of imperialism.

A crucial aspect of genealogy's counter-historical project, then, is the way in which it involves taking issue with the imperialist and *totalising* strategies of traditional historical writing. For Foucault, traditional history systematically works to suppress evidence of discontinuities, disjunctions and struggles between rival regimes of knowledge, because its overriding goal is to portray the present as the product of a clear and rational development. Taking an example from a very different area, the early science of alchemy, it is possible to see how this process of suppression operates. Looking at accounts of modern science, it is not difficult to show how alchemy's role as a major contributor to the development of chemistry and physics becomes erased from our history of the Enlightenment. In the dominant historical view, alchemy is subordinated as a fraudulent or crackpot science. Genealogy, by contrast, is actively concerned to uncover evidence of alternative and submerged knowledges. Thus, in Foucault's work there is a constant interest in foregrounding the marginal, the silenced and the unacceptable.

These 'subjugated knowledges' include erudite, scholarly and occult knowledges – systems of ideas which lost the ideological struggle against their rivals, and hence failed to institutionalise themselves as legitimate and 'scientific'. Here we can see the profound influence of the Argentinian writer Jorge Luis Borges on the development of Foucault's thought. Borges' work is constantly concerned with disrupting established systems of knowledge, by proposing provocative and fantastic alternatives. We will look at some of these in chapter 2. Foucault's work, meanwhile, is interested in uncovering not only lost scholarly traditions but:

> a whole set of knowledges that have been disqualified as inadequate to their task or insufficiently elaborated . . . such as that of the psychiatric patient, of the ill person, of the nurse, of the doctor – parallel and marginal as they are to the knowledge of medicine – that of the delinquent etc.
>
> (Foucault, 1980, p. 82)

Drawing on Nietzsche's work a century before, Foucault's genealogies seek to frustrate attempts by traditional academics and writers to present history as a well-understood, rational development towards civilised enlightenment. Instead he tries to show a much messier series of struggles, a series of ideological and bodily coercions and subjugations, by means of which dominant discourses secure their own emergence as 'rational', 'true' and 'right'. Thus the kinds of things he is interested in uncovering are 'not a decision, a treaty, a reign, or a battle, but the reversal of a relationship of forces, the usurpation of power, the appropriation of a vocabulary turned against those who had once used it, a feeble domination that poisons itself as it grows lax' (Foucault, 1971, p. 88). Just as a biochemist might attempt to trace the evolution and, perhaps, marginalisation and extinction of a particular micro-organism, so genealogy involves tracing the development of discourses and power relations, and their struggle to institutionalise themselves and to colonise bodies and subjects.

In literary studies, Foucauldian methods of analysis have been amongst the most influential of the past three decades. Developed by critics such as Stephen Greenblatt, they formed one of the key co-ordinates of the movement known as New Historicism. Within feminism and gender studies too, whilst Foucault has been critiqued by figures such as the African American scholar Barbara Christian for the way he problematises traditional notions of emancipation, his work has been taken up and developed by others in some extremely fruitful directions. Judith Butler, to whom I will return in chapter 3, provides a notable example of post-Foucauldian feminist work.

In the field of contemporary literature, similarly, it is often possible to see the influence of Foucault's writing. In their study *Literatures of Memory: History, Time and Space in Postwar Writing* (2000), Peter Middleton and Tim Woods distinguish sharply between postmodernist fiction and the older realist mode in terms that clearly echo Foucauldian analysis:

> Postmodern historical fiction is unconvinced that there is a single unitary truth of the past waiting to be recovered, and is more interested in who has or had the power to compose 'truths' about it, whereas historical realist fiction tends to assume that the literary narrative has

a special power to present the past in a language of the present and give direct access to the thoughts, speech and events of that other time without distorting their significance.

(p. 21)

Instead of presuming that the past is accessible as 'truth', they suggest, postmodernist fictions seek to uncover the relations of power inherent in the processes of history-making.

Although Foucault is not an acknowledged influence on Toni Morrison's work, in chapter 8 we will be looking precisely at the way her texts attempt to uncover 'subjugated knowledges' of struggles which are elided by dominant histories of the United States. Perhaps the most important ideological problem she and other African American writers encounter is how to mitigate the generalised suppression of black-authored texts within the canons of historical documentation. Together with that, they face the problem of how to deal with the strongly conventionalised form of those texts that do reach visibility. The majority of published slave writings, for example, either are penned by the representatives of white organisations 'on behalf of' their subjects, or else their discourse is tightly restricted by the conventions and proprieties of contemporary abolitionist literature. Morrison's work poses a direct challenge to those shaping and silencing forces.

As we will see similarly in chapter 6, the representation of Asian American memory attempted by Maxine Hong Kingston is again one punctuated by silence and suppression. Writers like Kingston, Frank Chin and others have dedicated their writing to countering the wilful amnesia of mainstream American culture towards the legacy of Asian immigration to the United States. From a different cultural position to Morrison's, Kingston exploits the contradictory narrative conventions of English and Chinese literature to provide a many-sided image of history in the process of its formation. Like Morrison's, Kingston's work concerns itself with the gaps and boundaries of history, the relationships between power and insti-tutionalised knowledge, and the ramifications of these for marginalised communities. In one way or another, almost all of the fictions explored in this book could be described as 'genealogical' in the sense that they work to raise questions about the construction of stable pasts in narrative, and the role of such constructions in the formation of national, gender and ethnic identities. For Angela Carter, as we will see in chapter 10, the construction of the sexed body becomes the target. For Salman Rushdie, it is the manufacture of nations.

The general movement in contemporary fiction towards what we could call a 'genealogical' consciousness cannot, of course, be ascribed to the work of one figure. Rather, it reflects a vaster shift of confidence away from what the French theorist Jean-François Lyotard (1979) describes as 'grand narratives' of history. This is not simply a matter of intellectual fashion. The liberal grand narrative of progress, civilisation and consensus has, he suggests, simply been overtaken by the sheer ideological heterogeneity of the postmodern period, with its plurality of voices, perspectives and knowledges. Likewise, we could argue, the ideological assurance of an older European imperialism has been comprehensively problematised by the diverse challenges of postcoloniality. And in a different but parallel way, Marxism, imperialism's great revolutionary counter-narrative, has struggled to defend the coherence of its vision against the changing demands of the contemporary period.

The 'End of History'

Earlier in this chapter, I mentioned the demand for clear historical understanding associated with the Marxist tradition, picking out the example of Georg Lukács. For several generations of socially committed theorists and critics, Lukács among them, Marxism has been an immensely important resource, because of the power and breadth of historical vision it enabled. Towards the end of the twentieth century, however, the adaptations of and retrenchments from Marxist orthodoxy – which had always been a feature of the leftist intellectual tradition – seemed to be giving way to a general diversification of methods and assumptions. Foucault's work, which I have briefly outlined, signalled the emergence of one strand of dissident leftist thought. In literary studies, cultural materialism, which proposes a more complex relationship between culture and historical change than earlier thinkers like Lukács would ever have allowed, represented another post-Marxist development.

For many people, it was probably the retreat of the Soviet bloc from its European satellite states in the late 1980s, and the dis-establishment of the USSR itself in 1991, which most dramatically seemed to encapsulate the retrenchment from Marxist orthodoxies in this period. On closer examination, it is easy to see that for several decades the relationship between the Soviet establishment and the various Marxisms in the West had been a pretty problematic and distant one. In the Trotskyist tradition particularly, intellectuals had taken a critical line towards Moscow throughout the whole of the Soviet era. In that sense, the events of 1989 to 1991, to which one could add the breaching of the Berlin Wall and (in a Chinese context) the Tiananmen Square massacre in Beijing, did not in themselves precipitate any major 'crisis of orthodoxy' amongst socially committed thinkers in the West, who were already deeply critical of the

Soviet and Chinese communist regimes. Nevertheless it is still fair to say that the climactic developments of this period, in which the balance of world power seemed to be changing almost by the day, seemed once again to demand a reassessment of historical and political assumptions.

In their introduction to Jacques Derrida's study *Specters of Marx* (1994), Bernd Magnus and Stephen Cullenberg put their finger on the mood in this period, when they argue that

> it seemed to many that the collapse of communism in Eastern Europe and the Soviet Union, as well as democratic insurgencies in China, had created a new world order. Politicians from George Bush to Václav Havel had proclaimed that the ideological and political alliances which structured the global community prior to 1989 must now be rethought and restructured . . . The meaning and consequences of these changes are of vital importance to us all; no discipline or sector of culture has a monopoly on potential analyses, much less a monopoly on answers.
>
> (p. viii)

Amongst the more complacent of Western commentators, the apparent victory of free market capitalism against state socialism in the former Soviet Union led to a rash of fresh pronouncements about the 'End of History' in the early 1990s. According to the influential political theorist Francis Fukuyama, writing in 1989, the triumph of capitalism and liberal democracy at the end of the Cold War meant that history was simply over, because we had reached a point beyond which nothing more of significance was going to happen. In Europe too, amongst philosophers like Gianni Vattimo, the same phrase was adopted as one of the central slogans of postmodernism. For him, the whole notion of postmodernity is premised in terms of history's redundancy. 'What is finished is not simply a certain view (or set of views) of history but history itself' (Vattimo, 1991, p. 134).

On the evidence of continuing world conflict, it is now plain that pronouncements of the End of History were as over-hasty in their turn as the 'death of the novel' thesis had turned out to be a decade before. Let it be said, too, that Fukuyama's presumption that historical questions had permanently disappeared from the agenda of serious thinkers and writers was simply mistaken. What certainly has happened, though, is that the representation of history has become more complex and paradoxical than it seemed to writers two or three generations ago.

Nowhere is this more evident than in contemporary fiction. On the one hand, there is an obvious reluctance to abandon the responsibilities of the novel as a medium for shaping our pasts and giving them public meaning. But on the other hand, as we have seen, there is a widespread recognition amongst writers that the narrative constructions of history must always be partial and problematic. In the very different work of contemporary writers like Carter or Rushdie, for example, we see a common use of stylisation, pastiche and disjunction, jarring the reader into a kind of self-reflexive, post-historical awareness. In influential novels like Toni Morrison's *Beloved* (1987), meanwhile, historical amnesia frequently emerges as a reminder of the tortuousness of memory. Clearly, this is far from saying that such writing is disengaged from historical questions. A text like *Beloved*, as much as Rushdie's *Midnight's Children* or Carter's *The Passion of New Eve* (1977), seems rather to be overflowing with historical contents, with all their contradictory and uncomfortable demands.

In his collection of essays *Specters of Marx* (1994), the philosopher Jacques Derrida attempts to theorise the relation of contemporary culture to its histories in terms of what he calls 'hauntology'. Showing how, in Marx's own writing, the past is often figured as a kind of haunting, Derrida's text suggests some interesting ways in which we might consider the tortuous relation of contemporary culture to its pasts. By virtue of its passing, what we call the past cannot exist, and yet as Derrida says it continues to assert itself in the present in innumerable ways. Like a haunting, a past returns as a half-presence, something which is simultaneously remembered and known, and at the same time strange and unknowable. Certainly, Toni Morrison's character Beloved could be considered as a revenant in a sense similar to this. She is a past that will not lie down to sleep, a reminder of a history that no one wants retold, and an old wound which must be treated, if there is to be a healing. Using a kind of hauntology, what Morrison's writing does here is to open up a sense of 'histories' whose buried-ness and half-knowability, in Marx's (1852) own memorable phrase, 'weighs like a nightmare on the brains of the living'.

The presumption in Derrida's *Specters*, as in Morrison's novel, is that collective memory needs to be thought of in more complex ways than are offered in traditional, linear historical narrative. Instead, as Derrida says, we need to consider our cultural and historical legacies – our most intimate inheritance – in terms of their multiplicity and ambiguity:

> An inheritance is never gathered together, it is never one with itself. Its presumed unity, if there is one, can consist only in the *injunction* to *reaffirm by choosing*. 'One must' means *one must* filter, sift, criticize, one must sort out several different possibles that inhabit the same injunction. And inhabit it in a contradictory fashion around a secret. If the readability of a legacy were given, natural, transparent, univocal, if it did not call for and at the same time defy interpretation, we would never have anything to inherit from it. One always inherits from a secret

– which says 'read me, will you ever be able to do so?' . . . The injunction itself (it always says 'choose, and decide from among what you inherit') can only be one by dividing itself, tearing itself apart, differing/deferring itself, by speaking at the same time several times – and in different voices.

(p. 16, italics in original)

Certainly, in many of the fictions we will be exploring in this book, the past is uncovered not as a known tale but as an enigma or a secret. In work like Morrison's, one is certainly discomfited by the cacophony of the dead. Responding to the difficulty and complexity of contemporary history, such texts refuse to address our cultural inheritance in tidy and closed forms. Rather, they require us to be responsive to narrative invention, inversion and decomposition, denying us the discipline of linear narration. It is for good reasons that they are disruptive and disturbing – disallowing the past from sliding quietly into history.

2 Time and narrative

Chapter 1 outlined some of the ways in which attention has turned to the representation of history in contemporary culture. In the work of a number of writers, as we have seen, this has led to a connected set of questions about the construction of social time. From a critical point of view, then, time has emerged as one of the central issues that need to be grappled with in contemporary fiction.

Like the questioning of historical representation, the problematisation of conventional assumptions about time has arisen not simply in a vacuum, but in the context of wider cultural transitions. Many of the writers explored in this book draw on an extraordinary range of work, from seventeenth-century philosophy to twentieth-century quantum physics. The purpose of this chapter is to sketch in some of that context, showing the ways in which writers have exploited fiction's particular possibilities to shed light on time, that most inescapable of human concerns.

In the twentieth century, one of the most important influences on literature's exploration of time was the collection of radical sciences grouped under the term 'the New Physics'. For many writers of both modernist and postmodernist fiction, indeed, the shattering of conventional wisdom by Albert Einstein, Niels Bohr, Werner Heisenberg and others has been seen as an immense imaginative challenge. It has become a popular mythology of the twentieth century that in 1905, with the emergence of Einstein's Special Theory of Relativity, the conception of time in Western society 'suddenly changed'. In one sense, the importance of Einstein's work was certainly immense, supplanting Newton's conception of a universal, abstract, mechanistic time with Relativity's quite different model of a flexible four-dimensional space-time. Across many of the disciplines of science, Relativity did change the face of the older Newtonian universe. As far as theoretical physics is concerned, the publication of Einstein's Special Theory was one of the most revolutionary events of the century. But it needs to be recognised, too, that Einstein himself was only one amongst a variety of thinkers in the twentieth century and before who have sought to question the 'truth' of absolute time.

In a number of other areas of thought, alternative conceptions of time to that of Newton had, in fact, been in play for a long period. For Immanuel Kant writing in the 1780s, for example, time was certainly not conceived as something absolute. Rather, time experience could only be considered as 'objective' in the sense that it was a function shared by all human consciousness. As Kant argued in 1781: 'Time is therefore a merely subjective condition of our (human) intuition . . . and in itself, independently of the mind or subject, is nothing' (p. 31). For Henri Bergson in the late nineteenth century, moreover, the exploration of lived time or 'duration' already involved a critique of the reductive, mechanistic treatment of time in Newtonian science. Bergson's *Time and Free Will: Essay on the Immediate Data of Consciousness* (1889) was a huge influence on writers like Marcel Proust, whose seven-volume *A la Recherche du Temps Perdu* (1913–27, translated as *Remembrance of Things Past*) was one of the twentieth century's most monumental studies of internal time consciousness.

For Edmund Husserl (1905), one of Einstein's contemporaries, time is again far from absolute, becoming meaningful only in the formation of the self. Reciprocally, for Husserl the self only has meaning as a creation in time. And similarly, according to the influential German philosopher Martin Heidegger (1927), the entire question of time is inextricable from the question of human 'being' (his notion of *Dasein*). According to Heidegger, it is only owing to our ultimate anticipation of death that any 'authentic' experience of being-in-time becomes possible. As we can see from these few examples, then, in philosophy as well as physics the notion of absolute time has been in question for much of the modern period.

In Jonathan Boyarin's 1994 collection *Remapping Memory: The Politics of Timespace*, an important question flows from this. Why, despite the efforts of such influential thinkers, does the 'common-sense' notion of time which we encounter almost everywhere in Western societies continue to reflect a dehumanised and abstract, Newtonian understanding of time? As Boyarin asks, 'why is it that our physics are now those of Einsteinian relativity and quantum mechanics, whereas our politics and our rhetorics still assume a world as described by Newton and Descartes?' (p. 4). One possible answer to this question is provided by the political theorist Dan Thu Nguyen, in his analysis of the emergence of standardised time in Europe and America.

In 'The Spatialization of Metric Time' (1992) Nguyen undertakes the apparently paradoxical task of narrating a history of modern time. His essay traces the rapid colonisation of the West by a new standard of chronometric time, which occurred with the coming of the railways in the late nineteenth century. Where previously, a whole diversity of localised times had been reckoned on observation of the sun, and the seasonal variation of its orbit, the railway made it necessary to adopt a more rigorous time regime that had not been required for other industries. In Britain, in order for the rail network to run effectively, an abstract, universal system of timings and timetables was established, with a system of telegraph wires along the railway tracks used to distribute time signals from London across the country. In the same period, cable links were established to Europe and to North America, whilst in the United States, the institution of standardised time zones was being formalised. In 1880 the Statutes (Definition of Time) Bill became law in Britain, and over the next decade the 'mean time' issued by Greenwich began its rapid colonisation of the globe. Thus according to Nguyen:

> As gradually all countries began to adopt the time zone system based on the prime meridian of Greenwich, the specifically Western temporal regime which had emerged with the invention of the clock in medieval Europe became the universal standard of time measurement. Indeed, its hegemonic deployment signified the irreversible destruction of all other temporal regimes in the world, the last vestiges of which remain only in the form of historical and anthropological curiosities.
>
> No longer determined by either organic or cosmic cycles of time, 'Greenwich time' is a mathematical fiction which signals the collapse of human experience of space and time into a mathematical formula . . .
>
> (p. 33)

The adoption of a reliable and standardised time can certainly be argued to have brought benefits of convenience and efficiency along with it. But at the same time, sociologists like W. F. Cottrell in the United States were showing, as early as the 1930s, the ways in which its application by industry brought profoundly alienating effects as well. Cottrell's study 'Of Time and the Railworker' (1939) took the railway as its focus, examining the ways in which train drivers had become enslaved by the industry's intricately timetabled regime, working a sixteen-hour day governed by constant clock-watching.

Whilst Frederick Taylor's theories of 'scientific' time management were being more and more widely adopted in the design of mass production lines, figures like Cottrell were trying to show the debilitating effects of such regimes on the social and personal lives of working people. More recently, theorists like Michael Shanks and Christopher Tilley (1987) in archaeology, and Helga Nowotny (1984) in social theory have developed this argument further, showing the ways in which capitalist production has instituted more and more complex systems for the utilisation and management of time.

In the late nineteenth and early twentieth centuries, then, we can already draw out two contradictory developments. On the one hand, in various areas of advanced thinking, we see a series of critiques of universal and absolute time being taken up, of which Einstein's is only the most notorious. And on the other hand, in workplaces around the industrialised world, we see the determined imposition of just such an abstract, absolute, dehumanised model of time on millions of ordinary people. In 'Greenwich Meanings: Clocks and Things in Modernist and Postmodernist Fiction' (2000), Randall Stevenson draws out the struggle over time in this period in exactly these kinds of terms. As he suggests, it is precisely at the moment when science and business interests begin to rigorously enforce a standardised time regime at both the local and global level, that in radical science, in philosophy, in sociology and in literature, many of the most profound re-evaluations of the nature of time are taking hold. This is, of course, no coincidence. As we can see in fictional texts of the period, writers' explorations of desire and the imagination are often schematically opposed to the inhuman rigidity of industrial time. In Stevenson's essay, D. H. Lawrence's *Women in Love* (1920) and Aldous Huxley's *Brave New World* (1932) are offered as two examples of texts in which Fordist industrial organisation and time management form a dark backdrop to the narrative. In this sense, it is possible to see how writers easily find themselves in a position of resistance to the dominant culture of time.

Narrative strategies

In the novels of this period, we see a whole series of attempts to break with the straitjacket of chronometric time, to show the diversity of time experience, the many notions of desire and of memory, different and dissident conceptions of the past, and the implications of speculating on fantastic utopian and dystopian futures. In his 1895 novel *The Time Machine*, H. G. Wells' vision of the end of time, as a tentacled leviathan at the shore of a blood-red sea and 'a terrible dread of lying helpless in that remote and awful twilight' took us much closer to desolation than most of his sci-fi descendants would be willing to boldly go. But amongst socially engaged writers we might also think of William Morris' *News From Nowhere* (1891) and George Orwell's *1984* (1949). Within the modernist canon, novels like Virginia Woolf's *Mrs Dalloway* (1925) and James Joyce's *Ulysses* (1922) raise the complexity of our internal time experience as an increasingly important concern. Later, in postmodernist fictions such as Angela Carter's *The Passion of New Eve* (1977), the rethinking of time is transformed into a lurid exploration of nostalgia and apocalypse.

Amongst all the literary explorers of time in the twentieth century who have influenced contemporary fiction, however, the Argentinian writer

Jorge Luis Borges has been of special significance. In stories such as 'Tlön, Uqbar, Orbis Tertius' (1941), Borges invites the reader to imagine a place in which time, memory, history and even language itself are structured in a radically different way. 'One night in Lucerne or in London, in the early seventeenth century, the splendid history has its beginning. A secret and benevolent society (among whose members were Dalgarno and later George Berkeley) arose to invent a country . . .' (p. 39). With a few finely honed pages, his text begins to slice away at all sorts of unexamined assumptions about the nature of time and the real.

In this text and others, the imaginative audacity of Borges' work has been an enormously influential example to subsequent writers. Looking at the work of leading late twentieth-century intellectuals such as Michel Foucault and Umberto Eco particularly, the influence is quite explicit. Eco's best-known text, *The Name of the Rose* (1981), reads almost like a novel-length reworking of Borges' collection *Ficciones* (1956), featuring a malignant blind monk who is clearly a caricature of the Argentinian writer. Meanwhile, in the opening of Foucault's groundbreaking *The Order of Things* (1966) the radical spark that first ignited his work is acknowledged from the same source:

> This book first arose out of a passage in Borges, out of the laughter that shattered, as I read the passage, all the familiar landmarks of my thought – *our* thought, the thought that bears the stamp of our age and our geography – breaking up all the ordered surfaces and all the planes with which we are accustomed to tame the wild profusion of existing things.
>
> (p. xv)

The ideas of power and knowledge which Foucault deploys in his genealogical project, which I outlined in chapter 1, are clearly prefigured in many of Borges' texts. Thus Borges' influence has been important in two crucial respects. The first of these is the way in which his texts work to put the whole notion of conventional rationality in question. Certainly this is a major theme that Eco develops in *The Name of the Rose*. The second is the way his writings show the possibility of exploring new and alternative models of social time.

Perhaps surprisingly, Borges' own *œuvre* does not consist of a series of hefty philosophic tomes, but instead a collection of short fictions, essays, poems and parables, often no more than a couple of pages apiece. Rather than writing great books, elucidating grand systems of knowledge, he seems to prefer simply to sketch out their outlines. For example, at the centre of the story 'The Garden of Forking Paths' (1941) is a description of a fantastic book written by the narrator's great-grandfather Ts'ui Pên. The extraordinary quality of this book, the narrator explains, is that it is also a labyrinth. Unlike the majority of labyrinths one might have encountered before – which exist as a maze in physical *space* – the peculiar quality of this work is that it is a labyrinth for the mind, a labyrinth in *time*:

> In all fictional works, each time a man is confronted with several alternatives, he chooses one and eliminates the others; in the fiction of Ts'ui Pên, he chooses – simultaneously – all of them. *He creates*, in this way, diverse futures, diverse times which themselves also proliferate and fork . . . In contrast to Newton and Schopenhauer, your ancestor did not believe in a uniform, absolute time. He believed in an infinite series of times, in a growing, dizzying net of divergent, convergent and parallel times. This network of times which approached one another, forked, broke off, or were unaware of each other for centuries, embraces *all* possibilities of time. We do not exist in the majority of these times; in some you exist, and not I; in others I, and not you; in others, both of us. In the present one, which a favourable fate has granted me, you have arrived at my house, in another, while crossing the garden, you found me dead; in still another, I utter these same words, but I am a mistake, a ghost . . . Time forks perpetually towards innumerable futures. In one of them I am your enemy.
>
> (pp. 51–3, italics in original)

In this story, time, meaning and desire are connected in a particular kind of way, through the irreducible proliferation of *possibility*. As in the experience of passing through a labyrinth, the idea of living through time is envisaged as a series of alternate paths and choices that sometimes may be retraced, and sometimes may not. In some of Borges' other stories, the concept of time is approached in quite different ways. In 'The Lottery in Babylon' (1941), for example, the reader is invited to consider the idea of a society governed entirely by *chance*. Meanwhile, the story 'Funes the Memorious' (1944) differs again in that it attempts to describe the worldview of a man whose *memory* is total. Borges' classic short piece 'The Library of Babel' (1941), on the other hand, describes a system of knowledge in which all possible thoughts and arguments – and their refutations – have *always already* been recorded in advance. The universe here is envisaged as a library, a repository of knowledge so vast that, paradoxically, all searching for truth amongst its endless archives has become futile.

In all of these texts, there is a common interest in the possibilities of rethinking the everyday notion of time as something singular and absolute. Crucially, time is conceptualised as a culturally determined framework of understanding, rather than as an independently existing entity. In pursuing this line of thinking, Borges follows clearly in the tradition of the eighteenth-century idealist philosopher George Berkeley. If time is thought of not as a tangibly existing 'thing' but as a system of perception, he reasons, then like any other such system it could be open to refutation. If the notion of time were to be refuted, what further consequences might that have for other basic concepts like change, memory or even death?

Perhaps inevitably, even in his most explicit articulation of this argument, in the essay 'A New Refutation of Time' (1947) Borges is unable to pursue this philosophy of time to its ultimate conclusions. Thus finally, in his writings, time remains a psychic labyrinth from which one cannot escape:

> Time is the substance I am made of. Time is a river which sweeps me along, but I am the river; it is a tiger which destroys me, but I am the tiger; it is a fire which consumes me, but I am the fire. The world, unfortunately, is real; I, unfortunately, am Borges.
>
> (p. 269)

The work of Borges and of the other writers I have mentioned needs to be understood, as I suggested earlier, in the context of a broad range of attempts to explore alternate conceptions of time and experience. In post-Einsteinian science, perhaps the most important reflection of these concerns is to be found in the insights of Quantum Theory. As we will see in Part II of this book, writers such as Ian McEwan have attempted to respond directly to the notions of uncertainty and complementarity, or necessary contradiction, which Quantum Theory enshrines. And more widely, the rethinking of social time has fed symbiotically into reflections on the nature of collective memory and its reconstitution in historical narrative, some of which we have already encountered.

In Holocaust novels particularly, questions of historical responsibility are often approached in a tortuous way, and this frequently finds expression in disjunctive techniques of narration in which the fabric of time is shown unravelling. In this regard, I referred to D. M. Thomas' *The White Hotel* in chapter 1. Compared with that novel, the strategy for manipulating narrative time which we see in Martin Amis' *Time's Arrow* (1991) is a comparatively uncomplicated one. Unlike Thomas' text, Amis takes us right into Auschwitz, into the gas chambers themselves, and into the laboratory. This is clearly extremely difficult material. But his text allows itself a 'safe' distance from the Holocaust by means of a simple but effective narrative device: a wholesale reversal of time. Beginning with the death of its protagonist and ending with his birth, the effect of *Time's Arrow*'s narrative is to invert the meaning of each and every experience we encounter in the protagonist's life.

Not all of Amis' novel dwells on the representation of atrocity; in fact much of it is witty and light-hearted. Even activities as everyday as eating and shopping, backward-wound like a film strip, become the subject of clever set-pieces:

> you select a soiled dish, collect some scraps from the garbage, and settle down for a short wait. Various items get gulped up into my mouth, and after skilful massage with tongue and teeth I transfer them to the plate for additional sculpture with knife and fork and spoon. That bit's quite therapeutic at least, unless you're having soup or something, which can be a real sentence. Next you face the laborious business of cooling, of reassembly, of storage, before the return of these foodstuffs to the Superette, where, admittedly, I am promptly and generously reimbursed for my pains. Then you tool down the aisles with trolley or basket, returning each can or packet to its rightful place.
>
> (p. 19)

As 'the past' gradually approaches, the major realisation we face is that Amis' main character Tod/John/Odilo is an ex-Nazi. A war criminal, it eventually unfolds, he knows all about the Final Solution, to the extent of being responsible for the Zyclon pellets that were placed in the gas chambers. As a doctor he has assisted in breathtakingly sadistic medical experimentation on the Jewish victims of Auschwitz.

Describing Odilo's career backwards, it is notable that Amis' novel avoids direct engagement with the questions of motivation and remorse by means of two major narrative devices. Firstly, the narrator's voice is not the doctor's own, but that of a disembodied personality who, whilst residing in Odilo's body, has virtually no access to his thoughts and feelings. Secondly, the reversed movement of time in the novel has the profound effect of inverting the moral implications of everything he does and sees. As readers we are continually having to 'decode' the action by reversing its effect. In the case of the passage quoted above, this may appear as a witty piece of metafictional play. When the novel's attention turns to the death camps, the effect is more unsettling and problematic. Genocide, turned upside down, becomes a grand and magical gift of life:

> Our preternatural purpose? To dream a race. To make a people from the weather. From thunder and from lightning. With gas, with electricity, with shit, with fire . . . Sometimes, my face rippling peculiarly with smiles and frowns, I would monitor proceedings through the viewing slit. There was usually a long wait while the gas was invisibly introduced by the ventilation grilles. The dead look so dead. Dead bodies have their

own dead body language. It says nothing. I always felt a gorgeous relief at the moment of first stirring. Then it was ugly again. Well, we cry and twist and are naked at both ends of life. We cry at both ends of life, while the doctor watches.

(pp. 128–9)

Here we can see how the manipulation of time in Amis' text directly facilitates access to its ethical and historical concerns. In this particular case, Amis' metafictional manipulation of time works as a kind of prophylactic which enables us to face the unbearable.

In his three-volume study *Time and Narrative* (1984–8), the theorist Paul Ricoeur analyses the relationship between narrative and the experience of time in a way that throws the disjunctive strategies of contemporary fiction into relief. For Ricoeur, the crucial role of narrative in our everyday social and personal lives is essentially to affirm the *coherence* of our temporal impressions. Thus 'time becomes human to the extent that it is articulated through a narrative mode, and narrative attains its full meaning when it becomes a condition of temporal existence' (vol. I, p. 52). Like other theorists we have met with, Ricoeur argues that time should not be seen as a linear continuum, but rather as a multi-level construction. Between the vast scheme of cosmic time, the public plane of historical time and the private, fluctuating experience of personal time, he suggests, our experience of time can easily be discordant and unsettling. Narrative's function, then, is to mediate between these different levels of time consciousness, creating a sense of comforting continuity.

A good example of this function at work is provided by the genre of classical Greek tragedy, in which the (cosmic) forces of fate, the epic dramas of history, and the loves and lives of individuals are woven together into a meaningful narrative whole. In Ricoeur's theory, then, we could argue that narrative's role is fundamentally a conservative one. Arising from 'a pre-understanding of the world of action, its meaningful structures, its symbolic resources' (vol. I, p. 54) and mediating between these and the experience of the reader or viewer, what narrative is supposed to do, over and over again, is to rehearse the coherence of conventional time. Its duty is to ensure a comfortable continuum between our understanding of the cosmic or absolute, our sense of our historical placing and the texture of our everyday experience.

In contemporary fiction, it is useful to consider Ricoeur's analysis of narrative's classic function as a healer of time, because it helps us to see the extent to which this function has been abandoned in recent writing. As we will see in chapter 7 with the work of Jeanette Winterson, the comforting, coherent, linear-historical frames characteristic of realist fiction have often been replaced by more fractured and unsettling narrative forms, in which meditations on the nature of the quantum universe work not to calm but to disturb the surface of personal time. Amongst writers who deal with the problems of collective memory, likewise, new ways of exploring the relations between time, history and subjectivity have had to be found.

In Kurt Vonnegut's novel *Slaughterhouse Five* (1969), for example, protagonist Billy Pilgrim, a prisoner of war and witness to the Allied destruction of Dresden in the Second World War, is constantly dislodged from a stable experience of time, identity and history:

> LISTEN:
> Billy Pilgrim has come unstuck in time. Billy has gone to sleep a senile widower and awakened on his wedding day. He has walked through a door in 1955 and come out another one in 1941. He has gone back through that door to find himself in 1963. He has seen his birth and death many times, he says, and pays random visits to all the events in between.
> He says.
> Billy is spastic in time . . .
>
> (p. 17)

Vonnegut's attempt to come to terms with the trauma of an atrocious fire-bombing cannot be contained within the bounds of a conventional narrative. Instead the text searches discontinuously amongst wartime recollection, space-travel fantasy, whimsical anecdote, quotation, reportage. *Slaughterhouse Five* is an attempt to understand and to bear witness to the paradox of mass killing for democracy. And it is for this reason that, in terms of narrative form, the novel so explicitly reproduces the sense of disorientation and loss of faith in time as something progressive, coherent and meaningful that we have come to recognise more and more in contemporary fiction.

For many writers and thinkers, as we have seen, it is not the memory of Dresden but that of Auschwitz which must stand as the most potent symbol of departure from modernity's optimistic faith in time as a benign force. In the writings of the German Marxist Theodor Adorno (1966), the idea of history as something positive and transcendent that can give meaning to each individual's life seems a pointless mockery in the face of that genocide:

> What the sadists in the camps foretold their victims, 'Tomorrow you'll be wiggling skyward as smoke from this chimney,' bespeaks the indifference of each individual life that is the direction of history. Even

in his formal freedom, the individual is as fungible and replaceable as he will be under the liquidators' boots.

(p. 362)

For others, especially in the literature of the Cold War, it is the first use of the atom bomb on the citizens of Hiroshima which stands as the most important event, dramatising the demise of the coherent, Newtonian universe, and the Enlightenment narrative of civilised progress to which it was so integral. Ian McEwan's oratorio *Or Shall We Die?* (1983) is a characteristic example of this sensibility in late twentieth-century writing. In this context, the fact that it is the *critique* of absolute time in Relativity Theory which makes nuclear technology possible is a paradox with which many writers have struggled. Contrary to the liberatory figuration of the New Physics in many modernist works, it is Einsteinian science which turns out to be responsible for the twentieth century's definitive technological atrocity. Clearly, then, the advent of the nuclear age has forced writers to confront time and change once again as problems which manifest themselves on ethical, historical and personal levels. This is not to say, by any means, that all post-war fictions are necessarily concerned with questions of atrocity. What it does mean, though, is that the questions of time and narrative which are explored in modernist fiction often return in late twentieth-century texts in different and intensified forms.

Relativity and chronotopicity

Ironically, one of the thinkers who have done most to illuminate the disjunctive remodelling of time in contemporary fiction is a figure whose major work precedes the Second World War, the Russian dissident writer Mikhail Bakhtin. In his seminal study *The Dialogic Imagination* (1934–41), which enjoyed a major revival amongst postmodernist theorists in the 1990s, Bakhtin developed the notion of the 'chronotope' to open up the complex exploration of time that is possible in literary texts. The notion of the chronotope parallels Albert Einstein's famous texts 'On the Electrodynamics of Moving Bodies' (1905) and 'The Foundation of the General Theory of Relativity' (1916) which, as we have already seen, sought to overturn the idea that space and time can be considered as separate entities.

In his work on relativity, Einstein explicitly refutes the idea that chronometric time (the time of the clock) progresses evenly in all circumstances. This leads to the conclusion that the structure of the universe can only be understood in terms of a single four-dimensional continuum, spacetime. In a similar way, Bakhtin's chronotope brings together the prefix 'chrono' (indicating time) with the suffix 'tope' (indicating space or place) as a single idea. For Bakhtin:

> In the literary artistic chronotope, spatial and temporal indicators are fused into one carefully thought-out, concrete whole. Time, as it were, thickens, takes on flesh, becomes artistically visible; likewise, space becomes charged and responsive to the movements of time, plot and history.
>
> (Pearce, 1994, p. 67)

For Einstein space-time is a single universal continuum. Bakhtin's chronotope is more radical than this in one important respect: in his theory, *multiple* chronotopes or models of the time/space horizon are possible. Even within a single literary work, more than one chronotope may be in play. And looking from a historical perspective, Bakhtin argues that great shifts in perception can be understood in terms of the transition between different chronotopes.

In his work as a whole, then, Bakhtin can be argued to be far more relativist than relativity itself. The most important example Bakhtin uses to illustrate the transition between rival chronotopes is drawn from the end of the Middle Ages. In this period of cultural and ideological change, he argues, particular kinds of revolutionary energies began to build out of the need for a new chronotope – a new temporal and spatial, historical and social worldview. In *Rabelais and His World* (1965) he shows how this revolutionary pressure manifested itself in cycles of popular revolt and carnivalesque disorder.

The Dialogic Imagination argues that, in the wake of 'the dissolution of the medieval world view' (p. 205) in which the theological doctrine of the Last Judgement had been so dominant, a fundamentally new conception of time and space was needed, which could 'permit one to link real life (history) to the real earth. It was necessary to oppose to eschatology a creative and generative time, a time measured by creative acts, by growth and not by destruction' (p. 206). It is to popular folklore that Bakhtin looks in search of this new chronotope, showing how carnival instituted itself as an antidote to the ordered, official culture of medieval society.

In chapter 7 we will be examining the work of Jeanette Winterson specifically through the lens of Bakhtin's chronotope. In texts such as *The Passion* (1987) and increasingly throughout her *œuvre* Winterson makes self-conscious use of contrasting chronotopic horizons, often deploying the conceptual models of Relativity and Quantum Theory against the grain of linear narration. In *The Passion* particularly, the city of Venice is set up as a carnivalesque space of uncertainty, set apart from the arid linearity of history, and in contradistinction to it. Applying Bakhtin's analysis to Winterson's work, we can see how both the questioning of time and the insertion of alternative imaginary, mythical and fairytale spaces in her texts open up possibilities for re-imagination and resistance in ways which would not be possible within the parameters of realist narration.

Returning to Martin Amis' *Time's Arrow*, meanwhile, we can see how this text operates in a parallel way through the disjunction between the forward movement of the reader's experience through the novel, and the reversed dynamic of its action. In Bakhtin's terms, it is again useful to think of this as a chronotopic opposition. In Borges' various stories, likewise, the way absolute time is subverted is precisely through the proposition of alternative temporal universes. In texts such as those of Maxine Hong Kingston which seek to foreground their cultural hybridity, on the other hand, the use of dissonant chronotopes or horizons of time/space can be seen working again, to different kinds of effect. Kingston's work is the focus of chapter 6. In each of these examples, it is possible to see how many contemporary fictions function through a refusal of the canonical, conservative relationship between time and narrative, as Ricoeur describes it.

In this chapter, I have suggested that one of the most important challenges for post-war and contemporary writers has been to find ways of responding to the unravelling of absolute time in this period, and to understand its implications for the representation of collective memory. As I began by saying, the exploration of time in contemporary fiction is something that has taken place not in isolation, but rather against the background of a whole set of explorations in different fields and disciplines. In the area of literary and cultural studies, these debates have been at least as vigorous as elsewhere. For theorists of postmodernism such as Jean-François Lyotard in his collection *The Inhuman: Reflections on Time* (1988), for example, the fact that contemporary texts retain the power to radically surprise and confound us is seen in itself as one answer to the colonising, terroristic tendencies of modern time. Others, such as Fredric Jameson in his influential study *Postmodernism* (1991), are much more pessimistic. For Jameson, postmodern culture, with its shiny surfaces and historical amnesia, is seen ultimately as a threat to our self-liberation and self-determination. In a way that recalls the earlier work of Georg Lukács, which was discussed in chapter 1, what is needed, according to Jameson, is a restoration of grounded historical consciousness in contemporary culture. These debates, it hardly needs to be said, are ongoing.

It could be argued, in defence of fiction, that the novel's flexibility and imaginative dynamics make it an unusually effective vehicle for exploring concerns about time, memory and history which are widespread throughout many areas of culture and society. The questions which are asked in the work of Ian McEwan, Maxine Hong Kingston, Toni Morrison, Salman Rushdie, Angela Carter and many others are becoming more and more familiar. In the wake of changing perceptions of time and social space, how are we to reconceive and reconstruct our personal and collective histories? How are we to envisage positive futures when our ability to navigate past and present seems radically uncertain? What is the nature of a future? What is the nature of a past? What are the responsibilities of the novel as a framework for representing our times? As we will see many times in Part II of this book, these are not questions with simple, single answers.

3 Bodies, genders

Having considered the abstraction of time, we need now to turn our attention to more fleshly concerns. The aim of this chapter is to suggest some of the ways in which contemporary fiction has framed questions of the body and of gender. Over the past three or four decades, the body has transmuted in anglophone writing into a range of grotesque and sublime manifestations, from many-breasted fertility goddesses, through the undecidable unborn, through the scarred bodies of slaves to the image of dancers composed only of light. In order to make sense of the strategies through which the body, gender and sexual identity are refigured in some of these texts, it is necessary to outline some of the wider context out of which these strategies arise.

In the contemporary period there has been a sea change in understandings of the body and its relation to identity. Arguably the most important moment in this transition is the emergence of a formal distinction between 'sex' and 'gender' in the 1960s. As the gender theorist Anna Tripp (2000) suggests, the text which most definitively institutionalised the sex/gender opposition is probably American psychoanalyst Robert Stoller's influential study *Sex and Gender: On the Development of Masculinity and Femininity* (1968). Obviously, though, Stoller did not 'invent' gender. Indeed, well before this it is possible to see how a notion of culturally constructed gender is nascent in the work of many writers. As early as 1929 Virginia Woolf discusses the construction of 'woman' in male-authored literature in *A Room of One's Own*. In the same period, psychoanalyst Joan Riviere was already arguing that the notion of 'womanliness' might be reconsidered as a socially necessary 'masquerade' rather than some pure expression of feminine identity. In *The Second Sex* (1949), similarly, the French feminist theorist Simone de Beauvoir laid much of the groundwork for later thinking on the construction of gender identities and norms:

> One is not born, but rather becomes a woman. No biological, psychological, or economic fate determines the figure that the human female

presents in society: it is civilization as a whole that produces this creature, intermediate between male and eunuch, which is described as feminine.
(p. 249)

In each of these earlier texts, in different ways, the sex/gender distinction is comparatively slippery and uncertain. Conventionally, then, the 1960s are read as the period in which it becomes more formalised and widely applied. As David Glover and Cora Kaplan (2000) illustrate, for example, where in the first (1950) edition of Alex Comfort's influential *Sexual Behaviour in Society*, the notion of gender does not enter the frame of analysis, by the second (1963) edition, the distinction between 'physical sex' and 'gender roles' has become a significant one. In 1968, Robert Stoller's work consolidates and institutionalises this emerging framework.

The fundamental importance of the sex/gender opposition for thinkers and writers lies in the way it frees thinking about gender identity from the assumption – encapsulated in the famous phrase 'biology is destiny' – that the subordinate social status and ideological positioning of women in society could be 'naturally' attributed to differences in biological formation. As a consequence, the 'second wave' feminism which emerged in this period has sometimes been seen as a movement 'in flight from' the body and biology. In her study *Feminism and the Biological Body* (1999), for example, the biologist Lynda Birke outlines what she sees as a continuing reluctance in feminism to engage with bodily systems and processes, a reluctance she traces directly to the critique of biological determinism initiated by theorists such as Simone de Beauvoir. Birke wants to take issue with 'theories of social construction that ignore my bodily pain and bleeding, or that ignore the ways that desire (however constructed) finds expression through my material body' (p. 25).

What is certainly true is that, in 'French feminism' particularly, the representation of the body has been subjected to a rigorous re-examination. Theorists such as Monique Wittig, for example, have become notorious for their polemical refusal to accept the received terminologies of sex. Wittig (1992) begins from a position of radical scepticism towards canonical assumptions, developing de Beauvoir's analysis in order to question the stability of basic labels like 'man' and 'woman'. This is not to say that Wittig is a proponent of androgyny. Rather, drawing on Marxist analysis, she emphasises the ways in which women can be considered as a group unified by factors other than biology, namely their common experience of social and economic subordination. According to Wittig,

it is our historical task, and only ours, to define what we call oppression in Materialist terms, to make it evident that women are a class, which is to say that the category 'woman' as well as the category 'man' are political and economic categories not eternal ones.

(p. 313)

Even in Wittig's case, however, it is wrong to see recent writing about gender as defined by a loss of interest in the body. Rather, what we see in contemporary writing is a polymorphous rethinking of the body and its relationships to identity and experience. This rethinking extends across the whole range of theoretical and literary writing. Overall, rather than closing down the body as a terrain for thinkers and writers, the distinction of sexual morphology from gender identity which first became popular in the 1960s – and which has been critically revised many times in the period since then – has not closed the body down, but on the contrary opened it up for a whole range of new kinds of exploration. Amongst the most radical re-figurations of the body by contemporary intellectuals is Donna Haraway's 'Cyborg Manifesto' (1991) in which the figure of the cyborg – half organism, half machine – is offered as a paradigm for a new post-gendered, post-humanist identity.

In fictional texts from the 1970s such as Angela Carter's *The Passion of New Eve* (1977) there is huge amount of playful experimentation with body construction and alteration. The twin protagonists of Carter's novel are a young misogynist male who is captured and surgically transformed into a woman by a radical cult, and a female screen icon, modelled on Greta Garbo, who turns out to be a man in drag. Initially dismissed as a piece of titillating 'soft-core', *The Passion of New Eve* has been read more recently as one of Carter's most interrogative and interesting texts. Whilst notions of androgyny had already been explored in texts such as Virginia Woolf's *Orlando* (1928), Carter's text pursues its transvestite and intersexed interests to much more radical extremes. The novel tracks the adventures of its problematic protagonists through a number of contrasting psycho-sexual scenarios, including a rape, a love affair and a pregnancy, to explore the complex and ambivalent ways in which images of sex and gender are mediated through contemporary culture.

The contrast between *The Passion of New Eve* and a very different text like Alice Walker's *Possessing the Secret of Joy* (1992) illustrates the variety of ways in which issues of gender and embodiment are raised in contemporary writing. Dealing with the issue of female circumcision in the fictional African state of Olinka, Walker's text interrogates notions of social, psychic and bodily 'normality' in a much more difficult political context. In a way which contrasts sharply with the portrayal of Carter's almost cartoon-like characters and remodellable bodies, Walker's protagonist Tashi is irreparably wounded by the modification of her biological apparatus during the 'initiation' ceremony. Moving between Africa, Europe and North America, Walker's text urges us to consider cosmetic surgery in the West and female circumcision in African 'Olinka' as part of a continuum of bodily abuse which needs to be resisted. In so doing, it forces the reader into a critical confrontation with overly relativist notions of the body as an infinitely redefinable construction. Bodies may be remodellable, the novel suggests, but they are also lived organisms, just as genders are lived identities which cannot be abstracted from social and cultural experience.

This interest in the complex relation between the body and culture has been a common feature of both theoretical and literary writing, as well as work which blurs the boundary between them. Looking at writers like the feminist theorist Luce Irigaray and the novelist Jeanette Winterson, we can see a mutual interest in reworking the metaphors within which the body and femininity have been inscribed in Western culture. Each of them is heavily influenced by poststructuralism and its stress on the constitutive role of language in structuring perception. For each of them, there is a concern to show how language, anatomy and pleasure can be seen as co-extensive with each other. Both writers display a sophisticated awareness of the range of critiques of essential (biologistic) sex categories from Riviere and de Beauvoir onwards. At the same time, though, both writers constantly play with the sexed body, and even with the metaphors which have traditionally designated femaleness in terms of weakness and instability.

In the language of Irigaray's *This Sex Which Is Not One* (1977) therefore, what we see, in an important sense, is a reclamation of the sexed body and its pleasures:

> Let's hurry and invent our own phrases. So that everywhere and always we can continue to embrace. We are so subtle that nothing can stand in our way, nothing can stop us from reaching each other, even fleetingly, if we can find means of communication that have *our* density. We shall pass imperceptibly through every barrier, unharmed, to find each other. No one will see a thing. Our strength lies in the very weakness of our resistance. For a long time they have appreciated what our suppleness is worth for their own embraces and impressions. Why not enjoy it ourselves? Rather than letting ourselves be subjected to their branding. Rather than being fixed, stabilised, immobilised. Separated.
>
> Don't cry. One day we'll manage to say ourselves. And what we say will be even lovelier than our tears. Wholly fluent.
>
> Already, I carry you with me everywhere. Not like a child, a burden, a weight, however beloved and precious. You are not *in me*. I do not contain you or retain you in my stomach, my arms, my head. Nor in my

memory, my mind, my language. You are there, like my skin. With you I am certain of existing beyond all appearances, all disguises, all designations.

(Irigaray, 1985, pp. 215–16)

In Jeanette Winterson's *Written on the Body* (1992), which will be examined in chapter 7, there is a parallel attempt to reclaim the body. Just as Irigaray does in *This Sex Which Is Not One*, Winterson approaches the body as a fleshly text in the process of rewriting. Her novel contrasts two lovers, one of whom, Louise, is obsessively over-defined by the language of objectifying eroticism, and the other of whom, the narrator, remains provocatively undefined and un-sexed. Like Irigaray's writing, Winterson's texts play with sexed representations of the body, in order to subtly undermine and overturn them. In the work of both, the body is celebrated for its contours, processes and pleasures, at the same time as its lines are being redrawn.

In thinking about gender and the body, as we can see here, contemporary women's writing has been crucial in the development of new and radical perspectives. In the light of this, it is perhaps ironic, then, that one of the most important influences on thinking about the body in contemporary writing has been the work of Michel Foucault, who is much criticised by feminists for his lack of attention to questions of gender.

In chapter 1, I discussed Foucault's exploration of the inter-relatedness of power/knowledge, in texts such as *Discipline and Punish* (1975) and *The History of Sexuality* (1976–84). For Foucault, as I suggested there, power is not conceived as a 'top-down' exercise of authority, but rather as something which is dispersed throughout society, operating through institutionalised discourses such as medicine, criminology, psychiatry and so on. What needs to be stressed for our purposes here, then, is Foucault's concern with the very specific ways in which power operates, at the base level, on the body itself.

Both of the studies cited above are primarily concerned with tracing the development of modern society in terms of the particular ways in which it seeks to control subjects and their bodies. *Discipline and Punish* (1975), for example, starts with the spectacle of public torture and execution as traditional means of popular control, and then goes on to explore their decline and replacement by modern forms of disciplinary control in the seventeenth and eighteenth centuries. In this later period, Foucault traces the emergence of the highly rationalised modern prison system, in which an intricate and precise regulation of the prisoner's regime, coupled with the constant awareness of surveillance, is designed to remould the mind and body of the prisoner into that of a healthy and legal subject. In place of violent bodily retribution, the intricate control and regulation of the prisoner's body is used to 'rehabilitate' them into circumscribed patterns of 'legal/healthy/normal' behaviour.

Importantly, in this study as a whole, Foucault's examination of the penal system becomes a metaphor for his analysis of the disciplining of the body in society at large. At the centre of this conception of power and the body, the notion of oppressive authority has been displaced by notions of power/knowledge, surveillance and self-regulation. These become the key dynamics of control in what Foucault calls disciplinary society. In this text, the word 'discipline' is particularly significant. Foucault uses it to point simultaneously to questions of knowledge and to questions of the body. In an academic sense it refers to the emergence of circumscribed, institution-alised 'disciplines' of knowledge. At the same time, on the level of the body, 'discipline' carries senses both of training and of self-control. In this way Foucault suggests what he sees as the intimate relationship between the institutionalisation of discourses and the regulation of subjects and their bodies.

In a range of areas, Foucault's thinking around the body and its regulation by discourses and institutions has been immensely influential. In medical sociology, for example, interest in his texts has enabled many thinkers to take a step back from the perspectives and assumptions of bio-medical science, towards an interrogation of the ways in which notions of health and illness, normality and deviance are inscribed and policed within clinical practice. Here, as Bryan Turner (1997) suggests, Foucault has thus been the major intellectual contributor to a new perspective on the body as a terrain on which discourses of moral and social control seek to establish themselves, on the level of both individuals and populations.

One specific example of work which straddles bio-medical concerns and those of gender theory is that of Anne Fausto-Sterling, who examines the practice of sexual surgery on children born with atypical sexual apparatus. Her essay 'How to Build a Man' (1995) explores the ways in which arbitrary gender norms are routinely enforced through the surgical alteration of male children who are not deemed to have sufficiently 'masculine' genitalia. In this way she provides an insight into the ways in which penile size becomes fetishised as the single defining marker of a satisfactory masculinity. Using evidence from substantial organs such as the *Johns Hopkins Medical Journal*, she shows that boys born with otherwise 'healthy' physiology but with penises measuring less than three-fifths of an inch at birth will be considered candidates for castration and sex reassignment. Possession of a large penis is thus taken axiomatically as the necessary condition of maleness.

By the same token, the small penis becomes a marker of deviancy that must be excised, regardless of the fact that castration and the manufacture of a makeshift vagina may severely compromise the capacity of the subject for sexual pleasure later on, as well as eliminating the possibility of reproduction. Where surgeons assume the task of 'normalising' the female body, by contrast, Fausto-Sterling finds that the rules have changed. In these cases, the future capacity for child-bearing is privileged, no matter what lasting effects the surgical and pharmaceutical interventions needed to secure this function might have. Here Fausto-Sterling quotes Patricia Donahue et al. (1991) in the professional journal *Current Problems in Surgery*, indicating 'best practice' for working surgical teams:

> Genetic females should always be raised as females, preserving reproductive potential, regardless of how severely the patients are virilised. In the genetic male, however, the gender of assignment is based on the infant's anatomy, predominantly the size of the phallus.
>
> (Fausto-Sterling, p. 112)

Like Foucault's work on the penal system, Fausto-Sterling's discussion of gender reassignment stands as a particularly graphic illustration of a much wider analysis of the ways in which the medical sciences can be understood as disciplines of the body. As the creatures of those discourses, the work of physicians and surgeons becomes that of substantiating *culturally defined* categories of the healthy and the unhealthy, the normal and the abnormal, and intervening to normalise bodies within those discursive frameworks.

Amongst the variety of figures in gender studies who have been influenced by Foucault's work, the American theorist Judith Butler is especially important to mention. Like Irigaray's, although in different ways, Butler's work returns to the opposition of (biological) sex and (cultural) gender which was formalised in the late 1960s. In questioning the sex/gender framework, Butler focuses on the unexamined assumptions about the body that the notion of biological 'sex' continues to hold in place. In contrast to the notion of gender, she suggests, sex seems by definition to denote a body that *is not* formed and disciplined within culture. What Butler does in her book *Gender Trouble* (1990), then, is to examine the ways in which the ideology of fixed biological 'sex' has become the pretext for presenting discriminatory ideas about gender and sexuality as 'natural' and 'unchangeable'. If 'woman', for example, is defined in terms of an anatomical facility for reproduction, then a certain model of fertile heterosexual femininity becomes idealised as a norm, a benchmark against which all women come to be measured. One can see, then, how a huge range of people – who are perhaps infertile, single, post-menopausal, gay, transsexual, intersexual, and so on and so on – become defined as somehow less than a full(filled) woman.

Because these kinds of assumptions are clearly produced within culture, Butler argues that the whole idea of 'sex' can be considered to be a part of the cultural articulation of identity designated by Robert Stoller and others as 'gender'. Rather than assuming that a person is born 'into' a sex, or a gender or a sexuality, she suggests that we need to think of historically produced categories like sex, gender and sexuality as part of the cultural apparatus with which we *discipline, interpret and articulate* the body and desire.

Importantly, for Butler, inherited gender and sex identities are not irresistible. What we need to do is to examine the ways in which they are (re)produced through time, by means of example and constant repetition. One of the most important themes of her work, therefore, is to disrupt the assumed 'naturalness' and 'inevitability' of these processes:

> And what is 'sex' anyway? Is it natural, anatomical, chromosomal, or hormonal, and how is a feminist critic to assess the scientific discourses which purport to establish such 'facts' for us? Does sex have a history? Does each sex have a different history, or histories? Is there a history of how the duality of sex was established, a genealogy that might expose the binary options as a variable construction? Are the ostensibly natural facts of sex discursively produced by various scientific discourses in the service of some other political and social interests?
>
> (pp. 6–7)

In contemporary fiction, the interest in the disciplining of the body which we see in Foucault's and Butler's work is frequently reflected. Like Butler, many recent writers have been interested in the disruptive possibilities of disguise, performance, body modification and particularly of grotesqueness. The emergence of magic realism as a style of writing, in which bizarre and fantastic characters and events are incorporated alongside realistic ones, has been especially important for writers working in this area. In Angela Carter's *Nights at the Circus* (1984), for example, the protagonist Fevvers takes the form of an enormous winged woman. Disrupting conventional bodily definitions, she is simultaneously angelic and carnal, sublime and grotesque, virginal and whorish. Importantly, throughout this novel Carter makes Fevvers' 'real' identity and her performance co-extensive with each other, so that we can never finally know whether she is real or fake, a freak or a fraud. From the opening chapter, Fevvers' ambiguity works to disrupt stable notions of inner, 'essential' gender identity. As the novel progresses, Carter transports us into a series of different regimes and environments, beginning in late Victorian London and ending in the wastes of Siberia, exploring the destabilising effects of her ambiguously endowed protagonist.

We have already seen that in the earlier novel, *The Passion of New Eve*, similar strategies are in play. Minds are deliberately mismatched with bodies, and bodies disciplined into a series of foreign regimes of power/knowledge.

In both texts, there is a consistent effort to disrupt commonsensical assumptions about the 'natural' relationships of bodies, pleasures and performed identities. Earlier, I contrasted the cartoonish quality of *The Passion of New Eve* with Alice Walker's *Possessing the Secret of Joy*, where questions of power and the body are taken up in a less abstracted context. But a text like this, too, can usefully be considered in Foucauldian and Butlerian terms. After all, what Walker's text explores is precisely the ways in which bodies are violently disciplined through a particular framework of 'virtuous' femininity. Walker uses African 'Olinka' as the setting for much of her novel. But turning her attention to the United States as well, in this and other texts Walker shows how the modification of body shapes – from painful cosmetic surgeries, to regimes of exercise, to forms of restrictive dress – become part of the societally imposed discipline of the desirable/healthy/attractive individual. For Walker as much as for Carter, though writing in very different ways, it is important to consider the body not just as a 'given' fact of life, but as a parchment on which dominant values are written.

Raced bodies

In many contemporary fictions, then, the disciplining and disruption of the sexed body is pursued in different ways. Jeanette Winterson's *Sexing the Cherry* (1989), for example, has its two protagonists, Jordan and 'Dog Woman', inhabit a series of different bodies – and different historical periods – during the course of the text. For many writers, moreover, this interest in the interrogation of 'sex' is intimately tied to the contestation of 'race'. Salman Rushdie's *The Satanic Verses*, for example, has one of its main characters, Saladin Chamcha, undergo a spontaneous metamorphosis some way into the novel. Detained as an illegal immigrant in England, the Indian Chamcha finds himself transforming under the gaze of his captors. Here Rushdie plays wittily on a history of racist discourses about African and Asian men as hugely endowed and sexually rapacious:

> The three immigration officers were in particularly high spirits, and it was one of these . . . who had 'debagged' Saladin with a merry cry of, 'Opening time, Packy; let's see what you're made of!' Red and white stripes were dragged off the protesting Chamcha, who was reclining on the floor of the van with two stout policemen holding each arm and a fifth constable's boot placed firmly on his chest . . .
> His thighs had grown uncommonly wide and powerful, as well as hairy. Below the knee the hairiness came to a halt, and his legs narrowed into tough, bony, almost fleshless calves, terminating in a pair of shiny,

cloven hooves, such as one might find on any billy-goat. Saladin was also taken aback by the size of his phallus, greatly enlarged and embarrassingly erect, an organ that he had the greatest difficulty in acknowledging as his own.

(p. 157)

Whilst Chamcha is alarmed and disorientated by his transformation, to the English police and immigration officers there is nothing odd about it. In a provocative narrative device, Rushdie allows his Indian character to metamorphose into a fantasy of the racist imagination, a hyper-embodied figure that is half demonic, half animal.

In the United States, in the work of many writers, we see a dual focus on combating the racial stereotypes perpetuated in much canonical literature, and on offering a range of positive counter-images of the body. In Maxine Hong Kingston's work, which we will be exploring in chapter 6, the first move in this process is simply to populate the literary landscape with the figures of the Chinese Americans which have consistently been erased by the white gaze. In this way novels like *China Men* (1980) seek to flesh out Chinese American-ness, combating images of the 'inscrutable oriental' which had become so entrenched in American popular culture.

Amongst African American writers, on the other hand, the figuration of the black body in narrative takes place against a different historical backdrop. As we will see in the next chapter, debates over slavery in the nineteenth century featured a series of attempts to classify blacks and whites as biologically different beings. And as Carla Peterson (2000) suggests, this often hinged on the representation of slaves as bodies without souls, lacking higher intellectual faculties or an imaginative interior life. For abolitionists, the demonstration that blacks were 'fully human' frequently involved the citation of slave writings, such as *The Life and Adventures of Henry Bibb, An American Slave, Written by Himself* (1849), in which the author's moral and imaginative capacities were made manifest. In pro-slavery writings, on the other hand, great efforts are made to deny the 'Negro' any kind of reflective interiority. This denial then becomes a key element of the ideological framework which allows black people to be conceptualised as a lower form of life. In contrast to the morally and intellectually cultivated white, in such writings, blackness becomes a sign of hyper-embodiment. Denied souls, slave bodies become layered over with representations of brute corporeality and especially of sexuality.

Focusing on black women, Vanessa Dickerson (Dickerson and Bennett, 2000) is one of a number of scholars who have traced the ways in which, historically, black bodies have been inscribed within these racist discourses in terms of debasement and animality:

Historically relegated to the auction block instead of the pedestal, the black female body has been constructed as the ugly end of a wearisome Western dialectic: not sacred but profane, not angelic but demonic, not fair lady but ugly darky. Along with her male counterpart, the black woman has belonged to one of those races 'perceived as more animal-like and less god-like'.

(p. 196)

Again, in an essay entitled 'Selling Hot Pussy: Representations of Black Female Sexuality in the Cultural Marketplace' (1992), the theorist and critic bel hooks examines the representation of bodies in nineteenth- and twentieth-century Europe and America in a similar way. Moving then to contemporary culture, hooks' work goes on to explore how contemporary singers and film-makers have responded to the disciplining of their bodies by the white gaze. Using examples like Aretha Franklin and Tina Turner, hooks shows how self-representations by African American artists often in fact seem to be caught between resisting and exploiting the representation of black women in terms of a debased sexuality. In the work of the singer Tina Turner, for example, we can see how suggestions of strength and autonomy are at the same time bound up with notions of sexual victimhood. In an effort to contrast Turner and Franklin with more unambiguously affirmative representations of black female embodiment, hooks points to films such as *Dreaming Rivers* by the British black film collective Sankofa. Far from a rejection of the black female body, she finally argues, what is needed is much more extensive exploration of bodies, sexualities and representations:

> This is certainly the challenge facing black women, who must confront the old painful representations still haunting the present. We must make the oppositional space where our sexuality can be named and repre-sented, where we are sexual subjects – no longer bound and trapped.
>
> (p. 128)

In contemporary fictions by African American women, there certainly are attempts to engage with black female embodiment and black female sexuality in the way bel hooks outlines. Alice Walker's work is a case in point. As it happens, in her writing hooks has been critical of *The Color Purple* (1983), focusing on the character of Sofia to argue that the novel is luke warm in its support for resistance by black women. In Walker's defence, however, I would argue that over the course of her *œuvre* there is a whole range of liberatory strategies, not all of them based on the positive representation of one character or another. The later novel *The Temple of*

My Familiar (1989), for example, attempts a radical liberation from the disciplined body, invoking notions of reincarnation and animism which cut directly across the assumptions of the Judaeo-Christian tradition. The groundwork for this is laid out clearly in *The Color Purple* through the characters of Celie and Shug.

Notably, the exploration of blackness through Lissie's reincarnated consciousness in *The Temple of My Familiar* involves a refiguring of the white body as well. Walker's re-working of the Eden myth, in particular, involves a highly self-conscious reverse pathologisation of the white man. As he awakes from the loss of his virginity in a forest garden, the white man first discovers his freakish pallor when he looks in horror at his penis, which has been rubbed clean through intercourse. Invoking the biblical Adam's discovery of his shaming nakedness in Genesis, Walker clearly figures the emergence of whiteness as a Fall. Shifting from an Adam figure to a Cain figure, the pale man makes himself an outcast in her novel. Clothing himself in animal hides which reek of death, he becomes the archetypal vagabond.

Alongside Alice Walker, the efforts of writers such as Toni Morrison to rework dominant representations of the body have been immensely influential. In framing counter-narratives against the grain of white history, part of the work done by their writing is to reclaim the black body as valuable and beautiful. In Morrison's *œuvre*, it is possible to see how this imperative gains force in subsequent texts, so that the desolate self-delusions of Pecola in *The Bluest Eye* (1970) gradually give way to the affirmative rhetoric of Baby Suggs in *Beloved* (1987), for whom a celebratory, fleshly enjoyment of the black body becomes the way to salvation.

In this, Morrison's and Walker's texts are of a piece with a wide range of writing, which returns to the body with the aim of reforming and rewriting it. As I have suggested, much of this writing meshes with recent thinking, within both feminism and elsewhere, which has sought to combat the biological determinism that, for years, dominated the horizon of public discourse in the West. Beginning in the 1960s, influenced by the Civil Rights movement in the United States and by second-wave feminism in France, we can see how a new set of questions about the disciplining and representation of the body begin to be raised in contemporary fiction. Frequently, as I have suggested, these questions are intimately linked to issues of history and its rewriting. As we have seen too, they are also inextricably connected to questions of 'race'. Indeed it is to this last, crucial problematic that I want to turn in more detail, in the concluding chapter of Part I.

4   Writing and race

In contemporary writing, the question of 'race' remains one of the most complex and difficult to handle. This chapter attempts to unravel some of that complexity, exploring race's status as and in fiction. Certainly, many leading writers in the post-war period have worked explicitly to combat the ideologies of racism, exploring their expression in the atrocities of American slavery and the Nazi Holocaust. At the same time, however, it is not difficult to find instances in which notions of racial identity and racial community are affirmed by writers in apparently positive and affirmatory ways. There is a paradox here which needs to be understood.

For more than half a century, the vast majority of scientists and sociologists have agreed that the notion of 'race' is so problematic that it can no longer be regarded as a useful term. As an ideology, racism can be traced to the middle of the nineteenth century, when it developed in association with debates over colonial expansion and the abolition of the slave trade. A century and more later, in the postcolonial period, though, race-thinking has been almost universally rejected by writers and academics.

In popular culture more generally, however, this consensus is far from being reflected. 'Race' has continued to entrench itself across all sorts of areas, ranging from casual language use to the culture of institutions. In the media we hear the word on the lips of public figures every day. As thinkers such as Howard Winant (1998) have argued, then, 'race' is fundamentally paradoxical. It is 'not only real, but also illusory. Not only is it common sense; it is also common nonsense. Not only does it establish our identity; it also denies us our identity' (p. 90). In order to unravel these apparent contradictions and understand how they are manifested in contemporary fiction, it is necessary to provide a genealogical sketch of the emergence of 'race' as a concept.

Tracing race

It is in the mid-nineteenth century that the idea of 'race' first emerges as a form of human classification, in relation to debates over slavery in France, Britain and the United States. From the late eighteenth century, however, it is possible to see how efforts are being made to develop a 'scientific' language for discrimination, deploying biological and anthropological categories to justify the economic exploitation of non-white populations around the world. In his study *Colonial Desire* (1995) Robert Young quotes the Jamaican slave-owner Edward Long, as early as 1774, arguing that 'for my own part, I think there are extremely potent reasons for believing that the White and the Negro are two distinct species' (p. 7). The classification of 'the Negro' as a subordinate species, here, works very clearly to set the groundwork for justifying the use of black slaves in forced labour.

In less directly 'interested' publications, even in the mid-nineteenth century, biologistic racism is by no means consistently reflected. In the British *Imperial Dictionary, English, Technological, & Scientific* (1848), based on Webster's *American Dictionary of the English Language* (1841), for example, 'race' is defined in terms of the idea of family lineage, using the idea of an ancestor from which subsequent generations 'run'. In contrast to the emergent scientific racism of the period, the use of 'race' here is both wide ranging and metaphorical in its usage: 'Thus all mankind are called the *race* of Adam; the Israelites are of the *race* of Abraham and Jacob. Thus we speak of a *race* of kings, the *race* of Clovis or Charlemagne; a *race* of nobles, &c.' (Ogilvie, 1848, vol. II, p. 522, italics in original).

In texts of the same period which specifically set themselves to justifying the use of slaves in colonial labour forces, on the other hand, we can see race-thinking developed in a very much harder form. Thomas Carlyle's notorious 1853 pamphlet 'Occasional Discourse on the Nigger Question' is a case in point. Carlyle's defence of slavery (and rejection of democracy) in the West Indies is built on the explicit assertion of a racist hierarchy, in which the educated, land-owning, white European is necessarily and naturally superior to his black worker. White supremacism is promoted everywhere in Carlyle's text, from his deployment of the derogatory 'nigger' in the title, to the anti-immigration rhetoric of his conclusion. Moreover, it is impossible not to notice the flavour of violence and abuse that lurks around the edges of his writing:

> Do I, then, hate the negro? No, except when the soul is killed out of him, I decidedly like poor Quashee; and find him a pretty kind of man. With a pennyworth of oil, you can make a handsome glossy thing of Quashee, when the soul is not killed in him . . .

> (p. 308)

Carlyle offers a range of justifications for the continuance of slavery, ranging from divine authority to the 'heroism' of the British soldier. At the same time, his characterisation of the 'oozy' and 'reeking' world of the black man is one of repulsive, diabolical primitivism:

> For countless ages, since they first mounted oozy, on the back of earthquakes, from their dark bed in the ocean deeps, and reeking saluted the tropical sun, and ever onwards till the European white man first saw them some three short centuries ago, those islands had produced mere jungle, savagery, poison-reptiles, and swamp-malaria. Till the white European first saw them, they were as if not yet created – their noble elements of cinnamon, sugar, coffee, pepper, black and grey, lying all asleep, waiting the white enchanter who should say to them, awake! Till the end of human history and the sounding of the trump of doom, they might have lain so, had Quashee and the like of him been the only artists in the game. Swamps, fever-jungles, man-eating Caribs, rattlesnakes, and reeking waste and putrefaction, this had been the produce of them under the incompetent Caribal (what we call Cannibal) possessors, till that time . . .
>
> (p. 373)

In the nineteenth century, it is possible to trace 'race's development in all sorts of works. A good example of this is provided by Harriet Beecher Stowe's anti-slavery novel, *Uncle Tom's Cabin* (1852). Even as it draws on the author's close observations of slave exploitation and attempts to oppose them, Stowe's novel continually affirms the naturalness of 'racial difference', attributing emotional, intellectual and 'instinctive' capacities and limitations directly to it. Whilst Stowe's 'negro' is the subject of 'rude' and 'untrained' passions, for example, the 'white race' is marked for its 'cold and correct' thinking. Clearly, the strategies of Stowe's work are very different from those of someone like Carlyle. But her caricature of 'racial' types still shares many of the same, increasingly prevalent ideological assumptions. Here for example we see her comparison of two developing specimens:

> There stood the two children representatives of the two extremes of society. The fair, high-bred child, with her golden head, her deep eyes, her spiritual, noble brow, and prince-like movements; and her black, keen, subtle, cringing, yet acute neighbour. They stood the representatives of their races. The Saxon, born of ages of cultivation, command, education, physical and moral eminence; the Afric, born of ages of oppression, submission, ignorance, toil and vice!
>
> (pp. 361–2)

As we can see in this case, where race-thinking is paradoxically mixed in with the cause of abolitionism, the indirect influence of racial theory is extraordinarily diffuse in the nineteenth century. Charles Darwin's enormously influential *The Descent of Man* (1871), for example, includes a lengthy meditation on the suitability or unsuitability of 'race' for classifying humans, a point on which Darwin is clearly ambivalent. In terms of understanding the particular forms of racist thinking that develop into the twentieth and twenty-first centuries, however, the work of the French ethnologist Joseph-Arthur de Gobineau is particularly significant.

Like many subsequent racisms, Gobineau's thought is based on a certain kind of historical fiction. The notorious 'Essay on the Inequality of the Human Races' (1853–5) theorises that early man was separated into three different 'races': the white, the yellow and the black. All human civilisations in history are then claimed as the work of the 'white race', which enjoys a fundamental racial superiority. In subsequent centuries, according to Gobineau's thesis, migrations of peoples and the reformation of nations have each led to all kinds of sexual experimentation between the three 'races', and this has brought the danger that 'white' blood may become fatally 'adulterated' with 'foreign elements'. For Gobineau, such adulteration and cross-breeding must inevitably bring with it the degeneration and death of the 'white race'.

The fundamental importance of this kind of hard race-thinking in the nineteenth century lies in the way it sets the framework for modern racism. Firstly, it uses the term 'race' to suggest a fundamental biological and historical division between people, usually (although not always) along lines of skin colour. Secondly, it attributes civilisation/culture to the 'white race' and degeneration and contagion to the 'non-white'. As Young (1995) shows, later texts which draw on Gobineau's work provide graphic illustrations of his particular brand of racism (see Table 1).

In the United States before the Civil War, Gobineau's work provided much of the ideological justification for the perpetuation of slavery. Again paradoxically, though, for a long period after Abolition the language of 'race'

Table 1 Hotze's summary of the characteristics of the races according to Gobineau (1856)

	Black races	Yellow races	White races
Intellect	Feeble	Mediocre	Vigorous
Animal propensities	Very Strong	Moderate	Strong
Moral manifestations	Partially latent	Comparatively developed	Highly cultivated

Source: Young, 1995, p. 94.

continued to be deployed by a number of African American thinkers, in campaigns for unity and autonomy. For W. E. B. Du Bois, whose work will be mentioned in chapter 8, the *positive* affirmation of 'race' was developed as a response to the social subjugation of African Americans. In an examination of his work, Anthony Appiah (1985) quotes Du Bois' 1897 essay 'The Conservation of Races':

> What, then, is a race? It is a vast family of human beings, generally of common blood and language, always of common history, traditions and impulses, who are both voluntarily and involuntarily striving together for the accomplishment of certain more or less vividly conceived ideals of life.

It is important to note, as Appiah does, that even in this early piece, we can see how Du Bois is attempting to shift the notion of 'race' away from biological categories, and towards the idea of social and cultural community. As we will see later in the discussion of Toni Morrison, the ambivalence we find here in Du Bois' re-appropriation of 'race' continues to be reflected in the work of many African American writers.

In the activist Marcus Garvey's *Declaration of Rights of the Negro Peoples of the World* (1920), a notion of 'race' is still in play. And in Langston Hughes' writing in the Harlem Renaissance, too, there are references to 'racial culture'. In 'The Negro Artist and the Racial Mountain' (1926) Hughes refers to the threat of 'pour[ing] racial individuality into the mold of American standardization'. Writers of the same period, such as Zora Neale Hurston, were much more wary of the dangers of race-thinking. As Hurston wrote in her autobiography *Dust Tracks on a Road* (1942): 'Race consciousness . . . is a deadly explosive on the tongues of men.' For many writers, similarly, whilst 'race' might have some uses as a unifying metaphor, the legacy of discrimination it carries with it makes such usages deeply problematic.

In Europe, as the Nigerian writer Chinua Achebe (1975) shows similarly, nineteenth-century race-thinking continues to reassert itself in various different forms in a wide range of subsequent writing. In his famous essay on Joseph Conrad's 1899 novella *Heart of Darkness*, Achebe takes a strong line on this, questioning the privileged position such texts continue to enjoy in the curricula of universities and colleges throughout the anglophone world.

Taking Achebe's example, if we read Conrad's text directly against nineteenth-century racial theory, it is possible to see that the caricatures of 'blackness' and 'African-ness' it offers are not, in fact, presented explicitly in terms of 'racial' difference. Certainly, 'blackness' is associated in *Heart of Darkness* with primitive-ness and animality. But at the same time (as critics have frequently argued), what really disturbs Conrad's narrator, Marlowe, is not the fundamental 'alien-ness' of the Congo, but rather the opposite: the absence of a secure distinction between his own white, supposedly civilised identity and the apparent 'darkness' of Africa. His journey is precisely towards their meeting point. So one could argue that, in setting out to explore the colonial encounter, what Conrad's text does is to problematise the concept of essential 'racial difference' as it exists in the nineteenth-century tradition of Gobineau and others. In this sense, we can see *Heart of Darkness* very much as a text of its time, in which the ideological foundations of European imperialism are beginning at least to shift, if not to crumble.

In the early twentieth century there is a whole range of texts which (at least) problematise nineteenth-century understandings of 'racial' difference. If we look at the way a slightly later text like Joyce's *Ulysses* (1922) deploys the language of 'race', for example, it is possible to see how far the term has blurred. In Joyce's representation of the Irish, the term 'race' is used repeatedly. But already it is possible to see here how the word has come to be used in a more metaphoric way than fifty years previously, so that the terms 'race' and 'nation' are deployed almost interchangeably, and are cut across in complex ways by issues of culture, history and religion.

Race in the post-war period

Particularly in the second half of the twentieth century, of course, there is an enormous amount of postcolonial writing in which the reappraisal of racist and imperialist ideology is a central concern. Achebe's classic 1958 novel *Things Fall Apart*, for example, can be read in one sense as a direct reply to *Heart of Darkness*, which sets out to critique many of its Euro-centric assumptions from a West African perspective. Later still, in Buchi Emecheta's work, we see a gendered reworking of the same theme.

Her novel *The Rape of Shavi* (1983), published twenty-five years after Achebe's text, turns the colonial encounter into a kind of mythology. Emecheta focuses on a traditional community, and a large proportion of her text is given over to exploring its cultural and economic relationships. As in *Things Fall Apart*, this equilibrium is broken by the arrival of the white man. As in Achebe's text, too, she leaves the identities of the invaders comparatively undefined. In this sense both texts work self-consciously to reverse the chiaroscuro of *Heart of Darkness*, in which white is always highlighted and black continually obscured. In a deliberate reversal of colonial race-thinking, it is the white invaders in Emecheta's novel, and particularly the Dane Ronje, who soon begin to display Gobineau's 'animal propensities' and weak 'moral manifestations', whilst for most of the novel, the ethical and intellectual fabric of Shavi remains resilient. In its conclusion, however, Emecheta's novel goes further than *Things Fall Apart* in terms of its portrayal of the demise of the traditional community. Most importantly, the destruction of Shavi through the ravages of disease, war and economic exploitation establishes an explicit connection between imperialist assumptions and patriarchal masculinity. It is the meeting of these two elements in the characters of Ronje, Mendoza and (importantly) in the African prince Asogba that precipitates Shavi's ruin. Buchi Emecheta's work will be discussed in more detail in chapter 12.

Throughout the post-war period there has been a succession of attempts by writers from all parts of the international community to interrogate the mythology of 'race'. Such writing complements the international efforts of scientists and sociologists working in their own spheres to refute the terms of nineteenth-century 'racial science'. Tzvetan Todorov (1986) of the Paris Centre National de la Recherche Scientifique summarises this intellectual consensus in clear and useful terms:

> There are a great number of physical differences among human groups, but these differences cannot be superimposed; we obtain completely divergent subdivisions of the human species according to whether we base our description of the 'races' on an analysis of their epiderms or their blood types, their genetic heritages or their bone structures. For contemporary biology, the concept of 'race' is therefore useless. This fact has no influence, however, on racist behaviour: to justify their contempt or aggressiveness, racists invoke not scientific analyses but the most superficial and striking of physical characteristics (which, unlike 'races,' do exist) – namely, differences in skin colour, pilosity [hair], and body structure.
>
> (p. 371)

From 1950 onwards the position of the United Nations is that, in sociological terms, the species *Homo sapiens* is divisible into groups and populations in various kinds of different ways, but that 'race' is not one of these. Indeed, UNESCO's first *Statement on Race* (1950) (Montagu, 1972) is the first of a series of authoritative refutations of nineteenth- and twentieth-century 'racial theory'. Here, the international community under the auspices of the UN explicitly rules out the possibility that any notion of differential intelligence or differences of culture, temperament or character could be ascribed to 'racial' biological difference. In subsequent decades, the international experts it brings together have consistently and unanimously concluded that the term 'race' can be regarded as having no scientific or intellectual value.

In 1967, it is worth noting, UNESCO's further developed *Statement on Race and Racial Prejudice* (Montagu, 1972) goes on to address the question of resistance movements around the world which have deployed the language of 'race' as part of their struggles against persecution or for national self-determination. Here, Black Nationalism is obviously one of the targets. According to the revised *Statement* in a very stark way, these movements, likewise, are purely 'the product of a political struggle and have no scientific foundation'.

In academic terms, this wholesale rejection of 'race' obviously raises the question of how to speak about cultural difference in a non-racist way. One answer to this question lies in the emergence of the notion of 'ethnicity'. In fact, it was at the same time in the late 1960s when the conceptual distinction between 'biological' sex and 'culturally constructed' gender was establishing itself in contemporary thought, that the term 'ethnicity' began to emerge as a cultural counterpoint to the biologism of 'race'. In place of 'race', 'ethnicity' offered a much less problematic way of describing the sense of cultural, religious and historical distinctiveness experienced by particular peoples and groups.

If Robert Stoller's *Sex and Gender* (1968) signalled the establishment of 'gender' as a key term in the academic lexicon, Max Weber's study *Economy and Society*, which emerged in English in the same year, heralded the institutional arrival of 'ethnicity'. In this text, which was in fact first published in German in 1922, the term 'ethnic' is borrowed from the Greek *ethnos* to designate 'those human groups that entertain a subjective belief in their common descent because of similarities of physical type or of customs or both, or because of memories of colonisation and migration' (p. 389). This focus on *historically produced* perceptions of kinship and community has been crucial in subsequent thinking and writing which seeks to think about the relations between groups and peoples without recourse to problematic notions of 'racial' difference.

For all this, however, the paradox with which I began this chapter remains. By the late twentieth century, there was a virtually unchallenged consensus in academic circles that 'race' is redundant as a means of social and biological categorisation. A huge amount of work has been done, exploring the complexity of ethnic and national identities. Benedict Anderson's (1983) and Homi Bhabha's (1990, 1994) work in this area has been particularly influential in the humanities. At the very same time, though, it is clear that in the public sphere more generally, race-thinking simply fails to go away. Despite the massive ideological adjustment which followed the Nazi Holocaust, when the destructive effects of 'racial theory' were first fully and internationally acknowledged, and the multiple challenges to race-thinking precipitated by de-colonisation, an idea of 'race' seems to have remained deeply embedded in language and culture.

Particularly in the United States, this paradox has not escaped the attention of commentators. Indeed in the 1990s, the extraordinary waves of reaction to the cases of Rodney King, whose severe beating by white police officers was caught on video and broadcast on national television, and of O. J. Simpson, a black football star who underwent a show trial following the murder of his white ex-wife and her lover, revealed the starkly 'racialised' divisions of American popular consciousness. According to some contemporary sociologists, such as Howard Winant (1998), we need to recognise that notions of race have become so historically embedded in Western culture that they cannot now be rooted out, however unstable and nonsensical such categories might ultimately be: 'All the evidence suggests that once created and institutionalised, once having evolved over many centuries, racial difference is a permanent, though flexible, attribute of human society' (p. 108). Provided that racial identities are recognised as *cultural* constructs that are the products of *history* and not of unchanging biology or human nature, Winant argues, they are categories which we need to work with, and not against.

Many contemporary writers, as we will see, have found themselves thinking along similar lines. At the beginning of her career as a writer, indeed, Toni Morrison was amongst those who have sought to work positively with notions of race. In the afterword to her first novel, *The Bluest Eye* (1970), for example, Morrison refers to the book's project in self-consciously raced language. In the much later essay 'Home' (1997) she describes herself again as 'an already- and always-raced writer' (p. 4). Here and elsewhere, there is an ambivalence towards the sedimented culture of racial identities, which carry with them both the lure of essential identity and the legacy of oppression: 'How to be both free and situated; how to convert a racist house into a race-specific yet non-racist home. How to enunciate race while depriving it of its lethal cling?' (p. 5).

On both sides of the Atlantic, of course, manifestations of a much less ambivalent, white-supremacist racism are also very much in evidence. In the British context, certainly, we need to think in terms of a continuum of racism, ranging from the unofficial 'canteen culture' of police forces in which racist assumptions have flourished under the surface, apparently against the grain of official policy, to areas where racist ideas are more explicitly acknowledged, for example in the British National Party. Like Oswald Mosley's earlier British Union of Fascists, the BNP's policies of segregation and forcible 'repatriation' of non-white Britons are still based explicitly on the ideas of national and blood 'purity' or 'health', developed in nineteenth-century racial theory. Notably, here, the major anxiety is to circumscribe whiteness in racial terms, in order to construct a raced, exclusionary model of British national identity. Towards the so-called 'white race' we see the same threat posed as in Gobineau's work. That is, progressive 'defeat' through biological degeneration:

> Today there is a threat to our national survival no less in gravity than those confronting us in the past when great foreign armies faced us across the channel. We must pay what it costs to deal with that threat for the alternative is national extinction.
>
> *British National Party Manifesto*, 1997

In recent years, events such as the murder of the London teenager Stephen Lawrence have forced official acknowledgement of the extent to which racism is not limited to such far-right groups, but has become institutionalised within the police force and other core public services. As the Metropolitan Police Commissioner Paul Condon made clear to the Lawrence Inquiry in 1998:

> racism in the police is much more than "bad apples". Racism, as you have pointed out, can occur through a lack of care and lack of understanding. The debate about defining this evil, promoted by the Inquiry, is cathartic in leading us to recognise that it can occur almost unknowingly, as a matter of neglect, in an institution. I acknowledge the danger of institutionalisation of racism.
>
> (Macpherson et al., 1999: para 6.25)

As the British sociologist Paul Gilroy (2000) has argued, then, to demonstrate the absurdity of 'race' within academia is not in itself enough. For Gilroy, there may indeed be 'no such thing' as race in real scientific and intellectual terms. But a very real job still remains in terms of coping with the destructive and dangerous effects of *racism* as it continues to exist within culture. Historically, the myth of 'race' has been complicit in a whole range of atrocities, ranging from American slavery through Asian and African colonisation to the Nazi Holocaust. It is for this reason that figures like Gilroy argue that race-thinking must at all costs be confronted and overcome, even in those contexts (such as the American Civil Rights movement) where it may seem to have positive and affirmatory effects. Clearly, writers have an important role to play in this task.

In the British context, one of the focuses of the second part of this book is to explore how some of the most interesting contemporary writers, including Hanif Kureishi and Buchi Emecheta, respond to this continuing spectre of 'race' in their work, and how each of them moves towards more complex and adequate representations of cultural difference. As writers like Salman

Rushdie and Caryl Phillips have shown, the idea of 'Britishness' itself is so saturated with imperialist histories as to be virtually inextricable from them. The changed conditions of postcoloniality have necessitated a difficult, and often reluctant rethinking of the political, economic, legal and adminis-trative structures that were the products of colonialism. As Hanif Kureishi suggests, the cultural diversity of modern society – in every sense – means that new ways of thinking are required about both national and personal identity. For him, likewise, a new concept of Britishness is needed based on inclusivity and plurality rather than parochialism and nostalgia. His work can be read as part of that project of deconstruction and, perhaps, rebuilding.

In the case of formerly colonised societies, the dismantling of racist ideology is made complex for parallel reasons. Thinking about Kenya, for example, it is difficult to consider the national identity of such an ethnically and linguistically diverse region in isolation from the history of colonialism. On another level, in countries such as Nigeria, it is naïve to assume that the ending of direct colonial domination necessarily spells the instant demise of imperialist ideologies. As Buchi Emecheta and other writers have argued, postcolonial liberation involves far more than a revision of economic and governmental infrastructure. Not only institutions and frontiers, but a whole raft of imposed and ingrained assumptions, especially about white 'culture' and 'advancement', may remain as a corrosive residue of the imperial worldview, long after independence itself. In the context of both Britain and Nigeria, Emecheta's writing explores the assumed 'superiority' of certain models of education, certain modes of social organisation, of literary expression, of language and dialect, interrogating canonical understandings of history based on notions of the 'civilised' and the 'savage', the 'developed' and the 'developing'.

In the specific context of the United States, once again, Toni Morrison (1997) bears witness to the difficulty of carving away 'the accretions of deceit, blindness, ignorance, paralysis, and sheer malevolence embedded in raced language', and the creative work that is required to make way for 'other kinds of perception' (p. 7). As Morrison's *œuvre* develops through texts like *Beloved* (1987), we can trace a progressive commitment to the ideal of a race-free society, however difficult or utopian such an ideal might seem. In relation to the later novel *Paradise* (1997) particularly, Morrison describes her writing explicitly as an attempt to engage 'the active complicity of a reader willing to step outside established boundaries of the racial imaginary'. As we have already seen, what this implies is not only a move against discrimination, but also a move away from the security of racially defined identity as it is entrenched in African American-ness. As she says: 'I want to imagine not the threat of freedom, or its tentative panting fragility, but the concrete thrill of borderlessness' (pp. 8–9).

On a further level of complexity, as writing like Morrison's and Emecheta's shows, it is never easy to divorce questions of race from those of gender and sexuality. As Young (1995) suggests, from the very beginnings of the Western obsession with 'race' it is impossible to fully separate issues of discrimination from issues of desire. And as we saw in chapter 3, bodies too have had to be recovered from the racial imaginary. In the work of the different writers who are explored in Part II of this book, the racing of the flesh and the relations between racism and desire are explored and contested in a range of different ways. In Salman Rushdie's and Angela Carter's texts, magic realist techniques are often deployed to explore the intimate relation between sexual desire and fantasies of 'barbarousness'. A text like Alice Walker's *Meridian* (1976), on the other hand, works in a very different way. Here, a style much closer to social realism is deployed to examine the ways in which 'race' thinking is often a function of anxieties around social and sexual adequacy. In the work of Hanif Kureishi, who will be discussed in chapter 11, on the other hand, sexuality seems to be framed quite differently again, as a means of escape from oppressive class and race divisions.

What needs to be stressed finally is that, in the work of all of these writers, the refusal of 'race' marks the beginning, not the end point, of fiction writing. For all our attempts to frame contemporary texts in terms of the changing ideological terrain of the post-war period, it should be remembered that the contemporary novel has become interesting and significant again, in a sense precisely because of its resistance to ideologisation. As we will see in the chapters that follow, the effect of contemporary fictions is not to schematise and police social identities, but to resist and problematise such schematisations. Disallowing the past from becoming a closed book, they open up our cultural inheritance to a plurality of understandings, raising new questions of historical responsibility. Rewriting our sexed and raced flesh, they offer a multifarious exploration of bodies, traumas and pleasures. If we approach contemporary fiction looking for a set of new orthodoxies, therefore, we are likely to be disappointed.

The texts which are examined in Part II of this book are part of the creative momentum that has taken the English language novel in this period and revitalised it as a global form. Certainly, they are by no means notable for the ways in which they define comfortable notions of cultural identity, as traditionally 'The English Novel' and 'The American Novel' were held to do. The *œuvre* of each of the writers I discuss demonstrates in different ways the complexity of the cultural shifts which have shaped the terrain of the past half century. Thinking back to the 'death of the novel' thesis of the post-war decades, it seems clear now that the parochial, 'national' novel that appeared to be gasping its last in the 1960s was unlikely to be able to make an adequate response to these changed and changing demands. In the face of the transitions and challenges of the contemporary period, we might say that it has been necessary for the novel, too, to divide and evolve.

Part II

Readings

5 Unravelling time in Ian McEwan's fiction

In chapter 2, we saw some of the ways in which contemporary writing engages with new thinking about time in the twentieth century and after. This chapter examines the work of Ian McEwan, and its response to this challenge. Most directly, his quasi-feminist oratorio *Or Shall We Die?* (1983), written at the height of the Cold War, seeks to build connections between the struggle against nuclear weapons in Britain and the insights of radical science in the form of Quantum Theory. Conventional modernistic science is aligned with masculinism and war, whilst the supposedly more ambivalent and holistic concerns of Quantum Theory signal the dawn of a different kind of 'womanly times'. The overtly political approach of this text is just one example out of a whole range of ways in which McEwan's writing works to destabilise the public conventions of time, history, memory and desire. More often, his work takes an intensely personal focus, on private, claustrophobic spaces in which the processes of psychological discovery can be studied in microcosm.

Particularly in the early years, McEwan's novels and short stories were often controversial. But there is an outstanding precision and freshness to McEwan's writing which enables apparently sordid and macabre subject matter to be turned into narratives that, at their best, are intensely affecting and disturbing. His later work certainly does deal with public and political issues, ranging from childcare to German unification. Here equally, however, it is by focusing narrative attention not on the general but on the particular, on the private psyche of individuals, the problems and disturbances of their thinking and feeling, that broader insights are captured.

For McEwan the actual process of writing is not a straightforward progress leading unproblematically from author's intention to finished product. Rather, it is experienced as a tension between his necessary moral, political and aesthetic projections as a writer and the subversive, independent life of the subject matter itself. Talking to John Haffenden (1985) about the development of what was to become *The Child in Time* (1987), for example, McEwan described an almost organic development: 'I can already feel that something is emerging, and it is not quite what I intended. So I hope that moral concerns will be balanced, or even undermined, by the fact that I still don't have complete control' (p. 174). Similarly, in writing his previous novel *The Comfort of Strangers* (1981) the idea of framing a work too system-atically around preconceived arguments and conclusions is artificial. For McEwan this over-controlled approach is incompatible with the intricate and complex dynamics of the novel form.

> These things are not entirely within one's control, and I don't think they should be. I am aware of the danger that in trying to write more politically, in the broadest sense . . . I could take up moral positions that might pre-empt or exclude that rather mysterious and unreflective element that is so important in fiction.
>
> (p. 173)

The Cement Garden

It is not only in the practical procedures of his writing, however, that McEwan's work disrupts the idea of narrative as something whose job it is to illustrate the controllability and knowability of events in time. His first novel, *The Cement Garden* (1978), for example, whose main theme is the metamorphosis of adolescent consciousness and sexuality, is more concerned with the stagnation than the progress of social time. The novel revolves, in the heat of a long dry summer, around a group of children who try to deny the death of their mother by encasing her body in cement in the cellar of their home. Instead of surrendering to the disintegration of their nuclear family unit the children attempt to suspend it. Gradually they assume the roles of mother, father and, in the case of the younger brother, babyhood.

At the climax of the novel the main character, Jack, and his older sister, Julie, complete this gesture of recuperation by consummating their relationship beside the cot of their (now) baby brother. The sense of time disrupted is powerful. 'Except for the times I go down into the cellar I feel like I'm asleep,' Jack says. 'Whole weeks go by without me noticing, and if you asked me what happened three days ago I wouldn't be able to tell you' (p. 123). They think about the creeping demolition of their street, and wonder what would happen when it reached their house. The destruction of the urban fabric around them accentuates the sense of their sexual and temporal dissidence. Appropriately, their lives in this period without time or convention will remain without record.

> 'Someone would come poking around,' I said, 'and all they would find would be a few broken bricks in the long grass.' Julie closed her eyes and

crossed her legs over my thigh. Part of my arm was against her breast and beneath it I could feel the thud of her heart.

(pp. 123–4)

McEwan's text is characteristically interwoven with a diversity of time-scales. The narrator's consciousness subtly modulates between memory, daydream and conventional narration. Jack is frequently paralysed: 'When a fly walked across my face I was determined not to move. I could not bear to remain on the bed, and yet any activity I thought of disgusted me in advance' (p. 68). This is skilfully counterpointed by the unwelcome intrusion of the elder sister's boyfriend, Derek, against whom Jack develops an intense jealousy. Like the appearance of the uniformed officer on the tropical island in William Golding's *Lord of the Flies* (1954), the blue revolving light Derek finally calls up from the outside world signals the breaking of the bubble, and the restoration of social time, with the arrival of the police.

More clearly than in Golding's novel, never do the experiences of the children in *The Cement Garden* really feel like freedom, because of our constant awareness as readers of the pre-set roles and narratives against which the characters are always pulling and chafing. Like the weeds which struggle in the back garden against the repressive layer of cement laid down by their father before his death, there is a continual sense of the limits within which the children are free to move. With McEwan's intriguing opening sentence – 'I did not kill my father, but I sometimes felt I had helped him on his way' – the reader is alerted to the possibility of some Oedipal pre-ordination in the events to come. Jack's sexual consummation with his sister/mother Julie becomes, in this light, not a bizarre perversion of events but a confirmation of what we have long suspected. Around the symbol of the cement garden, with its obsessively controlled rockery over-run by weeds, therefore, the book on one level narrates the rank destruction of bourgeois mores, and with that the children's attempts to abdicate a conventional social script. On an equally persuasive level, though, *The Cement Garden* is also the opposite of that: a study in constriction and the power of the prescribed.

If *The Cement Garden* makes explicit use of the notion of the Oedipal complex, the influence of mid-twentieth-century psychoanalytic thinking around the relationships between times and events is also evident in McEwan's later and more ambitious novels, *The Child in Time* (1987), *The Innocent* (1990) and *Black Dogs* (1992). In the background of this later work, the thinking of Sigmund Freud seems to be less of a shaping influence than that of Carl Jung, particularly in relation to synchronicity. What Jung proposes through the idea of synchronicity is quite a radical alternative to the conventional understanding of time. In conventional science – and conventional wisdom – time is understood to carry on in stable and predictable ways, and every event in the world is believed to be linked to other events by potentially identifiable processes of cause and effect. For Jung, however, there are many events and phenomena which simply cannot be explained through this universal belief in time and causality.

The occurrences Jung examines are precisely those relegated to the margins of science: rogue data, 'mystic' phenomena, premonitions, visions and meaningful coincidences in time. By studying what is dismissed by normal scientific procedures, he tries to show that, whilst it is true that many events do indeed seem to be governed by conventional causal relationships, there are nevertheless other areas in which this is not the case. What the ideologies of conventional science are desperate to show is the objectivity of time, its independence from human understanding. What Jung tries to show, by contrast, is the inter-relation between time and the psyche, the co-extensiveness of time and the creation of meaning. In terms of the processes of writing fiction, such ideas suggest far-reaching implications. McEwan's novel *The Child in Time*, in particular, needs to be understood partly as an attempt to explore some of these.

The Child in Time

Having said that, *The Child in Time* is by no means a dryly theoretical exposition, but is in fact a far more complexly imaginative and emotional story than any of McEwan's previous work. The novel's central event – the abduction of the main character Stephen's young daughter from a supermarket – forms a very human and immediate centre point around which many strands of time, memory, desire and experience are woven. After the trauma of his loss, Stephen is repeatedly caught between the apparent rigidity of time and its inseparability from belief and perception:

> Later, in the sorry months and years, Stephen was to make efforts to re-enter this moment, to burrow his way back through the folds between events, crawl between the covers, and reverse his decision. But time – not necessarily as it is, for who knows that, but as thought has constituted it – monomaniacally forbids second chances. There is no absolute time, his friend Thelma had told him on occasions, no independent entity. Only our particular and weak understanding.
>
> (p. 14)

In the oratorio *Or Shall We Die?* (1983), as we have seen, McEwan draws on a different kind of challenge to conventional scientific wisdom, Quantum

Theory. In contrast to the assumptions of Newtonian science, what Quantum Theorists such as Werner Heisenberg and Niels Bohr have shown is the inadequacy of conventional understandings of time, being and causality to explain the world at its fundamental level. Pioneering new concepts such as complementarity and quantum uncertainty, Quantum Theorists have forced a radical change of perception in a range of scientific areas. In particular, the notion of scientific objectivity is fundamentally questioned. Instead of standing objectively apart from his subject, for the Quantum Theorist 'the observer cannot exclude himself and faces the limits of what can be known' (Haffenden, 1985, p. 182). These insights become a significant element in *The Child in Time*, most explicitly through the figure of Stephen's friend Thelma, who is herself a theoretical physicist.

Part of the particular interest of this novel amongst McEwan's work is that it is able to introduce highly abstract ideas like 'complementarity' and 'relative time', as well as political themes such as childcare policy and the workings of government sub-committees, whilst managing to retain a compelling focus on the human experiences of Stephen and his closest family. The way this novel frames the internal struggles of its main character, in coming to terms with his own personal catastrophe, is within a larger debate between the repressive time regime enforced by the establishment and its institutions, and the more fractured and unstable time frames suggested by Quantum Theory, by thinkers such as Jung, and above all by the disjunctions of personal experience.

In his role as a member of the official committee on childcare, some of the most poignant moments of Stephen's psychological ordeal are set up by overlaying his vivid memories of his daughter, and the panic and pain of her loss, on to the arid linearity of the committee's long sessions, during which he daydreams and wanders. The disruption of conventional time flow which the novel continually enacts by mixing time-frames in this way, however, is radically intensified at certain moments in the narrative, for example when Stephen is involved in a near-death experience in a lorry crash. What emerges strongly in McEwan's handling of this scene is not just the changing speed of time but also its changing quality. Here, for example, we meet Stephen as his hire car, at forty-five miles per hour, is on the point of ploughing into the lorry's wreckage:

> Now, in this slowing of time, there was a sense of a fresh beginning. He had entered a much later period in which all the terms and conditions had changed. So these were the new rules, and he experienced something like awe, as though he were walking alone into a great city on a newly discovered planet.

(p. 94)

Afterwards too, when Stephen has miraculously managed to steer himself clear, there is a stress not only on the relativity of time but also on the imbrication of time with meaning and perception.

> He wanted applause, he wanted a passenger in the front seat turning to him now with shining eyes . . . The whole experience had lasted no longer than five seconds. Julie would have appreciated what had happened to time, how duration shaped itself around the intensity of the event. They would be talking about it now, thrilled to be alive, curious to understand . . .
>
> (p. 95)

Continually there is an attempt to dramatise the possibility of a time divorced from the bounds of banal predictability.

In the treatment of childhood and childcare, as well, the conventional novelistic idea of lived time as a passage from innocence to experience, from hope to disillusionment or from potential to achievement is continually problematised. The government's committee work and its corrupt shenanigans are on the one hand a reactionary attempt to master the future. The production of a future citizenry is to be shaped and directed through the education of the nation's children. Set against this, however, the pivotal political role played by Stephen's Conservative friend, Charles, is radically undermined by Charles' own dissident time consciousness. Whilst Stephen oscillates between obsession and catatonia, Charles ventures into a different universe of fantasy and nostalgia. Where Stephen seeks to conjure his lost child, Kate, from the strands of history and possibility, Charles too is engaged in prefabricating a childhood. Initially this manifests itself as a playful regression to pre-pubescent boyhood, but by the end of the novel Charles is depicted literally frozen in his childhood garden. Death lies down that wormhole of time.

In terms of its management of these various elements, the text of *The Child in Time* is structured not as a continuous narrative but as a series of carefully crafted vignettes, whose structural inter-relations increase in number and complexity the further the reader explores and re-reads. Amongst the clearest of these, perhaps, is the parallel between Stephen's safe delivery of the driver from the lorry wreckage in the wake of the crash, and his final reunion with his estranged wife, Julie, at the end, in which he delivers their new baby. Further narrative relationships around the idea of birth and new beginnings are also established in a scene outside a pub much earlier in the novel when Stephen witnesses or hallucinates his mother in a scene before his own birth as, unmarried in the 1940s, she contemplates his termination. At that moment McEwan ambitiously attempts to capture an experience of total severance from ordered time, and Stephen metamorphoses between man, unborn child and unfulfilled possibility, before finally awaking from unconsciousness in the marital bed:

> Perhaps he was crying as he backed away from the window, perhaps he was wailing like a baby waking in the night; to an observer he may have appeared silent and resigned. The air he moved through was dark and wet, he was light, made of nothing. He did not see himself walk back along the road. He fell back down, dropped helplessly through a void, was swept dumbly through invisible curves and rose above the trees, saw the horizon below him even as he was hurled through sinuous tunnels of undergrowth, dank, muscular sluices. His eyes grew large and round and lidless with desperate, protesting innocence, his knees rose under him and touched his chin . . . and for all the crying, calling sounds he thought were his own, he formed a single thought: he had nowhere to go, no moment that could embody him, he was not expected, no destination or time could be named; for while he moved forward violently, he was immobile, he was hurtling round a fixed point.
>
> (p. 60)

Talking to his fellow writer Martin Amis in 1987 soon after the publication of *The Child in Time*, McEwan cites William James' classic examination of ordinary people's diverse experiences of time in *The Varieties of Religious Experience* (1902) as a primary source for experimental elements in the novel, mixed in with more recent frameworks of understanding. 'I was keen to try and embody – since I was talking about children and [childhood] is something that occurs in time – as many of these subjective experiences of time [as possible] and yet place them within both a scientific and almost mystical frame' (McEwan, 1988). What emerges from this difficult undertaking is a collage of subtly mediated blocks of time and memory. Because of the fragmentariness of his understanding of childhood and time, it is not possible in the end for these to gel into the kind of fully coherent conclusion which seemed appropriate in the traditional novel. Arguably, *The Child in Time* does encourage the reader to expect some kind of holistic resolution of all the diverse strands of its narrative. But this is an expectation on which even the final moment of new birth is unlikely to be able to deliver.

If, traditionally, it has been the author's implicit responsibility to offer the promise of transcendent resolutions for narratives and lives, *The Child in Time* exemplifies the fact that for the contemporary writer this is very clearly a problem. In McEwan's earlier novel *The Comfort of Strangers* (1981), narrative closure was provided by a moment of horrifying violence, but in a sense one could argue that this was only possible and satisfactory because of the claustrophobia of the story, and the narrowness of the canvas on which its action is painted. With the increasing interest in time in his later novels, however, comes a more forceful questioning of the role played by memory and desire in the making of meaning out of the excess of modern experience. Moreover, in all of McEwan's work after *The Child in Time*, the whole idea or possibility of narrative (and psychic) resolution becomes a central question.

Black Dogs

In terms of psychological exploration, *Black Dogs* (1992) differs from the protagonist-centred *The Child in Time* in that its focus is divided around its narrator, Jeremy, and the relationship of his estranged parents-in-law, on whom a memoir is to be written. Making his narrator juggle with the different memories and versions of their story, therefore, McEwan is much more easily able to engineer his text as a negotiation between rival worldviews: logic and rationalism on one side; holism and faith on the other. In some of McEwan's earlier work as we have seen, there is a demand for some kind of newly open or even 'womanly' thinking to provide an alternative to the patriarchal, received regime of ideas, from childcare to national security. Here however we have a reformulated and more even-handed opposition of ideas. 'Rationalist and mystic, commissar and yogi, joiner and abstainer, scientist and intuitionist, Bernard and June are the extremities, the twin poles along whose slippery axis my own unbelief slithers and never comes to rest' (p. 19).

Through this opposition *Black Dogs* can be viewed in the context of a great deal of McEwan's *œuvre*, as a re-engagement with the tension between innocence and experience. In stories such as 'Homemade' and 'Butterflies' in *First Love, Last Rites* (1975), the treatment of childhood and innocence was disturbingly mixed with themes of incest and abuse. Through the later stories in the collection *In Between the Sheets* (1978) and the first novels, these concerns certainly remained, but with a focus increasingly altered to love, loss and anguish. By the time of *The Comfort of Strangers*, themes that had been established in *The Cement Garden*, of innocence, manipulation and initiation, were being translated into a more adult context. In the 1981 screenplay *The Imitation Game* (1981), likewise, the boundaries between knowledge and naïvety had become the arena in which the adult politics of sex and sexuality could be explored. McEwan's portrayal here of a young woman working on the boundaries of espionage, who is ultimately imprisoned because of the combination of her own illicit knowledge and her boyfriend's sexual naïvety, represents the clearest development of feminist thinking within McEwan's fiction. In the structure of the 1990 novel *The Innocent*, meanwhile, we can also see a development of this key analogy between espionage, sexual initiation and colonisation. Here the innocence/ experience opposition is inscribed in a more complex way, however, not only through the main character Leonard's transition from virginity to sexual experience, but beyond that through the sense of a more vastly historical tension between the finally impotent, quaint atmosphere of the old-school establishment and the chillier climate of the Cold War.

In McEwan's later work as much as his earliest stories, the method by which all of these ideas and conflicts are explored is not abstract analysis but the observation of lives and the intricate patterns of human interaction. Consistently, the primary thrust of his writing is its rootedness in attention to detail, rendering potentially unremarkable encounters both surprising and suspenseful. Because of the fragmentary character of McEwan's technique, further, he is frequently able to suggest patterns of significance between the different events of the novel in ways that go beyond what would be possible within the cause-and-effect dynamics of a more straightforward, linear narrative. Around the motif of the black dogs in particular, the accumulation of both menace and meaning in the novel is something that happens quite unexpectedly across a number of experiential and temporal levels.

As we have seen, one of the central themes of *Black Dogs* is Jeremy's attempts to construct a particular personal history, that of June and her turbulent relationship with Bernard. It is through the specific problems of a biography, therefore, that the vaster relationships between time, history and memory are placed in question. The characteristic McEwan move – to invest such concerns in personal experiences – can be seen in the course of Jeremy's interviews with the now elderly June in a hospice for the terminally ill. Here the concept of memory loss is introduced. Writing a biography or memoir precisely implies a task of making June produce her past 'organised' (p. 32), to create history where now there are only broken memories. In the course of this effort June quite often drifts into sleep, and it is the treatment of her awakenings that opens the novel's central agenda:

> June woke from a five-minute doze to find a balding man of severe expression sitting by her bed, notebook in hand. Where was she? Who was this person? What did he want? That widening, panicky surprise in her eyes communicated itself to me, constricting my responses so that I could not immediately find the reassuring words, and stumbled over them when I did. But already, before I had finished, she had the lines of causality restored to her, she had her story again, and she had remembered that her son-in-law had come to record it.
>
> (p. 49)

A fear is suggested here at the tendency of time and memory – and hence meaning itself – to slip out of our familiar grasp. Both they and we as readers recognise the social imperative: actively to organise experience into temporally and biographically contextualised meaning. The point, though, is that in the later stages of her illness this has become more difficult for June, something that cannot be regarded as 'given' but which requires conscious effort. The making of memory itself has become a problem. As the familiar figure of Jeremy first approaches she can only gape at him without recognition:

> She had been buried in a sleep that had itself been smothered in an illness. I thought I should leave her to collect herself, but it was too late now. In the few seconds that it took to approach slowly and set down my bag, she had to reconstruct her whole existence, who and where she was, how and why she came to be in this small white-walled room.
>
> (p. 33)

Accentuating this question mark around the nature of memory and biography, the props McEwan gives June for psychological defence are, cleverly, the paraphernalia of writing and scholarship: 'today she was taking longer to come to. A few books and several sheets of blank paper lay across the bed. She ordered them feebly, playing for time' (p. 33). The dialogue between past and present is an uncertain, fluctuating thing that must be secured by writing down.

The idea of 'playing for time' is strongly suggestive of certain strategies in contemporary fiction which parody and display the problems of biographical and historical writing. What this novel illustrates, however, is the fact that amnesia, the loss of time, is something far closer to fear than to play. In psychological and neuroscientific studies of memory it is easy to find illustrations of memory loss, associated with Alzheimer's disease, Korsakow's syndrome or accidental brain damage, which show amnesia as profoundly disabling. Inability to construct a stable past radically compromises our ability to form a meaningful present, and equally, to conceive of a liveable future.

For many contemporary writers, as we saw in chapter 2, the assumption of stable, absolute time has become an increasing problem. Part of this intellectual drift has been a linkage between the idea of personal memory loss and the crisis of historical representation associated with the contemporary period. According to the cultural theorist Andreas Huyssen in *Twilight Memories* (1995), for example, as we move forwards historically 'our gaze turns backwards ever more frequently in an attempt to take stock and to assess where we stand in the course of time. Simultaneously, however, there is a deepening sense of crisis often articulated in the reproach that our culture is terminally ill with amnesia' (p. 1). Moving as it does between different experiences of memory and historical narrative, *Black Dogs* can be read as an exploration through the medium of fiction of precisely these sorts of concerns.

A bewildering complex of disparate time-scales are suggested in the novel. All of them spiral in various ways around June's horrifying confrontation with a pair of enormous black dogs on a mountain path during her honeymoon in southern France. This incident is thus deeply enmeshed in multiple tissues of time. On a personal level, we have June's sense of a new beginning and the biological time-horizon of her recently discovered first pregnancy. The mountain landscape inscribes a powerful sense of geological age. And a vast sense of human time hangs over the area because it is a prehistoric burial site. On a historical level, this is also the newly liberated landscape of post-war France, with its sense of fresh, immediate possibilities. June's physical fight for survival is further framed in memory within a fundamental teleological debate. For Bernard, the future lies in the power of historical materialism to explain and to create social change through rational analysis. For June what matters ultimately is a more essential spiritual power, promising an ultimate salvation that is outside time and history.

McEwan's basic narrative framework of a memoir-within-a-memoir is thus set further within the complex time-scales of a narrative which, on a level beyond that again, also has its own multiple time-sites of telling and remembering. The older June's 'clinical' amnesia, then, is in a sense only the most literal disclosure of the personal and social memory crisis of which *Black Dogs* is an exploration. To put this differently, the presentation of this 'clinical' amnesia in the novel is intimately intertwined with the sense of a far wider argument about the difficulty of expressing our pasts in adequate and meaningful ways.

In the loss of a comfortable, confident knowledge of history, nevertheless, lies a very significant threat, the novel importantly suggests. The black dogs at its centre, with their cycle of attack and retreat, can be read as representing a number of things, particularly in relation to the defeat of Fascism and the fear of its recurrence. This specific anxiety can, in itself, be read as a reflection of concerns that are very contemporary to the early 1990s, in which the dis-establishment of the Soviet bloc and the re-unification of a resurgent Germany promised to change the power balance of Europe in profound, unpredictable, perhaps dangerous ways. In this context, above all, what the black dogs direct us towards is the threat of complacency and complicity – and through that the imperative of remembering.

It is through a build-up of small and discreet narrative moments, rather than some epically proportioned grand narrative, however, that this threat and this imperative are represented. As Jeremy and his father-in-law witness the oddly uneventful breaching of the Berlin Wall, for example, a group of kids who threaten to kick Bernard to death in an outburst of hatred and boredom are used as a linkage between the animal brutality we will later see in the dogs on the mountain path and the spectre of organised racism:

> Collectively they exuded a runtish viciousness, an extravagant air of underprivilege, with their acned pallor, shaved heads, and loose wet mouths . . . The kids had stopped short and were bunched up in a pack, breathing heavily, heads and tongues lolling in bemusement at this beanpole, this scarecrow in a coat who stood in their way. I saw that two of them had silver swastikas pinned to their lapels. Another had a swastika tattoo on his knuckle.
>
> (pp. 96–7)

These child Nazis do not appear spontaneously in McEwan's narrative, notably. Instead they are enticed into the foreground by the casual antagonism of 'a mixed bunch . . . what I saw in that first instant were two men in suits – business types or solicitors' (pp. 95–6) against a Turkish protester. Whilst McEwan offers no packaged moral here, his writing is clearly motivated by the anxieties of a period in which history-making is in the air, but also profound uncertainty. In chapter 1, we saw how many contemporary writers have confronted history as a paradoxical imperative – as something which refuses satisfactory representation, but which at the same time demands to be accounted for. *Black Dogs* seems to be caught in exactly this double-bind, as it confronts the processes of history-making. Unable to offer a full or coherent historical account, the novel seems possessed nevertheless by a sense of historical responsibility, that is, by the concern that historical lessons have been learned.

In a parallel instance, as Jeremy and his soon-to-be-lover Jenny take a working visit to the concentration camp at Majdanek in Poland, the memorial notice we are shown omits any mention of the Jews exterminated there. Again, though, it is where we do not expect it, in the narrative gaze itself, that the danger of complicity is implied.

> We were strolling like tourists . . . We were on the other side, we walked here freely as the commandant once did, or his political master, poking into this or that, knowing the way out, in the full certainty of our next meal. Either you came here and despaired, or you put your hands deeper into your pockets and gripped your warm loose change . . .
>
> (p. 111)

The ease with which the camp's status as a historical monument can become subverted is shown clearly: in the blink of an eye it is no longer a refusal to forget, but a disturbingly undefined connivance in atrocity.

As, later, Jeremy unexpectedly finds himself hitting out at a man whose violence against a child he has just witnessed, there is a similar instance of recognition: 'Immediately I knew that the elation driving me had nothing to do with revenge and justice. Horrified with myself, I stepped back' (p. 131). The narrator himself is brought to heel by the words used to dogs: 'Ça suffit' (p. 131). As we can see here, the way McEwan's narrative uses the black dogs is not as a realist device but instead as a linking motif, a means of articulating meaningful relationships between moments not connected by simple cause and effect. The novel's central 'storyline', certainly, is simple enough to be said in a few sentences. June is attacked by two dogs. She finds that they may have been used during the war in the rape of an ostracised village girl. But the local authorities, for their own reasons, remain unwilling to have the dogs tracked and killed. This simplicity, arguably, is central. It is a parable about creeping complicity and vested interests, a little narrative around which a whole set of *causally unconnected* ideas about organised and disorganised hatred, violence and compliance can be knitted together.

If *The Cement Garden* is an exploration of the suspension of social and personal time, therefore, what *The Child in Time* seeks to examine, in quite a positive way, is the experience of their more radical disruption. *Black Dogs* can certainly be read as a continuation of these themes. Within the fragmentation and ephemerality of history and memory, however, it also attempts to show the dangers that must be inherent in losing the ability to remember. Thus it is disturbingly appropriate that the threat at the heart of the novel is represented through the conventions of neither biography nor chronology, but instead through the recurring, uncontrollable form of a dream:

> But it is the black dogs I return to most often . . . June told me that throughout her life she sometimes used to see them, really see them, on the retina in the giddy seconds before sleep. They are running down the path into the Gorge of the Vis, the bigger one trailing blood on the white stones. They are crossing the shadow line and going deeper where the sun never reaches, and the amiable drunken mayor will not be sending his men in pursuit for the dogs are crossing the river in the dead of night, and forcing a way up the other side to cross the Causse; and as sleep rolls in they are receding from her, black stains in the grey of the dawn, fading as they move into the foothills of the mountains from where they will return to haunt us, somewhere in Europe, in another time.

(pp. 173–4)

6 Memory blocks: the fictional autobiography of Maxine Hong Kingston

Set alongside the new-scientific and psychoanalytic ideas of Ian McEwan, the narrative strategies of Chinese American writer Maxine Hong Kingston push the exploration of time and memory in a different direction. Her approach is distinct from that of a writer like McEwan, first of all, in the particular sense that it emerges out of the creative tension between two extremely powerful cultural traditions. As for a number of noted British Asian and Asian American authors, Kingston deploys this 'inter-cultural' positioning extremely effectively in her work.

In terms of texture, Kingston's texts are fashioned out of a considerably more variegated linguistic and ideological fabric than is often the case in the *Bildungsroman* or novel of self-discovery. In terms of form, too, she uses a range of narrative styles and voices in a particularly intricate and fluid way. Specifically, her approach to the questions of time and collective memory is not to reinforce the divide between history and fiction, or between the real and the imagined. Rather, what we see in these texts is the patch-working of a new kind of narrative form out of the multifarious materials of biography and nostalgia, literature and rumour, history and mythology.

One of the mistakes made by some white Western readers of Kingston is to imagine her work to be representative of 'authentic Chinese tradition'. In fact, almost all of the borrowings of tales from the Cantonese tradition with which her texts are embroidered have been criticised in some degree by critics as inaccurate or distorted. From a different direction, her status as a serious (auto)biographer has been challenged by English and American biographical scholars who would like to classify her work as (mere) fiction by comparison with their allegedly more rigorous and serious trade. This two-pronged attack has not, however, prevented Maxine Hong Kingston from becoming the most anthologised living writer in the United States. In the American college curriculum *The Woman Warrior* (1976) has deservedly come to be regarded as a modern classic. For the wider reading publics of much of the Western world, moreover, it is fair to say that she has become one of the seminal voices of Chinese America. There is perhaps some postmodern irony in the idea that a writer so concerned with re-imagination and counter-memory should be adopted as the unofficial historian of a nation.

The Woman Warrior and *China Men* (1980) were originally conceived as one book. As her material began to develop and proliferate in the process of writing, Kingston ultimately had no choice but to find some principle of division. It is for this pragmatic reason that the two texts are divided as they are for publication, by means of a convenient gender divide. Thus the former text elucidates the stories of female relatives whilst the latter deals with those of the males. Despite this obvious split, both texts need to be considered fundamentally as feminist texts. As Kingston says quite simply, 'Growing up as I did as a kid, I don't see how I could not have been a feminist. In Chinese culture, people always talk about how girls are bad. Right away, it makes you radical like anything' (Kubota/Kingston, 1998, p. 3).

The Woman Warrior

In the 1975 feminist short story 'No Name Woman', which later became the opening of *The Woman Warrior*, time is already of central importance. As in McEwan's *Black Dogs*, it is memory and amnesia which provide the keys to the formation or annihilation of personal identity. For Kingston as much as for McEwan, moreover, the personal narratives she explores lead inevitably to a number of larger historical and political questions. Rather than revolving around the pasts and futures of Europe, of course, in Kingston's work these impinge centrally on the formation and constitution of the United States.

'No Name Woman' begins with an orgy of violence and revenge, against an aunt in China who had become pregnant whilst her husband was out on the road. In Kingston's account of her ancestral village, it is a place of gossip, but also a place of curious silence. Throughout the nine months of gestation, no comments are passed about unfaithfulness, and no questions are asked about rape or illicit lovers. Instead, at the end of them, the neighbours come after dark and in masks to smash the family possessions, ruin their crops and splash the walls of the family home with blood. During the night, the young woman delivers her baby in the pigsty. In the morning a pair of waterlogged and bloated bodies are found blocking up the family well.

On the surface, Kingston's narrative concerns adultery, morality and retribution. But it is crucially concerned too with the way these ideas are imbricated within the temporal horizon of the community. On one level, it is a cautionary tale, a warning from a mother to a girl at the biological milestone of her first menstruation. In time-honoured fashion, Maxine's mother recalls her aunt's story as a warning against straying from the straight-and-narrow. On another level, it is about the power of memory and forgetting as weapons of deterrence. The mother makes it clear that the ultimate punishment for such a family dishonour is neither humiliation nor even death but something even more disturbing: banishment from time itself. On the insistence of her father and his family the woman's name is never to be mentioned again, or her existence acknowledged. 'We say that your father has all brothers because it is as if she had never been born' (p. 11). No Name Aunt's existence is never to be admitted, and yet it is: in her sister-in-law's story, and again in her niece's written text. In this sense Kingston's narrative begins by outlining its pivotal opposition: between amnesia as a weapon of oppression, and re-memory as its means of resistance.

Amnesia and re-memory are not the only ways in which Kingston's text invokes the problem of time. Indeed it is important to consider the ways in which her writing works to construct a whole temporal economy for the ancestral village. By temporal economy I mean the entire complex of ways in which a culture articulates its life in relation to time: the ways in which it conceives of the unfolding of its possible futures; of the root-like branching narratives that articulate its history; of its cycles of regeneration and rebirth; of the values it carves deep against the eroding force of change. Certainly, No Name Aunt's fate needs to be read in these temporal terms. As a virtuous wife, first of all, her appointed role is to be one who waits. Pending the uncertain return of her husband and his brothers from the West, she is to be a fixed point, a co-ordinate of constancy. In this passive presence, secondly, as a young woman chosen as the carrier of the next generation, she is also supposed to stand as a living guarantee of the village's continuation. In these two senses No Name Aunt's adulterous pregnancy not only constitutes a disruption in the local, present moment. Nor is it simply an offence against tradition. Beyond such past and present concerns it is a threat to the stasis of the family and, through that, to the principle of the village's futurity.

In the circular equilibrium of the village, maternity's place and function is more tightly circumscribed than any other institution. *Timely* maternity is integral to its cycles of self-preservation. In this sense, what Kingston's story suggests is the violence with which this economy of timeliness is inscribed and enforced:

> The round moon cakes and round doorways, the round tables of graduated sizes that fit one roundness inside another, round windows and rice bowls – these talismans had lost their power to warn this family of the law: a family must be whole, faithfully keeping the descent line by having sons to feed the old and the dead, who in turn look after the family. The villagers came to show my aunt and her lover-in-hiding a

broken house. The villagers were speeding up the circling of events because she was too short-sighted to see that her infidelity had already harmed the village, that waves of consequences would return unpredictably, sometimes in disguise, as now, to hurt her. This roundness had to be made coin-sized so that she would see its circumference: punish her at the birth of her baby.

(pp. 19–20)

Stripping the woman of a name, denying her a place in time and memory, represents an attempt by the village to sustain its traditional, patriarchal economy. That is, to sustain a gendered division of labour in which the values of innovation, progression and the new are allocated to masculinity, whilst femininity becomes the receptacle of tradition, conservatism and perpetuation.

All of the stories in *The Woman Warrior*, from that of the legendary swordswoman Fa Mu Lan to the story of Kingston's mother, Brave Orchid, herself, converge upon the reconstruction of this gendered temporal economy. Frequently Brave Orchid's talk-story involves an equation of Chinese girls to slaves, or livestock to be sold off or killed at birth. If girls do not shoulder the burden of tradition, they are treated as consumables. Where they do not embody the ideal of domesticity, they become a symbol of waste. In this extraordinarily stark way, the thin line between daughterly obedience and the threat of erasure is constantly being re-sketched.

Clearly, *The Woman Warrior* partly concerns the narrator's apprehension of, and rebellion against this misogynistic scenario. At the same time, however, she is quick to recognise its repressive complement in the sexual standards of America, where feminine submissiveness is prized in different ways. 'Normal Chinese women's voices are strong and bossy. We American-Chinese girls had to whisper to make ourselves American-feminine' (p. 155). Kingston's highly crafted reworking of mythological and biographical sources in the text as a whole is underpinned by a desire to move through and beyond these limiting constructions. In her reappropriation of the Fa Mu Lan mythology, particularly, she can be seen as attempting to construct a new narrative of femininity that is neither 'traditionally' Chinese nor 'traditionally' American, combining the assertion of female strength and resourcefulness with the celebration of passion and maternity. By equating the battles of her reappropriated Fa Mu Lan with the author's own struggles of writing, moreover, she explicitly seeks to identify her own use of story-telling as the weaponry of a contemporary woman warrior:

The swordswoman and I are not so dissimilar. May my people understand the resemblance soon so that I can return to them. What we have in common are the words at our backs. The idioms for *revenge* are 'report a crime' and 'report to five families'. The reporting is the vengeance – not the beheading, not the gutting, but the words. And I have so many words – 'chink' words and 'gook' words too – that they do not fit on my skin.

(p. 53)

There certainly is a major argumentative thrust to both *The Woman Warrior* and *China Men*: the unacceptability of amnesia. But the solution to amnesia is not necessarily the monomania of received historical memory. By contrast to her father, who participates in the conspiracy of silence of which he is ultimately the victim, the narrator Maxine is intent on understanding her distinctively Chinese American heritage on many different levels. Although she has never even been there, the temporal economy of the ancestral village – its memories, traditions, mythologies and desires – is a constant pull on her imagination. The time of America, the tangible time of the school day, is intermixed and disturbed by the created time of her mother's tales, the undefined desire for 'back home', the collective past of a mythical China and a plethora of half-known literatures. In the 'White Tigers' section of *The Woman Warrior*, her narration is almost dreamlike, stepping out of American real-time through the looking-glass of mythology:

I heard high Javanese bells deepen in midring to Indian bells, Hindu Indian, American Indian . . . I am watching the centuries pass in moments because suddenly I understand time, which is spinning and fixed like the north star. And I understand how working and hoeing are dancing . . .

(pp. 31–2)

In a similar way, it is possible to see how the narrative parameters of Kingston's texts are redefined through her use of the Cantonese tradition that she refers to as 'talk-story'. Although she substantially modifies the aesthetic form of talk-story itself by amalgamating it with the canonically Western/Christian form of the (written) autobiography, important elements of Cantonese practice are retained. In this particular tradition of oral composition, special aesthetic importance is attached to the establishment of creative continuities between different times and places, between contemporary and ancient tales, and between family experiences and traditional myths. As a cultural practice talk-story is thus partially performance, partially commemoration, partially repetition, partially embroidery. In the mouth of an appropriately skilled practitioner all of these elements may be threaded together into a highly intricate process of storytelling. Clearly, as we have already seen, it would be wrong to say that Kingston's writing fits squarely into this aesthetic tradition. To a significant extent, her choice of creative medium renders her subject to the Western conventions in which writing is a fundamentally solitary and meditative activity, in contra-distinction to the social, improvisatory and interactive characteristics of the oral tradition. Reading her as an American writer, however, it is certainly possible to see the ways in which the use of key themes and characteristics from this Cantonese tradition aids her texts in their necessary extension of biographical and literary conventions.

Describing her childhood in Stockton, California, Kingston certainly does try to claim some kind of veracity or authenticity for her portrayal of Chinese literary tradition. 'I was constantly listening to [my parents] and my relatives talk-story. Their recollections of myths, fables and Chinese history turned out to be amazingly accurate. After the book was published, several people pointed out the presence of these stories in anthropology and art books' (Skenazy and Martin, 1998: p. 2). In fact, however, there is far more distortion, mis- and re-appropriation of Chinese sources in her work than this would seem to imply. As Sau-Ling Cynthia Wong (1992) has shown, looking at Kingston's treatment of her heroine Fa Mu Lan, for example, Kingston's texts not only play with various references from Cantonese and Mandarin works but also draw freely on other mythologies, radically changing their meaning in the process:

> The tutoring of the Woman Warrior is based on the well-known tale of Yue Fei, whose mother carved four characters (not entire passages) onto his back, exhorting him to be loyal to his country. Also, the spirit-marriage to the waiting childhood sweetheart, a wish-fulfilling inversion of the No Name Woman's fate, is utterly unlikely in ancient China, considering the lowly place of women. The traditional Fa Mu Lan is never described as having been pregnant and giving birth to a child while in male disguise ... The Fa Mu Lan of 'Mulan Shi' is a defender of the establishment, her spirit patriarchal as well as patriotic, a far cry from the peasant rebel in the vein of the heroes of *Outlaws of the Marsh*.
>
> (p. 253)

Notwithstanding some of her own suggestions, then, one of the most interesting and challenging aspects of Kingston's writing is the way she freely manipulates and appropriates elements from different historical and biograph-ical locations, from traditional Chinese and from American and European culture. Indeed, the self-consciously embroidered, multi-dimensional character of her texts is central to their wider project. Far from purporting to offer 'reliable' recollection, her texts are characteristically framed to exclude the possibility of coherent memory. As we have seen, two or more versions of events are often placed side by side, or interspersed throughout the work, creating a texture of provocative ambiguity. In the opening of *The Woman Warrior*, two mutually exclusive accounts are offered of No Name Aunt's story, one depicting systematic rape and the other illicit love. In *China Men* the narrator's father enters America *both* as a stowaway *and* as a legal immigrant detained on Angel Island. Ultimately in the course of the text, his journey to the United States is framed in as many as five different ways. In this way, clearly, Kingston actively forestalls the possibility of reading her texts as conventional (auto)biography or conventional historical narration. Personalities, memories, histories are never stable and single, always provisional constructions, each with its particular historical and political implications.

The realisation that concludes *The Woman Warrior* is that the narrator should have thought and listened more carefully. In the Western *Bildungsroman* novel, we have been conditioned as readers to expect that, as we follow the protagonists' progress towards maturity, we will ultimately come to a fuller understanding. If anything, Kingston's first novel suggests the opposite. As Maxine's mother says, 'Can't you take a joke? You can't even tell a joke from real life. You're not so smart. Can't even tell real from false' (p. 180). In a reversal of the conventional novel form, what we are left with at the end of the text is not fulfilment but disjuncture, and the awareness of more questions to be asked.

China Men

Throughout her texts Kingston constantly works to open up the temporal economy of the United States, forcing cross-infections and cross-fertilisations between the lived time of America and the remembered or imagined time of the ancestral land. Living in America, neither Maxine nor her mother can bear to participate in the erasure of No Name Aunt from the collective memory. But the attitude of her father is a very different one, and not only towards his female relatives. For Baba in *China Men*, to live in the West as an immigrant involves a severing of oneself from both history and memory. As the narrator says to him, 'there are no photographs of you in Chinese clothes nor against Chinese landscapes . . . Do you mean to give us a chance at being real Americans by forgetting the Chinese past?' (p. 18). Baba's strategy for resolving the problem of translation, between his sense of Cantonese-ness and his sense of Californian-ness, is to ravage his consciousness of all desires and memories which do not readily fit within the discourse of America. For him, in ways that the young Maxine doesn't fully under-

stand, the exactitude and abstractness of the American present become a
method of escape from the entangled roots of Chinese memory:

> On New Year's Eve, you phone the Time Lady and listen to her tell the
> minutes and seconds, then adjust all the clocks in the house so their
> hands reach midnight together. You must like listening to the Time
> Lady because she is a recording you don't have to talk to. Also she
> distinctly names the present moment, never slipping into the past or
> sliding into the future. You fix yourself in the present, but I want to hear
> the stories about the rest of your life, the Chinese stories. I want to know
> what makes you scream and curse, and what you're thinking when you
> say nothing . . . I'll tell you what I suppose from your silences and few
> words, and you can tell me that I'm mistaken. You'll just have to speak
> up with the real stories if I've got you wrong.
>
> (p. 18)

In the text, there is a fascinating tension between Baba and his American-
born daughter Maxine, for whom such a strategy of denial is insupportable.
Instead her narrative continually tries to insert questions into the enforced
silences surrounding the ancestral village, the detention centre, the plantation, the labour camp. Whilst Baba seeks to collude in the erasure of his own
past, Maxine's discourse becomes an attack on the conspiracy of amnesia
surrounding the origins of Chinese America.

Even as it makes this attempt, however, the flow of her own narrative is
constantly punctuated with its own pauses and silences, motivated by the
old fear of persecution. A century and a half of racist persecution, physical
and economic exploitation and hostile legislation cannot be overcome in a
single generation. The very act of repeating her father's name still carries
a potential threat inside it: 'I hesitate to tell it; I don't want him traced and
deported' (p. 31). Of course, on the other side of the coin, there is a bitter
irony in the official certification of Maxine's brother as a true American,
when he becomes valuable for use as an interrogator of Viet Cong prisoners
in the Vietnam War. By exploring these difficult moments Kingston seeks
not just to fill silences with stories but also to bear witness to the kinds of
personal and political contradictions and coercions which underlie the
institutionalised silence of Chinese Americans in the inherited culture of
the United States.

As a recoverer of collective memory, as a cultural revisionist, Kingston's
project is far too large and multi-levelled to be accommodated within the
received form of the biography, or indeed within the conventions of
academic historical writing. Thus the formal innovation of Kingston's work
is as integral to its concerns as her subject matter. The multi-dimensional,

palimpsest form of *The Woman Warrior* and *China Men* is necessary as a means for bringing together not only the admitted, the legal and historical bits and pieces of discourse that exist to outline the story of the Gold Mountain pioneers, but also the diversity of silenced voices that resist collection and representation. In a pivotal moment of *China Men*, as the narrator stands contemplating the sugar fields of Hawaii, she tries to make herself an oracle for the plethora of stories they conceal – never related, much less remembered, stories of all the men and women who died reclaiming that stretch of land from the wilderness:

> I have gone east, that is, west, as far as Hawaii, where I have stood alongside the highway at the edge of the sugarcane and listened for the voices of the great grandfathers . . . The winds blowing in the long leaves do not whisper words I hear. Yet the rows and fields, organized like conveyor belts, hide murdered and raped bodies; this is a dumping ground . . .
>
> I have heard the land sing. I have seen the bright blue streaks of spirits whisking through the air. I again search for my American ancestors by listening in the cane.
>
> (pp. 89–92)

The procedure of research and writing Kingston uses here can neither be classified easily as fiction, nor as biography nor as history in the conventionally academic sense of those words. But it nevertheless needs to be thought of as an integral part of the creative struggle against what Toni Morrison calls dis-memory, the process of collective forgetting. In this sense, her work concurs with a wider body of Chinese American writing, including that of the playwright Frank Chin, whose career she satirises in the 1989 novel *Tripmaster Monkey: His Fake Book*. By contrast to Kingston's writing (which he vehemently criticised for what he sees as her negative and counterproductive depictions of Chinese American men) Chin's work fits into a more traditionally heroic literary canon, in which both Chinese and Chinese American manhood are celebrated. His enormously influential collection *Aiiieeeee! An Anthology of Asian-American Writers* (1974) and its sequel, *The Big Aiiieeeee!* (1991), consciously exclude established women writers such as Kingston and Amy Tan in an effort to build a united front in Asian American literature, focusing not only on strong and positive portrayals of Asian masculinity, but also on an appeal to 'authentic' rather than 'distorted' representations of Chinese and other East Asian cultural traditions.

In reply, groups of writers and activists such as Asian Women United of California have sought to combat what they see as the potentially limiting critical perspective of writers like Chin, Shawn Wong and other influential figures in the literary establishment. AWU's own anthology *Making Waves: An Anthology of Writing by and about Asian American Women* (1989) seeks to put on record a much greater heterogeneity of experience amongst women of Asian and Pacific origin in the United States. As the most successful of all Asian American women writers, Kingston's own work is certainly not shy of championing women's experience, or of identifying misogyny where she finds it either in China or in the United States. Nor has she been unwilling to appropriate a variety of literary and cultural traditions in the service of her own distinctive attempt to recreate the complex imaginative fabric of Chinese America.

In the formal construction of *China Men*, particularly, we can see how she uses Chinese literary conventions to depart from the familiar linear narrative form that is the staple of Western historical, biographical and novel writing. In this text, six chapters relating the experiences of different male relatives coming to America are interspersed with a dozen shorter sub-texts, in the same way that in traditional Chinese literature, short mythological and allegorical *hsieh-tzu* are used to frame more sustained sections of continuous narrative. The most important effect of this patterning of form and discourse throughout Kingston's text is, I suggest, to disallow the reader's response from being reduced down to the basic narrative level of 'what happens'. Instead the subtle allegorical and thematic parallelisms between the different sub-texts invite the reader to take a more proactive role in the creation of larger meaning in the text. Instead of being a passive recipient of narrative entertainment or instruction, we are placed in a position of repeated reinterpretation and rethinking, as different layers of discourse are laid down each on top of the next. Baba, for example, is both heroic and misogynist, both astute and naïve, and his story is shifting and multi-faceted. What are the implications of 'The Ghost Mate' or of '*Li Sao*' for reinterpreting his history? Consistently, we are asked as readers to jump between different temporal domains – personal history, traditional myth, childhood fantasy – and to weave our own networks of meaning among them. Similarly, instead of being invited simply to sit to attention and have the gaps plugged in our knowledge of US history, the reader of Kingston's texts is continually alerted to each narrative's provisionality and constructedness. In 'The Father from China' as much as in 'The Laws' the reader is made aware that all histories are written partially, and for a purpose.

Certainly, Kingston does at times make use of the privileged discourse of chronology and, indeed, linear-historical narration. Equally, however, much of her material is very consciously extrapolated from stories and half-known dreams. This patchworking and imaginative technique is a highly deliberate aspect of her approach: 'it's part of the Chinese American culture, to make fictive lives. As a writer, I'm just part of that. These are real people in my books, and to depict them as accurately as I can, I tell what they make up about themselves' (Bonetti/Kingston, 1998, p. 38). Without question, Kingston's texts are fundamentally about history and memory. As for a large number of postmodernist writers, however, it is often in the faultlines of conventional historicising that her most important insights begin to be uncovered.

In *The Woman Warrior* we are continually confronted with the question of what it is, in terms of experience and in terms of memory, to be an American. That is, what it is to have an affirmatively American sense of selfhood. On every level, Kingston shows how self-divided the sense of identity can be, and at the same time how complexly it is embedded, even in the very language of self-narration:

> I could not understand 'I'. The Chinese I has seven strokes, intricacies. How could the American 'I' assuredly wearing a hat like the Chinese, have only three strokes, the middle so straight? Was it out of politeness that this writer left off strokes the way a Chinese has to write her own name small and crooked? No, it was not politeness; 'I' is a capital and 'you' is a lower-case.
>
> (p. 50)

The 'I' that the white American takes for granted is formed out of a whole history of cultural assumptions about the meaning of individuality and the meaning of belonging. Paradoxically, as the passage above begins to indicate, it is also an 'I' built out of a rejection of subservience, even a rejection of tradition: a libertarian 'I'. Despite this, as *China Men* shows, the unpalatable truth is that inhabiting the American 'I' is far from being simply a personal matter, an embracing of liberty, a denial of oppression or an assertion of one's self-determination. On the contrary, in this novel's central section, 'The Laws', Kingston uses the starkest chronological format to list the ways in which the United States has systematically manoeuvred to exclude those of Asian origin from possession of a sense of free American selfhood.

Ultimately, the question of who is and who is not acceptable as an American is determined through the regulation of citizenship and natural-isation. And both of these processes are centred upon questions of history and origins. When did you cut off your pigtail? What was your affiliation to the 1912 Chinese Republic? Where were you born? What are your memories of your ancestral village? As all of Kingston's texts show, the representations of both history and memory are fundamentally intractable and equivocal. One could argue that it is partly for this reason that – in a deeply problematic way – the ideas of 'race' or 'skin colour' become a discriminatory shortcut to the assumption of an acceptable or unacceptable personal history. Americans of white European extraction have seldom been assumed to be a threat to the futurity of American-ness. But for those classified as 'Asian', historically the default strategy has been to exclude. As Sau-Ling Cynthia Wong (1993) has argued:

> The Naturalisation Act of 1790 passed by Congress employed specifi-
> cally racial criteria limiting citizenship to 'free white persons.' After this
> Act was successfully challenged on behalf of blacks after the Civil War,
> 'Asian American Immigrants became the most significant "other" in
> terms of citizenship eligibility.' In the *Ozawa v. United States* case (1922)
> the Supreme Court ruled against a Japan-born applicant to natural-
> isation (who had spent most of his life in the United States), arguing
> that 'had these particular races been suggested, the language of the
> Act would have been so varied as to include them in its privileges.'
> To circumvent the question of color, the Court defined 'white' as
> 'Caucasian.' However, when an immigrant from India, Bhagat Singh
> Thinde, attempted to gain citizenship by arguing that he was Caucasian,
> the Supreme Court changed its definition again . . . appealing to the
> popular meaning of the term 'white' . . . We may say that Asian
> Americans are put in the niche of 'unassimilable alien': despite being
> voluntary immigrants like the Europeans (and unlike the enslaved
> blacks), they are alleged to be self-disqualified from full American
> membership by materialistic motives, questionable political allegiance,
> and, above all, outlandish, overripe, 'Oriental' cultures.
>
> (pp. 5–6)

Here, we can see clearly the slippage by which deeply problematic notions of 'race', 'colour', history and allegiance are allowed to merge into each other, in the building of an exclusionary concept of American-ness.

Whilst much of *China Men* is concerned with history, the subject of 'The Laws' is much more closely focused on legislation. This distinction is an important one. To look back through the pages of histories is to see a repeated reshaping of the past, as the ideological struggles of the present produce new historical constructions of previous peoples and events. Much of *China Men* engages with historical discourse in this sense, in that it aims, retrospectively, to revise the popular understanding of the American past. In 'The Laws', on the other hand, Kingston's text deploys a strategy close to Foucauldian genealogy, which I outlined in chapters 1 and 3. Tracing the progress of legislation, she opens a window on the way in which that discourse has functioned to shape a certain model of American citizenry

– how the population is constituted and regulated, how certain sets of values are to be laid down for enforcement by the courts, the penal system, the immigration service. In this way 'The Laws' shows the slippery way in which the law has worked to ensure that the normative American subject remains white.

From the end of the eighteenth century onwards, 'The Laws' suggests, a whole economy of coercions and prohibitions has been brought into play in the United States, to ensure that the American subject be made out of a particular kind of Christian, European family history, not out of memories of a village in Canton. Thus, in *China Men*, the juxtaposition of official records with the many imaginative and counter-historical accounts of her forebears has an important effect. That is, to force a conflict between two different kinds of accounts of the making of America and of American-ness. In this way, the multi-level structure of *China Men* clearly attempts to facilitate an understanding of the ways in which Chinese Americans themselves have struggled to frustrate the intention that America should exclude them.

Unquestionably, then, the strand of institutionalised racism and political exclusion which runs through much of the legal constitution of American-ness is part of what Kingston seeks to contest in *China Men*. As we have seen, however, her struggle against 'national amnesia' also necessitates an extension beyond the level of public record. Beyond that, she is interested in the ways in which the recorded documentation of history shades into the less easily recoverable domains of memory, desire and personal experience. As contemporary scholars have sought to demonstrate, from the mid-nineteenth century onwards, not a mere handful but tens of thousands of Chinese Americans were employed in the mining and railway industries, as well as in other forms of construction and plantation building. Yet dispro-portionately few documentary records remain to stake their claims. The chapter which describes the building of the trans-continental railway, 'The Grandfather of the Sierra Nevada Mountains', provides one of several instances in which Kingston attempts to dramatise the meaning of this amnesia.

Here, she offers what is in one sense a classic 'nation-building' narrative. The text follows Grandfather Ah Goong's heroic labours, first with a sledgehammer and later with the aid of explosives, to burrow through the granite peaks of east California, and to lay the steel rails that will connect America together. In a decidedly un-Herculean way, he is routinely exploited. But Kingston's narrative is not only about nineteenth-century Chinese men's struggles to survive the trials of America, a foreign country. It is also about their struggles to build American-ness in their own image, their refusal to be consumed and to disappear:

'The Greatest Feat of the Nineteenth Century,' they said. 'The Greatest Feat in the History of Mankind,' they said. 'Only Americans could have done it,' they said, which is true. Even if Ah Goong had not spent half his gold on Citizenship Papers, he was an American for having built the railroad. A white demon in top hat tapped on the gold spike, and pulled it back out. Then one China Man held the real spike, the steel one, and another hammered it in.

While the demons posed for photographs, the China Men dispersed. It was dangerous to stay. The Driving Out had begun. Ah Goong does not appear in railroad photographs (p. 144) . . .

Good at hiding, disappearing – decades unaccounted for – he was not working in a mine when forty thousand chinamen were driven out of mining. He was not killed or kidnapped in the Los Angeles Massacre, though he gave money towards ransoming those whose toes and fingers, a digit per week, and ears grotesquely rotting or pickled, and scalped queues, were displayed in Chinatowns . . . He was lucky not to be in Colorado when the Denver demons burned all chinamen homes and businesses, nor in Rock Springs, Wyoming, when the miner demons killed twenty-eight or fifty chinamen . . . The count of the dead was inexact because bodies were mutilated and pieces scattered all over the Wyoming Territory. No white miners were indicted, but the government paid $150,000 in reparations to victims' families. There were many family men, then. There were settlers – abiding China Men. And China Women.

(p. 147)

If Chinese Americans are often subjugated to a position of marginality within the historical consciousness of the United States, Kingston seeks to account for this process of othering. Indeed, she explicitly describes *The Woman Warrior* and *China Men* as

a response to the legislation and racism that says we of Chinese origin do not belong here in America . . . When I say I am a native American with all the rights of an American, I am saying 'No, we're not outsiders, we belong here, this is our country, this is our history, and we are part of America. We are a part of American History. If it weren't for us, America would be a different place.

(Yalom and Kingston, 1988, p. 25)

In this revisionary sense, we can see the ways in which the politics of Kingston's texts crucially underpin and inform their postmodernist experimentation with narrative.

Certainly, her texts are far from articulating a sense of victimhood. Nor is she interested in painting crude caricatures of 'ethnic minorities', unfortunates who are 'caught between cultures'. Her books are not only concerned with the illustration of a certain kind of immigrant experience. In fact her writings are far more boldly transformative than any of these things. It is for very good reasons that they attempt to violate the assumed distinctions between 'Chinese-ness' and 'American-ness', to disrupt the received equation between 'historical fact' and 'historical record', and to destabilise the division between the officially recorded and the imaginatively restored. Her work is concerned not simply with 'setting the record straight' but with problematising the boundaries of memory, history and myth, and showing why those boundaries need to be problematised.

7 Jeanette Winterson: re-membering the body

As we have already seen, time and memory have become immensely important in contemporary fiction. In the very philosophic writing of Jorge Luis Borges, as we saw in chapter 2, time becomes a series of labyrinthine intellectual games. In Ian McEwan's and Maxine Hong Kingston's work, it ripples through culture and history, with memory and amnesia becoming crucial concerns. The focus of this chapter is on time and the body. Looking at some of Jeanette Winterson's texts, it explores how questions of time lead inevitably to questions of flesh.

Within feminism, time, sex and gender have long been inter-related. From the mid-twentieth century particularly, we see all sorts of efforts by feminists to interrogate the supposedly 'timeless facts' of female biology, and to separate them out from the variety of women's social identities. This separation of 'culturally constructed' gender from 'biological' sex has been very important in terms of the effort to overturn the traditional assumption that 'biology is destiny'.

Traditionally, as we see in Kingston's *The Woman Warrior*, 'virtuous' femininity has often been equated, in terms of time, with conservatism and the cyclical reproduction of the *status quo*. Meanwhile, to be a 'real man' has traditionally meant to adventure, colonise and progress. In the twentieth and twenty-first centuries, feminist writers have reconsidered this kind of gender division in terms of the way it is produced by particular kinds of cultural conditions and assumptions. Such work questions the anchorage of femininity to the reproductive functionality of the body. And it enables an understanding of gender as a changing thing that is radically affected by ethnicity, class, sexuality and history.

In chapter 3, I discussed the emergence of a formal sex/gender opposition in the 1960s, showing the ways in which feminist theorists such as Luce Irigaray and Judith Butler have returned to the spectre of the biological body in different ways. In Butler's work particularly, sex and gender identities are never seen as finally and completely formed, but acquired and maintained through an ongoing process of imitation, re-presentation and social performance. One of the concerns that Butler and Irigaray share with many contemporary feminist thinkers and writers, then, is to rework the historically produced conventions within which both gendered femininity(ies) and the female body itself have been inscribed. In this context, Jeanette Winterson stands out for the radicalism of her attempts to think beyond and to transform conventional notions of sex/gender. One of the keys to this achievement is that, like McEwan's and Kingston's, her work suggests that any serious re-imagining of sex and gender necessitates a rethink of the collective memory and the social time within which those two things take form.

The critical reaction to Winterson's work has often been hostile, and she has suffered numerous attacks in the media, in particular, for arrogance and hubris. But then, her work poses some awkward challenges to the *status quo*. Time and sex/gender are interlocking dimensions of the cultural and ideological complex that allow us to 'know our place'. They are prime constituents of the social narratives that enable us to articulate our identities, even to ourselves. In Winterson's dissection of structures so integral to the body of culture, it is hardly surprising that she uncovers some raw nerves.

Oranges are Not the Only Fruit

Oranges are Not the Only Fruit (1985) is often read as Winterson's autobiography. And certainly, the novel contains a great deal of autobiographical material. Like her narrator, Winterson was adopted by a Pentecostal evangelist and her husband in a mill town in Lancashire, in England's industrial north. From the age of eight, she was writing and delivering sermons, and in her adolescence emerged as a charismatic preacher in the mobile 'gospel tent' run by her church. Like her narrator, Winterson became an outcast from the church community and from her home when she admitted a lesbian affair to her parents at the age of fifteen. As in the novel, once again, Winterson's late teens were spent driving an ice-cream van and working as an undertaker's assistant. Despite all these references, however, it is a mistake to simply identify the narrator Jeanette 'as' Jeanette Winterson. *Oranges* is, on one level, an attempt by Winterson to explore her own early life, through the medium of fiction. But this is not all the novel does, and autobiography is only one of the reference points we can use in approaching it.

On a thematic level, clearly, it is also important to focus on the novel's approach to the question of heterosexuality and its 'compulsory' status within dominant culture. In this respect one of the most interesting episodes of the novel is Jeanette's portrait of her first lover, Melanie, who is 'saved' from 'unnatural passion' by marriage and the church. Using a technique that becomes more important in her later fiction, Winterson writes this transition on Melanie's body itself, which quite abruptly changes from that of a compelling and beautiful young woman to a passive and sexless figure of 'bovine' (p. 121) plumpness. Within the novel, the character of Jeanette does develop a thoroughgoing critique of heterosexuality *per se*, or even of the institution of marriage. Looking at the text's treatment of figures like Melanie, together with its presentation of the dysfunctionality of all the straight relationships it examines, however, it is helpful to think about *Oranges* as a lesbian text, in the sense that, in its various narratives, hetero-sexuality is consistently and comprehensively marginalised.

In order to understand this process of marginalisation, at the same time, it is necessary to consider *Oranges* as a text about Evangelism. Following the theology of St Paul, Evangelism's perspective is that even heterosexual marriage is very much a second best to the Christ-like ideal of celibacy. Within this perspective, indeed, marriage's 'carnal' implications are only grudgingly endorsed as a means to 'avoid fornication' (*1 Corinthians* 7:2). Thus, within the world of the church to which Jeanette belongs, not hetero-sexuality but sexlessness is the ideal. For Winterson, the policing of desire is an integral part of the ideological mission of the church. In her book *The Lesbian Postmodern* (1994), Laura Doan lends weight to this view by quoting the writer's own commentary on *Oranges*. According to Winterson, the text examines very precisely 'the way that the Church is offered up as a sacrament of love when really it is an exercise in power'. The church's prohibition on all non-heterosexual sex as 'unnatural passion', and on non-procreative heterosexual sex as 'fornication', forms part of a disciplinary framework in which *all* manifestations of the sexual body are more or less illicit.

When Jeanette admits her passion for Melanie, all of the community's resources are mobilised to exorcise these 'deviant' impulses. Initially, she is shut in a darkened room and starved into submission. But these authoritarian measures are in fact the least of the sanctions that are brought to bear against her. Far more important than this temporary incarceration is the way in which she is threatened with permanent exclusion from the community of the 'saved', the way in which her 'purity' and 'worthiness' are instantly revoked and replaced with a stigma of 'unnaturalness'. Even in Jeanette's own mind, her lesbian sexuality is imagined as a seductive little demon. At the age of fifteen, this sudden relegation to a position of social deviancy is infinitely more difficult to cope with than a period of starvation and imprisonment, and so the choice Winterson's character makes is to commence a public masquerade of 'normalcy'. Her sexuality becomes closeted, and we see how a radical split is opened, between her experience of lesbian desire, on the one hand, and her public performance of an accept-able, 'reformed' femininity, on the other.

If Evangelism's attitude towards gender and sexuality is presented in the novel as being particularly prescriptive and coercive, moreover, then this needs to be understood in terms of its Christian conception of time. By comparison with a secular-scientific perspective, time within Pentecostal Evangelism is over-laden with meaning. Human history, from the Creation to the Last Judgement, is knowable and finite, and there is little time remaining before history comes to its ultimate end. At the same time, the meaning of life for the individual is defined in an intimate relation to a divine plan. Even one's moment-to-moment progress through a lifetime is filled with a definite structure of prohibitions and obligations, by the constant expectation of judgement. The surveillance of an omniscient God is total, and there is no place of secrecy, no sinful act, no impure thought or illicit desire for which one will not ultimately be called to account.

Clearly, this conception of time – and its relation to identity and to desire – is very different from the view that has been dominant in secular society for the past hundred years. Within this secular-scientific perspective, the creation and destruction of the earth are envisaged as taking place over almost unimaginably vast spans of time, against the backdrop of a basically impassive universe. If we look at the Darwinian narrative of evolution, similarly, the role of any single individual in a species is virtually negligible. And in socio-political terms, even where 'apocalypse' is threatened – for example through nuclear war – most individuals' relation to those threats is usually quite peripheral. Clearly, this represents a significant contrast to the redemptive narrative of Evangelism, in which judgement is written directly into the life of each and every individual.

If we compare these two ideological schemas, it is clear that each implies quite a different narrativisation of gender and sex. Within a framework of Darwinian evolution, on the one hand, the position of the subject in relation to procreation (reproduction of the species) is usually privileged. And thus, the notion of futurity that evolution envisages has an obvious tendency to privilege reproductive heterosexuality as the proper 'goal' of the subject.

The judgement-laden time of Pentecostal Evangelism, on the other hand, puts a premium on the prohibition of sexual acts, and prizes a celibacy that is a continual refusal of the sexed body, a 'guarding against' its impulses. Destiny, within the matriarchal community of Jeanette's mother, is to be found in a rejection of biology. The novel uses this ideological schism to mount a witty satire on the culture of compulsory heterosexuality, and on the whole popular discourse of romantic love.

The most important place where this happens in the novel is in Jeanette's mother's affair with the semi-mythical Pierre. In this episode, Winterson plays on the motif of 'falling in love', exploiting the biological clichés by means of which it is customarily narrated. In an uncountable number of romantic novels, Hollywood movies, pop songs and fairytales, we are constantly referred to this mythical moment – when a sudden weakness of the female body (weak knees, 'butterflies' in the stomach, giddiness in the head) signals the approach of destiny in the figure of Mr Right. When Jeanette's mother experiences the requisite 'fizzing' and 'giddiness' with the Frenchman Pierre, she listens to her biology and (orthodoxly enough) assumes it is destiny calling. It is hugely ironic when, after the physical seduction is complete, she learns from the doctor that her fizzing and giddiness are not the symptoms of love but of a stomach ulcer. 'Imagine my mother's horror. She had given away her all for an ailment. She took the tablets, followed the diet, and refused Pierre's entreaties to visit her. Needless to say, the next time they met, again by chance, she felt nothing' (p. 85). Rather than rehearsing the conservative myth of female biological capitulation, the text instead renders it ridiculous.

In terms of sexuality, *Oranges* certainly does look at the way lesbianism is pathologised by the church as a manifestation of 'unnatural passions' (p. 7). But at the same time, as we can see, it also appropriates the perspective of the church community for its own ends, to cast a critical gaze on the symbolic narratives of heterosexuality. If 'falling in love' is an ulcer, marriage itself is little more than an irksome, social necessity, with the heterosexual male almost excluded from the frame. At the same time, the novel works to problematise the conventional linkage between marriage and maternity, again through the figure of Jeanette's mother. Immaculate conception, rather than the societal model of heterosexual parentage, is the standard the mother aspires to. Despite her own sexual history she is 'very bitter about the Virgin Mary getting there first' (p. 3). When the narrator's 'natural' mother appears, there is no drawn-out drama about the 'natural' bond of maternity. Instead she is summarily dismissed as 'a carrying case' (p. 99).

Formally, too, the novel works to subvert the narratives of compulsory heterosexuality. In the sense that *Oranges* tracks the fortunes of its protagonist from adolescence to adulthood, like *The Woman Warrior* it reflects the familiar conventions of the *Bildungsroman*, or novel of self-discovery. In the hands of the most-celebrated practitioners of the form, such as Charlotte Brontë, narrative closure for the *Bildungsroman* is invariably a marriage (if not a 'suitable' one). *Oranges* is narrated in a very different way, and not only in the sense that its main character emerges as a lesbian. More generally, the novel subverts the sense of *inevitability* that is so much a hallmark of the *Bildungsroman*'s gendered narrative, by adopting a spiralling structure, travelling round and round Jeanette and her mother, rather than recounting their experiences in a one-dimensional causal chain. At the same time

fabulous thing but not for a dog or a cock or the casual dice . . . Our rich
friend was clearly excited. His eyes looked past the faces and tables of
the gaming room into a space we could not inhabit; into the space
of pain and loss . . .

There were those that night who begged him not to go on with it,
who saw a sinister aspect in this unknown old man, who were perhaps
afraid of being made the same offer and of refusing.

What you risk reveals what you value.

(pp. 90–1)

Presenting it against the often-rehearsed narratives of the Napoleonic
wars, Winterson sets up Venice very specifically, then, as a space of indeter-
minacy. Escaping from the ravages of history, it is the place where Villanelle
and Henri go to hide, only to be confronted by their pasts in a different guise.
The city is not a blank canvas, on which history has yet to be written.
Rather, the opposite is the case. Just as, spatially, Winterson represents
Venice as multiple and labyrinthine, so, on a temporal level, the city is over-
saturated with the power of memories and desires. As Villanelle says,

The future is foretold from the past and the future is only possible
because of the past. Without past and future, the present is partial. All
time is eternally present and so all time is ours. There is no sense in
forgetting and every sense in dreaming. Thus the present is made rich.
Thus the present is made whole.

(p. 62)

On the Russian plains in the third section of the novel, we are offered a
vision of the blankness and aridity of history, where suffering and death seem
to be the inevitable destination of the individual. Life for Henri and
Villanelle, in their different places, is regulated by servile repetition of their
expected roles. Utterly disenfranchised, their lives and those of their
companions are almost completely subject to the capricious authority of
Napoleon.

The chronotope of Venice is precisely opposite to this – a model of
intimacy, uncertainty and possibility. And importantly, one of the effects
this has in the novel is to open up a set of subversive possibilities for the
representation of gender and sex. According to the critic Judith Seaboyer
(1997), Winterson's presentation of Venice as a whole in *The Passion* is
implicitly gendered:

For as long as cities have existed, they have been symbolically figured
as female; Venice's seductive, decorative beauty, its historical reputation

for duplicity, and its topography, at once contained and enclosed by water and penetrated by it, has rendered it an ideal vehicle for the historical and cultural burden of ambivalence that inheres in the female body and is mirrored in theories of urbanism.

(p. 485)

In Winterson's novel, as Seaboyer shows, familiar narratives of heterosexual development are provocatively displaced and problematised. Established conventions lose power in a city where the past and future are shifting and subject to reinvention. It is a place where one can get lost, elude the past or be recaptured by it, a place where the permeable boundaries of classes, genders and sexualities erotically interpenetrate in a carnivalesque masquerade.

By setting up Venice as a space of uncertainty/possibility, in other words, the text destabilises the constitution of sexes and genders as determinate, historically defined categories. Both Villanelle and Henri are marked by the instability of their gender identities. In the army, Henri finds it impossible to consummate his manhood with the Boulogne prostitutes in the violent manner of the other soldiers. Before he enters Venice with Villanelle, their exchange reveals that he is already engaged in a masquerade. '"When we get through this snow, I'll take you to the city of disguises and you'll find one that suits you." Another one. I'm already in disguise in these soldiers' clothes' (p. 100).

After stealing the clothes of a lover, the soldier's uniform is also one of Villanelle's many disguises. In the novel, her character is drawn in a way which plays about not only with masculine and feminine styles of dress and gesture, but also with styles of sexual pleasure. When she is sold into prostitution by her husband, she is forced by the army in Russia to adopt the canonical position of female sexual subordination. But in Venice, by contrast, the sexual and gender possibilities for her are multifarious. In the Venetian Masquerade 'there are women of every kind and not all of them are women' (p. 58). Sexual liaisons are temporary and anonymous. 'Passion is sweeter split strand by strand. Divided and re-divided like mercury then gathered up at the last moment' (p. 59). It is in Venice that her boatman's webbed feet become a sign of secret knowledge and power. Only in the city does the mark of hermaphroditism take on meaning, opening up multiple, undefined possibilities for adventure and escape.

Perhaps the most important motif though which the novel reworks the boundaries of gender and sexual identity is through the idea of passion itself. Throughout the text, passion recurs and recurs, always eluding definition. For Henri, locked in an asylum, 'words like passion and extasy, we learn them but they stay flat on the page' (p. 155). And for Villanelle too, passion can never be finally possessed. Early in the novel she seems to see it 'somewhere between fear and sex' (p. 55), but later passion has become indissoluble from risk. It is the 'valuable, fabulous thing' (p. 151) that, if it is not gambled, cannot be gained.

In the episode in which Villanelle literally loses her heart to her female lover, passion is manifested in the form of her disembodied organ. But the very cartoon-like presentation of this episode emphasises its parodic intent. The image of the woman reunited with her heart is, in itself, a joke about the traditional idea of biology-is-destiny. When Villanelle tasks the enamoured Henri with stealing her heart from her lover's villa, the novel twists up various heterosexual romance narratives. By hazarding himself for the fabulous object, the adventuring male hopes to re-animate his sleeping beauty, and in exchange, she will be his reward. Of course the novel offers no such canonical fairytale ending: Villanelle will not subordinate herself so easily, and Henri ends up trapped, like a Rapunzel in his tower. When he attempts to repeat his heroic gesture by handing her the bloody heart of her husband, the tableau we are presented with is the opposite of the fairytale ideal. At the 'heart' of the novel, then, it is possible to see how Winterson effectively de-couples the idea of passion from traditional narratives of gender and heterosexuality. Just as Villanelle's masquerades open up the possibility of a multiplicity of gender performances, so the unorthodox ending of the novel, resisting traditional closure, leaves open the possibility of a range of trajectories for desire.

Sexing the Cherry

In *Sexing the Cherry* Winterson pushes considerably further the re-narrativisation of time and sex that we see in *The Passion*. From the very beginning of the novel, she sets out to problematise the assumption of absolute and linear time. Before the main narrative has even commenced, we are introduced to the possibility of living within a totally different chronotopic environment:

> The Hopi, an Indian tribe, have a language as sophisticated as ours, but no tenses for past, present and future. The division does not exist. What does this say about time?
>
> (p. 8)

Alongside this anthropological strategy, like McEwan, Winterson is also interested in deploying insights from theoretical physics to re-present the parameters of space and time in her novel.

Chief among these insights is relativity, in which, as we saw in chapter 2, space and time are reconceptualised as inseparable aspects of a four-dimensional space-time. Within Relativity Theory, one of the characteristics of space-time, when compared with the fixity of the older Newtonian universe, is its capacity for curvature and deformation. *Sexing the Cherry* makes much of this possibility. Within the novel, moreover, it is also possible to see the influence of Quantum Theory. In this tradition, the principles of 'complementarity' and 'uncertainty' enshrine the idea that no object may be viewed in its entirety, but instead it presents different qualities to the observer in different circumstances.

In Winterson's novel, there are numerous explicit borrowings from these discourses. For the 'hero', Jordan, for example, it appears as no contradiction that the earth should be both round and flat at the same time. And within his worldview, the relationship between the observer and the observed is no longer a straightforward one. As far as time is concerned, Winterson takes maximum advantage of Einstein's critique, to radically open the field of temporal experience:

Lies 1: There is only the present and nothing to remember.

Lies 2: Time is a straight line.

Lies 3: The difference between the past and the future is that one has happened while the other has not.

One of the most immediately visible effects of this within the novel is that the characters of Jordan and Dog Woman are not confined to a single experience of time, a single century or even to a single body. With Jordan, we see an oscillation between a life as a seventeenth-century sea-goer, a fairytale quest for a dancer, and a life as a naval cadet in the late twentieth century. In a similar way, Dog Woman's existence by the water is multifaceted. As she says in her twentieth-century eco-warrior guise: 'if I have a spirit, a soul, any name will do, then it won't be single, it will be multiple. Its dimension will not be one of confinement but one of space. It may inhabit numerous changing decaying bodies in the future and in the past' (p. 216). For much of the novel she takes the form of a grotesque seventeenth-century giantess, and at a key moment, that of the goddess Artemis. In each life, there are thematic links, such as her oppressive experience of heterosexual desire. In each, a fire becomes the symbol of her dissidence. In the twentieth century, for example, she imagines herself 'stoking a great furnace with fat' (p. 125), whilst in the seventeenth century she helps the Great Fire of London take hold by pouring on a vat of oil. In the guise of Artemis, she is again ringed with fire, as she meditates on the shifting nature of being:

The fiery circle surrounding her held all the clues she needed to recognise that life is for a moment contained in one shape then released into another. Monuments and cities would fade away like the people who built them. No resting place or palace could survive the light years that lay ahead. There was no history that would not be rewritten and the earliest days were already too far away to see.

(p. 133)

As we can see, then, the way in which *Sexing the Cherry* experiments with space and time has important implications, once again, for its exploration of the notion of identity. Indeed, Dog Woman's opening statement foreshadows this very idea: 'I had a name but I have forgotten it' (p. 11). As Jordan's narrative opens too, we are made aware that his self-identity is to be divided and renegotiated: 'I began to walk with my hands stretched out in front of me, as do those troubled in sleep, and in this way, for the first time, I traced the lineaments of my own face opposite me' (p. 9).

An important effect of this splitting of time and identity is that, much more radically than in *The Passion*, it places a question mark over the supposed unity and 'in-dividability' of the 'individual' that underpins the idea of unified/determinate gender and sex. As in *The Passion*, one of the ways the novel explores this is by playing on the idea of masquerade, having its male protagonist pass as a female prostitute, as part of his romantic quest.

The idea of masquerade, in the prostitutes' house, becomes increasingly complex. Jordan learns that there is no fixed boundary between the company of prostitutes he meets and the community of nuns who inhabit a nearby convent. Instead, by cartoonish means, there is a constant movement and exchange of women between the two:

Their owner, being a short-sighted man of scant intelligence, never noticed that the women under his care were always different. There was an unspoken agreement in the city that any woman who wanted to amass a fortune quickly would go and work in the house and rob the clients and steal the ornaments . . . Some years later I heard that he had come into his pleasure chamber one day and found it absolutely empty of women and of treasures. He never fathomed the matter and made no connection between that event and the sudden increase in novitiates at the Convent of the Holy Mother.

(p. 31)

As in *The Passion*, the very notion of identity is belied by the possibility of disguise, as masquerades traverse multiple bodies.

To destabilise the narrative further, the form of *Sexing the Cherry* is again punctuated with interjections of fairytale and myth. Amongst these, one particular story is perhaps the most important. In the tale of 'The Twelve Dancing Princesses' made popular in the early nineteenth century by the Grimm brothers, twelve sisters escape from their bedchamber each night to an underground palace, in which each of them has a handsome prince. As time passes they foil the attempts by their father to discover where they are going, by drugging the wine of the various noblemen who watch over them at night. Eventually, when an old soldier foils their plan and discovers their secret, he is given the eldest in marriage and named as the king's heir.

In Jeanette Winterson's version, unsurprisingly, the princesses are somewhat less acquiescent in their fate than the Grimms would have it. As the novel visits them in turn, we see a series of little narratives in which the patriarchal assumptions that underpin the traditional tale are subverted in different ways. First of all, the twelve handsome princes become, in Winterson's version, twelve unwelcome husbands. The destinies of the princesses (who notably, in the Grimms' tale, are not recorded as living happily ever after, but left with uncertain futures) are wittily elaborated by Winterson. One begins an affair with a mermaid, and another with a woman in drag, another with Rapunzel. Five, after reasonable provocation, murder their husbands in a variety of ways, and three take their leave of husbands whose desires lie elsewhere. The twelfth princess is the Dancer of Jordan's fantasy, Fortunata. From a story about patriarchal control and the duplicity of women, Winterson turns the tale into a playful representation of the plural scenarios of sex and desire.

Throughout the text, Winterson constantly reworks images of femininity. As we have already seen, what this repeatedly involves is a freeing of the so-called 'individual' from the conventional representation of the sexed body. Just as she allows her characters to inhabit a plurality of times and bodies, so too her presentation of characters extends the boundaries of sexual representation – towards the grotesque, in the case of Dog Woman, and the sublime, in the case of Fortunata and her dancers.

One of the effects of this, of course, is once again to throw traditional assumptions about the 'timelessness' and 'naturalness' of the sexed body in question. The conservative culture which locates 'femaleness' in reproductive 'body parts' of course encourages a whole set of cultural anxieties about the attainment of successful heterosexual femininity, and particularly about the 'naturalness' or 'unnaturalness' of particular kinds of pleasures, bodies and individuals. *Sexing the Cherry* taps directly into those anxieties, playing on the potential instability and un-'naturalness' of 'sex' itself.

It is not accidental that the idea of 'sexing the cherry' provides the title of the novel. The section of the text to which this refers is the moment when again, one of the key resources on which Winterson draws is the New Physics. At the same time, it should be said that, in scientific terms, her attempts to use Quantum Theory and Relativity to place time in question have by no means always been orthodox. At one point, for example, there is a problematic reading of the 'event horizon' in astrophysics, with which Winterson attempts to introduce a notion of 'being outside time':

> Turn down the lights. This is outside of time. The edge of a black hole where we can go neither forward nor back. Physicists are speculating on what might happen if we could lodge ourselves on the crater sides of such a whole. It seems that due to the peculiarities of the event horizon we could watch history pass and never become history ourselves.
>
> (p. 72)

Certainly, the idea of all-seeing immortality Winterson describes here is not provided by any scientific theory of the 'event horizon'. As we will see, it is worth briefly outlining why. In astrophysics, a black hole is a collapsed star whose gravitational pull is so great that not even light can escape. The 'event horizon' is that orbit around it, beyond which everything is pulled to the centre. In Relativity Theory, time is not assumed to be a fixed and objective quality, and thus can only be thought of in terms of simultaneity or the gaps between observable events. Beyond the event horizon, there are no observable events. So if 'lodging ourselves on the event horizon' has any metaphoric value, it is more suggestive of sitting at the end of history, the point beyond which nothing further can be known. Whilst this is clearly a provocative idea in itself, it is not quite the omniscient position Winterson's novel is looking for.

Elsewhere in her work, it is possible to see similar kinds of misappropriations. In an interview about time conducted in 1997, for example, she makes the claim that, because it takes eight minutes for light to travel to earth from the sun, therefore everything we see happening around us is 'already eight minutes old' (Winterson 1997). Within the terms of Relativity Theory, which focuses on the experience of the observer, this statement does not hold water. Only from a God-position, again, does it begin to make sense. In each of these cases, we are not simply dealing with mistakes. Instead, these attempts by Winterson to go 'outside the envelope' of everyday understanding reveal how her texts try to map an over-arching ethical viewpoint on to the parameters of science.

In the interview cited above, indeed, Winterson describes herself as someone without family or bloodlines, for whom time precisely means the possibility of ethical self-invention:

There is no past, so you have to make it just as surely as you have to make your future. It affects your relationship to time. I mean you have to use the present in both directions — to build what you didn't have and to build what you want . . . It's not a question of what time it is on the clock, it's what you are doing with the time, how you are using it . . . Because there is so little time. We're here for a moment and then we're gone. So what are we going to get out of it, and what are we going to give back?

Here it is quite easy to see the legacy of Pentecostal Evangelism, with its meaning-laden model of time, and how Winterson is somehow seeking to amalgamate that with the relativity of the Einsteinian cosmos. In *Written on the Body* there is certainly a drive to make time meaningful, to reject the blankness of the secular universe. Rather than loading it with a prohibitive and oppressive morality (as in Evangelism), however, the ethics that are mapped on to time in this novel are concerned with sexual liberation.

In this attempt, Winterson is not alone. In the work of many feminist writers the attempt to re-imagine the notion of 'woman' goes hand in hand with the questioning of linear time. The theorist Julia Kristeva, whom Winterson claims as an influence, is one such example. For Judith Butler, as we have already seen, gender and sex identities are constantly reproduced in culture through processes of repetition, citation and imitation. The possibilities for resistance to the sexual *status quo* lie in the disruption of this cyclical reproduction of 'sex'.

Winterson's project in *Written on the Body* is very much in tune with this. In a fascinating way, it plays with the notion of the body without a past. With her black hole metaphor, we have already seen how the protagonist is positioned on the outside of history. Throughout the novel this idea is continually reinforced. The most obvious manifestation of this, of course, is the narrator's indeterminate gender. As the lover Louise says: 'I want you to come to me without a past. Those lines you've learned, forget them' (p. 54). When the narrator replies to her request several pages later, her/his words are resonant with the idea of being cleansed and born again. But the exchange is far from Evangelist:

I know what it will mean to redeem myself from the accumulations of a lifetime. I know and I don't care. You set before me a space uncluttered by association. It might be a void or it might be a release. Certainly I want to take the risk. I want to take the risk because the life I have stored up is going mouldy.

ice-cold prose of the medical textbook, and proceeds with the narrator's gradual reclamation of bodily structures and contours. But at the same time, in the text, another kind of rewriting of Louise is taking place, through the mutative, non-identical reproduction of the body that the term 'cancer' signifies.

Like Butler's 'parodic' mis-repetition of gender and sex, cancer represents precisely a self-generating mutation of the body, the text seems to suggest – a subtle malignancy that, indefinitely reproduced, threatens the very stability of the body itself. In the last part of the text, Louise undergoes a parallel, multiple mutation in the imagination of the narrator, in which she is both dead and alive, present and absent together. Much earlier in the text, this extraordinary narrative strategy has already been foreshadowed in a metaphor from biochemistry:

> Molecular docking is a serious challenge for bio-chemists. There are many ways to fit molecules together but only a few juxtapositions that bring them close enough to bond. On a molecular level success may mean discovering what synthetic structure, what chemical, will form a union with, say, the protein shape on a tumour cell. If you make this high-risk jigsaw work you may have found a cure for carcinoma. But molecules and the human beings they are a part of exist in a universe of possibility.
>
> (pp. 61–2)

In the novel as a whole, we are finally presented with a Louise who exists multiply, in memory and possibility. And clearly, this can be read as the novel's attempt to find an equation between the relativisation of time within the metaphors of physics, and the rethinking of gender and the sexed body within feminism and queer theory.

If this is a jigsaw, it is a fluid and shifting one in four dimensions, no less labyrinthine than the conundrums of Jorge Luis Borges or the talk-story of Maxine Hong Kingston. In a suitably provocative gesture, the final paragraph of *Written on the Body* is also its first: 'This is where the story starts, in this threadbare room' (p. 190). As in Ian McEwan's *Black Dogs*, we are left suspended on the borders of a dream. And of course, the last surprise of the novel is its perfect self-enclosure and circularity. Subverting the possibility of closure, we are back to the question of desire: 'Why is the measure of love loss?' (p. 9). As in Winterson's earlier work, we are not going to be allowed off the hook, into some formulaic romantic conclusion. Love is offered as the opposite of possession and submission, and passion as the inverse of mastery.

8 Toni Morrison: blackness and the historical imagination

Since the promulgation of its constitution in 1787 and its Bill of Rights in 1791, the United States has sought to define itself as a free nation, self-consciously distinct from the old powers of Europe. Compared with countries like Britain, there is a huge proliferation of American writing devoted to articulating the origins and goals of the nation, classically defined in terms of libertarianism. Even at the school level, study of the national constitution and of the freedoms enshrined within it, together with other texts like Abraham Lincoln's 'Gettysburg Address' (1863), is almost universal. For African Americans, however, it is not controversial to say that history remains a problem. There is an obvious difficulty in reconciling the national narrative of liberty, equality and justice with the conditions of internal colonisation and apartheid that have constituted much of their historical experience.

Undoubtedly, there is a disjuncture between the historical formation of African American-ness and the founding libertarian narratives of the United States. Compared with the grand narratives of white migration to North America, we saw in chapter 3 that the experiences of Asian Americans are relatively sparsely and partially recorded. The African American history of forced importation and enslavement represents a different context to either of these groups. Certainly, since the height of the Civil Rights movement in the 1960s, a huge amount of black scholarship has been devoted to documenting the histories of slavery and reconstruction. Thus it is wrong to read Morrison's novels, like many white critics, as a sudden 'breaking of silence'. What her work does represent, though, is an attempt to go beyond the limits of conventional, empirical historical scholarship, to a broader imaginative reclamation of African American-ness.

In the work of Michel Foucault, as we saw in chapter 1, the methods of conventional historiography, with its rhetoric of completion and authority, are superseded by methods closer to archaeology: the process of digging, reclamation and speculative reconstruction. In quite a literal sense,

Twenty, thirty years from now, he thought, all sorts of people will claim pivotal, controlling, defining positions in the rights movement. A few would be justified. Most would be frauds. What could not be gainsaid, but what would remain invisible in the newspapers and in the books he bought for his students, were the ordinary folk. The janitor who turned off the switch so the police couldn't see; the grandmother who kept all the babies so the mothers could march; the backwoods women with fresh towels in one hand and a shotgun in the other; the little children who carried batteries and food to secret meetings; the ministers who kept whole churchfuls of hunted protesters calm till help came; the old who gathered up the broken bodies of the young; the young who spread their arms wide to protect the old from batons they could not possibly survive; parents who wiped the spit and tears from their children's faces and said 'Never mind, honey. Never you mind. You are not and never will be a nigger, a coon, a jig, a jungle bunny nor any other thing white folk teach their children to say. What you are is God's.' Yes, twenty, thirty years from now, those people will be dead or forgotten, their small stories part of no grand record or even its footnotes, although they were the ones who formed the spine on which the televised ones stood.

(p. 212)

Throughout Morrison's fiction from *The Bluest Eye* (1970) onwards, her texts are interested in those with least ability to speak for themselves. In that sense, her work can be directly contrasted with the methods of conventional historiography which thinkers like Foucault attack. To draw on documents deemed 'reliable', to depend on commercially and institutionally preserved traces such as books and archived papers, as historians have frequently done, is almost inevitably to favour the literate, the published and the educated. Looking at pre-twentieth-century records, moreover, when literacy was denied to the vast majority of African Americans, is to deal almost exclusively with the white voice. Morrison's work is a challenge to this kind of historiography. In her portrayal of black experience, she continually moves away from 'important' and well-documented figures, towards those with less chance to be heard.

Even in the most celebrated areas of black cultural history, we see the same approach in Morrison's writing. In *Jazz* (1992), for example, the historic setting of the Harlem Renaissance could easily form the backdrop for a homage to great African American musicians and writers. But Morrison's novel is in fact a study of trauma and desire in the lives of individuals living far from the limelight. Indeed, as early as 1974, when Toni Morrison was co-editor of *The Black Book*, her focus was already moving away from the exclusionary habits and effects of traditional history, and towards a concern with the ordinary and the unrecorded. As Carolyn Denard (1993) has argued of *The Black Book*, 'she wanted to bring the lives of those who always got lost in the statistics to the forefront – to create a genuine black history book "that simply recollected life as lived"'.

The Bluest Eye

In her first novel, *The Bluest Eye*, we can clearly see the tension between two distinct elements in Morrison's project – quite a painful process of archaeology on the one hand, and a commitment to the affirmation of black experience on the other. The depiction of incest and child abuse which Morrison takes as her subject in this text gives an initial impression, certainly, of depression and anger. But this is, at the same time, a strangely positive and affirmatory text, an uncompromising but certainly not unbeautiful depiction of childhood vision and belief, adult guilt and desire.

> It was a long time before my sister and I admitted to ourselves that no green was going to spring from our seeds. Once we knew, our guilt was relieved only by fights and mutual accusations about who was to blame. For years I thought my sister was right: it was my fault. I had planted them too far down in the earth. It never occurred to either of us that the earth itself might have been unyielding. We had dropped our seeds in our own little plot of black dirt just as Pecola's father had dropped his seeds in his own plot of Black dirt. Our innocence and faith were no more productive than his lust or despair. What is clear now is that of all that hope, fear, lust, love, and grief, nothing remains but Pecola and the unyielding earth. Cholly Breedlove is dead; our innocence too. The seeds shrivelled and died; her baby too.
>
> There is really nothing more to say – except why. But since *why* is difficult to handle, one must take refuge in *how*.
>
> (p. 3)

The unproductive black dirt that is the lot of this African American community is more than sand and soil. It is the legacy of ingrown racism whose consequences these bright young girls only slowly and partially come to understand. Lack of opportunity is not simply a matter of poverty and clothing and housing; indeed these matters hardly seem to be of importance to the girls. At that age, their self-perception is not defined in those terms. Oppression, to them, is not the experience of authoritarian control or even the denial of civil rights. It is an inherited standard of beauty and worth, a racism-laden legacy of cultural assumptions which ensures that blackness can never measure up. In *The Bluest Eye*, then, the past is not recorded

tentativeness, doubt and inauthenticity that plagued him slithered away
without a trace, a sound.

(p. 183)

Milkman is caught in the forcefield of his father's success in the white world
of property and money. But at the same time he intuitively recognises Pilate's
traditional ways as the route to his freedom. His burning desire is *both* for the
flight he has always dreamed of *and* for the taste of salt that symbolises
the lust for possession and domination. In this way Morrison places Milkman
in a double-bind which he is only able to resolve by means of a quest for
roots.

Just as it is difficult to understand some important levels of meaning in
Joyce's *Ulysses* without a knowledge of the Homeric myths he draws on, then,
Morrison's work is also opened up significantly as soon as we turn to its
African American sources. Milkman again provides an obvious example. He
is born with a caul of skin and an excess of motherly love. He concludes the
novel by surrendering himself to the air. Each of these events can be read in
folkloric terms. As the women who tend his mother warn, the caul indicates
vulnerability to the seeing of ghosts, foreshadowing Milkman's coming
obsession with the myths of his family past. In the turmoil of contradictory
antagonisms and desires that surround him, moreover, the caul is also a kind
of protective straitjacket that symbolises his self-limitation and inward gaze.
Read in this way, the scene of baptism with the prostitute Sweet becomes a
pivotal moment of rebirth, as he finally starts to recognise the need to wash
away this 'skim of shame' that covered him 'thick and tight' (p. 300).

In this way Morrison's distinctive portrayal of the African American male
in terms of these four motifs – the caul or veil, the theme of second sight,
the desire for flight or freedom and the idea of divided desires – draws directly
on folkloric sources. At one and the same time, however, it can also be
connected directly to the African American philosophical tradition, and
especially the early twentieth-century work of Du Bois. In the same way that
African American folklore is creatively appropriated in *Song of Solomon* for
Morrison's particular narrative purposes, so too Du Bois' ideas are not simply
reiterated, but subtly woven into the dramatic structure of the text.

Du Bois' description of a particular, early twentieth-century moment in
African American emancipation is exactly what Milkman experiences. It is
the problem of living with a consciousness split between, firstly, the positive
sense of a black identity and, secondly, the negative self-image constructed
by a white-dominated society which consistently seeks to subjugate its black
population. Du Bois argues in *The Souls of Black Folk* (1903) that this double-
consciousness makes it necessary to find new ways of affirming blackness and
American-ness together:

After the Egyptian and Indian, the Greek and Roman, Teuton and Mongolian, the Negro is a sort of seventh son, born with a veil, and gifted with second-sight in this American world, – a world which yields him no true self-consciousness, but only lets him see himself through the revelation of the other world. It is a peculiar sensation, this double-consciousness, this sense of always looking at one's self through the eyes of others, of measuring one's soul by the tape of a world that looks on in amused contempt and pity. One ever feels his twoness, – an American, a Negro; two souls, two thoughts, two unreconciled strivings; two warring ideals in one dark body, whose dogged strength alone keeps it from being torn asunder.

The history of the American Negro is the history of this strife, – this longing to attain self-conscious manhood, to merge his double self into a better and truer self.

(pp. 10–11)

Part of the answer to this problem for Du Bois is through the values of education, professional achievement and social position. Another part of the answer is in the celebration of Black American culture and Black American history. A further part can certainly be found in Du Bois' vehement concern with issues of justice and civil rights. On each of these levels it is possible to draw parallels between Du Bois' work and that of Toni Morrison. In *Song of Solomon*, for example, Morrison sets up a structural opposition between Pilate's aura of independence, magic and tradition, and Macon Dead's embrace of the white world of control and possession. On one level this can certainly be read as a *gender* opposition, in which Pilate's feminine domain of 'peace . . . energy, singing, and . . . remembrances' (p. 301) becomes a haven from Macon's patriarchal control. As the stories of Milkman and his friend Guitar progress, however, the exploration of African American ethnicity becomes increasingly paramount.

Considered in terms of Du Bois' analysis, the journeys of the two young men can be read as representative attempts at a resolution of the problem of double-consciousness. For Guitar, the 'race' fundamentalist, the solution to oppression is the adoption of radical violence. Milkman, however, is far more strongly influenced by the cultural inheritances bound up in his family line. For him self-realisation demands a process of archaeology, searching back through the remains of culture for a simpler image of being black and a man. Ultimately, contact with the earth itself becomes the sign of arrival and belonging:

Laughing too, hard, loud, and long. Really laughing, and he found himself exhilarated by simply walking the earth. Walking it like he

belonged on it; like his legs were stalks, tree trunks, a part of his body
that extended down down into the rock and soil, and were comfortable
there – on the earth and on the place where he walked.

(pp. 280–1)

Song of Solomon could be seen as an African American odyssey. It is
fundamentally the story of Milkman's self-realisation though his discovery
of Solomon, the archetypal black father. Like the biblical *Song of Solomon*
and the *Odyssey* of Homer, the novel is indeed an exploration of ethnic,
social and sexual identity. But more precisely it is an argument for the
reclamation of an organic African American heritage, and with it a free and
rooted black masculinity. Importantly, it is not in the Good Book, much less
in the texts of canonical literature or history, that Solomon and his song are
to be found. Rather, it is in the voices of black country children that
Milkman ultimately discovers them: where his history and their own are
written in the sounds and rhythms of their play.

In a very important sense, *Song of Solomon* and *The Bluest Eye* in this way
provide us with a guide to reading Morrison's fiction as a whole. Working
both within and against established traditions of scholarship, it is sound,
rhythm and above all language that, for her, serve as the archive of the
African American. Certainly, texts like *Beloved* or *Jazz*, with their constantly
shifting speech registers and patterns of word and sound, are exemplary
models of linguistic artistry. Above all, though, what they attempt to
demonstrate is not how language can 'capture' experience, but the freedom
of both from ultimate definition and control. In her Nobel Prize acceptance
speech in Stockholm in 1993 Morrison argued exactly this: 'Language
can never "pin down" slavery, genocide, war. Nor should it yearn for the
arrogance to be able to do so. Its force, its felicity is in its reach toward
the ineffable' (pp. 207–1).

If we ask what a novel like *Jazz* (1992) is about, we might say that it is
about a period of racial oppression and violence, studied through the lives
of a few specific characters. But, in a similar way, these themes and plotlines
are only the backdrop to the novel's adventure with language, its celebration
of black words and voices. *Jazz* may have foundations in oppression, but it
is at least as strongly a novel of affirmation, whose medium is the lyrics and
rhythms of black music itself. In his essay 'Experiencing *Jazz*' (1997) Eusebio
Rodrigues illustrates this quality in Morrison's writing exactly. From *Jazz*'s
very first word, 'sth', teasing our ear 'like the muted soundsplash of a brush
against a snaredrum' (p. 245), Rodrigues traces the beat and rhythm of the
Harlem Renaissance throughout Morrison's text:

The harsh blare of the consonants, the staccato generated by the commas that insist on hesitations needed to accelerate the beat, the deliberate use of alliteration and of words repeated to speed up tempo – all come together to recreate the impact of jazz . . . sexual metaphors, charged with energy, leap into life. Language is made to syncopate, the printed words loosen up and begin to move, the syntax turns liquid and flows.

(p. 247)

Even in Morrison's first novel, *The Bluest Eye*, the aural qualities of language are immensely important. 'It was autumn too when Mr. Henry came. Our roomer. Our roomer. The word ballooned from the lips and hovered above our heads – silent, separate, and pleasantly mysterious' (p. 7). In this example, the stranger entering the girls' house is expressed firstly in terms of the qualities of sound he brings with him: 'too / our roomer / our roomer / ballooned'. In *Beloved*, chapter openings follow each other like a series of oral incantations.

BELOVED, she my daughter. She mine.

(p. 200)

BELOVED is my sister. I swallowed her blood.

(p. 205)

I AM BELOVED and she is mine. Sethe is the one that picked flowers.

(p. 214)

Eventually this text's fractured form resolves entirely into the simplicity of a chant, a statement of possession and belonging which – like the music of *Jazz* – cuts right across the novel's main narrative progression:

You forgot to smile
I loved you
You hurt me
You came back to me
You left me

I waited for you
You are mine
You are mine
You are mine

(p. 217)

As Barbara Hill Rigney (1991) suggests, often the use of language in Morrison's texts is guided by both the sense and sounds of words. 'One of the freedoms Morrison claims in her novels is to move beyond language, even while working *through* it, to incorporate significance beyond the denotation of words, to render experience and emotion, for example, as musicians do' (p. 7). The linguistic quality of Morrison's texts is characteristically fluid, filled with provocative undecidability. In *Beloved*, the songs sung by the chained black convicts are, as Rigney shows, 'subversive, garbled so they could not be understood' (p. 10). In defiance of a culture of discipline, they become a secret, oral archive of freedom. Here as elsewhere, the boundaries between different minds, speakers, levels of consciousness – between memory, daydream, desire – are also constantly in flux, with voices cutting across and merging into each other. Loves and atrocities are disclosed in glimpses. The text is never allowed to completely lie down or succumb to conceptual control.

All of these aspects of Morrison's techniques of language use are reflected in the approach outlined in her Nobel acceptance speech. Very clearly, here, she champions the freedom and energy of language against what Foucault would call disciplinary containment:

> Be it grand or slender, burrowing, blasting, or refusing to sanctify, whether it laughs out loud or is a cry without an alphabet, the choice word, the chosen silence, unmolested language surges towards knowledge, not its destruction. But who does not know of Literature banned because it is interrogative, discredited because it is critical, erased because alternate? And how many are outraged by the thought of a self-ravaged tongue?
>
> (p. 271)

Thus, again, it is not enough to see Morrison as simply trying to 'replace' older white-dominated histories with a fuller knowledge of the cruelty and exploitation in America's past, as one academic historiography supersedes another. Language, multi-voiced and multi-faceted, filled with lyric and rhythm, is the archive of trauma, but also freedom, within which she does her work: 'We die. That may be the meaning of life. But we do language. That may be the measure of our lives' (p. 271).

Beloved

Certainly, Morrison's writing has made a significant impact on the forms and means of the contemporary novel. Her fiction defines an aesthetic whose co-ordinates are language, the body and the earth itself. At the beginning

of *The Bluest Eye* the image of dirt or soil forms, as we have seen, a central metaphor for the negative constitution of blackness in American culture. In later novels, this metaphor is gradually but far-reachingly reworked, with the earth itself being reclaimed by Morrison as a source and site of value. In *Song of Solomon*, Milkman's discovery of himself is closely tied to his contact with the ground. In *Tar Baby* the opposition of beauty versus earth/dirt/ blackness has been reworked even further. As this novel progresses, the refined 'taste' of the privileged whites, Margaret and Valerian, becomes sickeningly effete and oppressive, as the choices represented by their black protégé, Jadine, and the poorer, more 'race-conscious' Son come increasingly into focus. Here, the task of reclaiming an unambivalent sense of African American identity hinges again on the rediscovery of the body and the earth together:

> By and by he walked steadier, now steadier. The mist lifted and the trees stepped back a bit, as if to make the way easier for a certain kind of man. Then he ran. Lickety-split. Lickety-split. Looking neither to the left nor to the right.
>
> (p. 309)

In *Beloved*, we see a return to this linkage between earth and flesh. Certainly, the ground is not always constituted as the friend to the black slave. In the hands of the white slave-holder it can be made literally into a prison. Perhaps the most harrowing descriptions in this text concern Paul D's physical and sexual abuse in a dirt cage, 'that grave calling itself quarters' (p. 106). Even here, though, the earth becomes the slaves' saviour, dissolving in the rain into mud thin enough to allow a collective dive under the bars of their prison. As Paul D heads for the Free North, it is the land itself, spreading pear and peach blossoms slowly northwards with the spring season, that points the way to liberation.

This redemptive connection between the land and the African American body, then, is central to Morrison's work. In *Song of Solomon* the search for the father ends not in the pages of scripture but in the backyard games of children. And similarly in *Beloved*, the redemptive language of Baby Suggs is drawn not from the church, but from the tactile reality of flesh:

> 'Here,' she said, 'in this here place, we flesh; flesh that weeps, laughs; flesh that dances on bare feet in grass. Love it Love it hard. Yonder they do not love your flesh. They despise it . . . No, they don't love your mouth. *You* got to love it. This is flesh I'm talking about here. Flesh that needs to be loved. Feet that need to rest and to dance; backs that need support; shoulders that need arms, strong arms I'm telling you. And O

my people, out yonder, hear me, they do not love your neck unnoosed and straight. So love your neck; put a hand on it, grace it, stroke it and hold it up. And all your inside parts that they'd just as soon slop for hogs, you got to love them. The dark, dark liver – love it, love it, and the beat and beating heart, love that too. More than eyes or feet. More than lungs that have yet to draw free air. More than your life-holding womb and your life-giving private parts, hear me now, love your heart. For this is the prize.'

(pp. 88–9)

As the leading African American scholar Barbara Christian (1997a) has argued, a constantly recurring theme of nineteenth-century slave narratives is their objectification of the black body. William Wells Brown's description of 'The Negro Sale' in the first published African American novel, *Clotel, or, The President's Daughter* (1853), is a classic example. The recording and evaluation of slaves as a function of their body parts – arms, legs, mouths, penises and even hymens – was felt as a process not just of examination, but of symbolic dismemberment.

The system of slavery, of course, was not just a means for exploiting workers economically. Beyond that, it was an entire regime organised around producing a continuous stock of usable bodies. As Christian argues, it is precisely 'because of their bodies, the appearance of their bodies, that African Americans were enslaved; it is their bodies on which slavery was written' (p. 40). As we saw in chapters 3 and 4, moreover, the stress on black corporeality in pro-slavery writing is part and parcel of the racist ideology which sought to justify this system for the subjugation of the 'soul-less' slave body. Looking at Baby Suggs' sermon, then, what we can see is precisely a rejection of this ideology – a *consecration* of black flesh. Rather than a refusal of embodiment, it is a liberatory reclamation of the body, *through* a redemptive affirmation of soul. In this sense, Morrison's text works to contest the legacy of race-thinking in America's past at the same time as it celebrates blackness itself.

In this context, of course, the key strategy of the novel is its use of the case of Margaret Garner, an escaped slave who killed her child rather than let it be returned into captivity. In the struggles over slavery that preceded the American Civil War, the Garner case was a crucial setback for Abolitionism, because it gave additional legal force to the status of slaves as items of property, who could not be credited with the moral responsibilities accepted by whites.

Morrison's primary source for Garner's story is the *Reminiscences* (1876) of Levi Coffin, an activist who worked on the underground railroad transporting escaped American slaves northwards to Canada. Coffin's text

describes how seventeen slaves, including the pregnant Garner and her husband and children, escaped from slavery in Kentucky and across the border into Ohio in 1856. Nine of the party successfully escaped to Canada, but the safe house where the Garner family were hiding was identified and surrounded by slave catchers. A battle ensued, and the door to the house was battered down. As Coffin says:

> At this moment, Margaret Garner, seeing that their hopes of freedom were vain, seized a butcher knife that lay on the table, and with one stroke cut the throat of her little daughter, whom she probably loved the best. She then attempted to take the life of the other children and to kill herself, but she was overpowered and hampered before she could complete her desperate work. The whole party was then arrested and lodged in jail.

(pp. 559–60)

Throughout the legal hearing that followed, Garner and her husband maintained that they would rather face the gallows than a return to slavery, and were defended by the well-known abolitionist speaker Lucy Stone. If Garner was to be formally tried for murder, she would have to remain in Ohio under the jurisdiction of state law. The claim of the slave-holders, under the 1850 Fugitive Slave Law, however, was that they were entitled to the return of their 'property' (p. 566) without reference to the courts. At the end of the hearing, the verdict of the United States Commissioner Pendery under American Law was that Garner should indeed be returned to slavery.

A postscript to these proceedings was provided when, on the return journey, Garner threw herself into the Ohio river, drowning another of her children in the process. Garner herself survived, and returned to Kentucky in bondage. As I have suggested, her case was a serious setback for the fight against slavery. Its effect was to establish the precedence of the infamous Fugitive Slave Law over the powers of individual states, even over questions of homicide. Put another way, the case confirmed that within American law, a slave's status as property overrode their status as a responsible being.

In *Beloved*, it is possible to see how Morrison uses but also modifies key aspects of the Garner case. Sethe's killing of Beloved clearly reflects Garner's story in its outlines. In the novel, however, Sethe is not taken for trial, and neither is she returned to slavery. Rather than being claimed by the slave-holder, Schoolteacher, she is written off as spoiled livestock: 'Right off it was clear, to Schoolteacher especially, that there was nothing there to claim . . . Two were lying open-eyed in sawdust; a third pumped blood down the dress of the main one' (p. 149).

Comparing the two texts, then, it is certainly possible to draw out significant differences. Looking at Levi Coffin's memoir and other accounts of the hearing, Angelita Reyes (1990) points out one particularly important aspect. All of them emphasise the skin colour of the child. As Coffin says, Garner's daughter was 'much lighter in colour than herself . . . The murdered child was almost white, a little girl of rare beauty' (1876, p. 563). The implication of this, in the light of well-established practices of slave-holding in the period, is that the child was probably fathered by Garner's white master. Barbara Christian picks up on Reyes' argument, noting that, once again, Morrison chooses to elide an important feature of the Garner narrative. In the novel Beloved is the result not of a rape, but of the quasi-marital relationship between Sethe and the black slave Halle. The effect of this narrative choice, importantly, is in fact to complicate, rather than to simplify Morrison's text. As Christian (1997a) argues, 'slave women who killed children who are the result of rape, or forced breeding, might be seen as striking out at the master/rapist and resisting the role of perpetuating the system of slavery through breeding' (pp. 41–2). The implications of Sethe's killing of Beloved, by comparison, are considerably less easy to cope with.

From a comparison of Morrison's text with her most important documentary source, therefore, some of the narrative strategies of *Beloved* come more clearly into focus. First of all, the text does not frame Sethe's narrative within the well-rehearsed dramatic form of the trial. Secondly, Morrison chooses not to literalise Sethe's struggle for emancipation in terms of a return to Schoolteacher's slave regime. And thirdly, the novel refuses to render Beloved's killing 'understandable' by making the child a product of institutionalised rape. Instead, *Beloved* deliberately avoids clarifying and objectifying the trauma of its protagonist, and more generally works to prevent her narrative becoming a kind of easily digestible précis of slavery 'as a whole'.

In terms of historical responsibility, then, the problem of the novel is not to demonstrate the inadequate 'fact' that slavery occurred, but rather to insist on the opposite: the impossibility of adequate historical representation in the face of genocide. Indeed, in an interview with Bonnie Angelo in 1989 during the writing of *Beloved* Morrison stresses her own difficulty with a subject that, reduced and sanitised by history, has been the subject of wilful forgetting:

> Then I realised I didn't know anything about it, really. And I was overwhelmed by how long it was. Suddenly the time – 300 years – began to drown me . . . I thought this has got to be the least read of all the books I'd written because it is about something that the characters don't

want to remember, I don't want to remember, black people don't want to remember. I mean, it's national amnesia.

(Matus, 1998, p. 103)

Within the novel itself, we see this process of forgetting in action. For the surviving daughter, Denver, the personal experience of slavery that led her mother to kill in front of her is, only a few years later, already obscured and confused. 'I don't know what it is, I don't know who it is . . . I need to know what that thing might be, but I don't want to' (p. 205). But once again in this novel there is a crucial counterpoint between the two daughters. In the remarkable memory sequence that forms the climax of the novel, Beloved's representation of the transportation of slaves in the Middle Passage is of quite a different order to Denver's experience. Beloved already occupies a space between life and death, actuality and the subconscious, her discourse caught between memory and the body. In this section her projected image of the slave ship becomes a kind of universal nightmare, a space of horror crammed with starved, convulsing bodies, where death is continually pressing. Here again, the text begins to invent its own conventions of narration, with horror coming as a pulse of recurring words and images: 'I am always crouching   the man on my face is dead   his face is not mine   his mouth smell sweet but his eyes are locked . . .   someone is thrashing but there is no room to do it in . . .' (p. 210).

In her essay 'The Site of Memory' (1990) Morrison likens memory to the overflowing of a river which, after a period of being diverted or 'straightened out', floods back eventually to reclaim its original path. 'Writers are like that,' she argues, 'remembering where we were, what valley we ran through . . . It is emotional memory – what the nerves and the skin remember as well as how it appeared' (p. 305). The novel uses a further metaphor, that of the footprint. As Beloved departs, the imprints made on the surface of the earth are not only her own, but those of everyone. 'Down by the stream in back of 124 her footprints come and go, come and go. They are so familiar. Should a child, an adult place his feet in them, they will fit. Take them out and they disappear again as though nobody ever walked there' (p. 275). If Denver's is the voice of collective amnesia, Beloved's is the voice of repressed memory. Like a haunting, like unfinished business, she returns irresistibly out of the margins of the past and the margins of contemporary consciousness.

Amongst all the proliferation of discourse in the United States about its origins and foundation in libertarianism, then, it is possible to see how Morrison's work contributes to the effort in African American writing to dig under the surface of those values. From her first novel, *The Bluest Eye*, onwards, the insights she finds there are not always palatable ones. As we have seen, Morrison's methods are unorthodox, making use of materials rejected by traditional historiography. Her texts are filled not only with allusions to established literary and other texts, but also as Foucault says, with 'naive knowledges, located low down on the hierarchy, beneath the required level of cognition or scientificity . . . unqualified, even directly disqualified knowledges' (Foucault, 1980, p. 82). Clearly, this is far from saying that her work represents a rejection of the lessons and legacies of the past. Rather, it alerts us to the dangers that can be implicit in the production of historical knowledge, and the overhasty desire for closure.

9 Imagining nations: Salman Rushdie's counter-histories

As we saw in chapter 1, the particular circumstances of the contemporary period have had a profound effect on writers' approaches to the framing of history. In the case of authors as various as Umberto Eco and Ian McEwan, the history of modern Europe is deeply problematic, no longer providing the assurance it did to a previous generation. For African writers like Ngugi wa Thiong'o, independence struggles and the decline of European colonialism have brought with them a whole raft of reassessments about the nature of historical, political and cultural development. In the United States, as we can see with both Maxine Hong Kingston and Toni Morrison, questions arise about collective amnesia, and the coercions and silences underlying the myth of America.

Rushdie differs from the authors we have encountered so far in three significant ways. Firstly, what is fascinating about him as a writer is partly the sense in which he himself has become a historical figure, and the ways in which 'Salman Rushdie' has been overwhelmed by a tide of fictional reconstruction. Secondly, Rushdie provides an interesting contrast to both Morrison and Kingston in that the major concern of his writing is not the loss or lack of history but its superabundance. His work is an overflowing cauldron of influences – Hindu cinema, Pakistani politics, English liberalism, Middle Eastern Islam, the writings of Joyce, Indian painting – because for Rushdie, history is forged not out of the silence of the past but out of its cacophony. Thirdly, although he deals with Britain and the United States, his primary focus is on the Indian subcontinent.

In February 1989 a decree calling for the death of Salman Rushdie was issued in his absence by the revolutionary leader of Iran, Ayatollah Khomeini. In the *fatwa* proclamation, 'All zealous Muslims' were called upon to carry out the execution of the author and his publishers, who were guilty of defaming Islam. In the furore over the publication of *The Satanic Verses* (1988), in September of the previous year, riots had already spread from England to Pakistan and Kashmir, resulting in the deaths of at least seven protesters against the novel. Rushdie himself was forced into hiding under the protection of the British Special Branch. Over the next decade, a reward of up to two and a half million dollars was offered by the Iranian foundation, 15 Khordad, for his assassination. His Japanese translator was stabbed and killed in 1991, whilst others involved with his work survived attempts on their lives. Although the Iranian government under the moderate President Mohammad Khatami disassociated itself from the death sentence in 1998, the Khordad bounty remained, and senior Iranian clerics continued to affirm the *fatwa*.

Of course the whole phenomenon of the *fatwa* against Rushdie can be understood in the context of Khomeini's own project to entrench himself as the patriarchal guardian of Iran. It also needs to be seen in the context of the large numbers of Muslims in the Middle East, the Indian subcontinent and the West, who voiced deep concern against this constitution of international Islam as the opponent of free speech. As we will see in Hanif Kureishi's fictional treatment of the affair discussed in chapter 11, moreover, the *fatwa* became the focus for a whole set of debates about ethnicity and religion in Britain and elsewhere.

The Satanic Verses itself is a novel about belief and the loss of belief, which deals closely with the figure of the Prophet and the ideas of Islam. It centres on a famous film actor called Gibreel Farishta, who undergoes a crisis of faith after he miraculously survives a plane crash. As in other magic realist fictions, such as Gabriel Garcia Marquez's *One Hundred Years of Solitude* (1967), historical reference is mixed with fantasy throughout the text. As the critic D. C. R. A. Goonetilleke points out in his book *Salman Rushdie* (1998), the air crash at the beginning of the novel is modelled on the blowing up of an Air India jet off south-west Ireland by Sikh extremists in 1985, for example, whilst the figure of the Imam in the novel can be read as a satire on Ayatollah Khomeini himself. However, the novel is far from being a historical novel in the realist sense. Indeed, in the sections that deal with religion especially, the text presents itself more as a kind of anti-text, or distorted fantasy of the history of Islam.

Despite this, as I have suggested, it is Rushdie's irreverent treatment of religion which made the novel the subject of such controversy. At times Gibreel (a variant of Gabriel, the archangel common to Christianity and Islam) believes that he is himself divine. At other times he is troubled by strange and prophetic dreams. In one of these, a young prophetess called Ayesha leads her whole village in a pilgrimage to Mecca, strengthening their faith through a series of miracles that culminate in the parting of the Arabian Sea. In this dramatic consummation, Gibreel finally envisages the attainment of Paradise through simple submission and belief. Earlier in the novel, though, he has had a different kind of vision. Here, he dreams of a prophet called Mahound in an illusory city called Jahilia, or doubt. As the narrator makes clear, it is not the story of the Prophet of Islam we see here as such, but rather a kind of fevered inversion of him:

> His name: a dream-name, changed by the vision. Pronounced correctly, it means he-for-whom-thanks-should-be-given, but he won't answer to that here . . . To turn insults into strengths, whigs, tories, Blacks all chose to wear with pride the names they were given in scorn; likewise, our mountain-climbing, prophet-motivated solitary is to be the medieval baby-frightener, the Devil's synonym: Mahound.
>
> That's him. Mahound the businessman, climbing his hot mountain in the Hijaz. The mirage of a city shines below him in the sun.
>
> (p. 93)

Constantly, the novel plays with the opposition of faith and blasphemy. In so doing it makes use of the controversial question of the 'satanic verses'. According to early Islamic sources such as the ninth-century scholar at-Tabari's *History of Prophets and Kings*, Mohammed's recitation initially contained a short series of lines which conceded the existence of three female goddesses, namely Al-Lat, Al-Uzza and Manat. Later, at-Tabari suggests, these 'satanic' interjections were rejected in favour of lines which affirmed the monotheism of Islam, calling the three goddesses 'nothing but names' and 'nothing but conjecture' (*Qur'an* 53: 23, 27). The significance of this sequence of events in Rushdie's novel is that it functions to portray his prophet-character Mahound as cynical and politically motivated, and to cast doubt on the integrity of his revelation, heightening the thematic dichotomy of faith/doubt that runs through the novel as a whole.

In a similar way, the divine/satanic opposition is almost cartoonishly reflected in the character of Gibreel, who spends his life portraying gods on the Bollywood screen but whose rank breath reeks demonically of sulphur. Saladin Chamcha, his friend/rival and fellow migrant, begins to become a goat-like, Beelzebub figure under the gaze of the conservative English. And Rushdie concludes by setting up a provocatively apt parallel between Gibreel's work and the writing of his own topsy-turvy text:

> Gibreel had embarked on a modern-dress remake of the Ramayana story in which the heroes and heroines had become corrupt and evil instead of pure and free from sin. Here was a lecherous, drunken Rama and a flighty Sita; while Ravana, the demon-king, was depicted as an upright and honest man. 'Gibreel is playing Ravana,' George explained in fascinated horror. 'Looks like he's trying deliberately to set up a final confrontation with religious sectarians, knowing he can't win, that he'll

be broken into bits.' Several members of the cast had already walked off the production, and given lurid interviews accusing Gibreel of 'blasphemy', 'satanism' and other misdemeanours.

(p. 539)

Perhaps because of the self-conscious fascination with narrative play and inversion that we can see here, *The Satanic Verses* has been the subject of radically divergent readings, from the militantly literal to the playfully postmodernist. In general, clearly, the interpretation of a text once it leaves an author's desk may often have little to do with his or her 'original' or 'intended' meaning. Readers always make texts their own, through the filter of their own circumstances and preconceptions. Certainly, writers have traditionally been assumed to be in control of their writings, and therefore to be responsible for the effects they have. What happened to Rushdie over *The Satanic Verses*, though, seems to demonstrate the reverse of this assumption. As the theorist and critic Gayatri Spivak (1990) argues, in many ways Rushdie became the creature of his text, rather than vice versa. In this sense his experience is not different in kind from that of many other writers, but simply an extreme example of what happens to authors continually.

Very quickly after the publication of *The Satanic Verses*, Rushdie came to be identified not only with the voices of his characters, but also by second- and third-hand accounts of their stories and ideas. For the vast majority of readers (and especially for Muslims who abstained from reading what they believed to be an offensive and blasphemous text) *The Satanic Verses* and Rushdie became refracted through the lens of the controversy itself. Everyone knew in 1989, didn't they, that Rushdie claimed that Mohammed's wives were prostitutes? A close reader of the novel might find it difficult to fix that claim, but this fact did not affect its popular currency.

With the same rapidity that *The Satanic Verses* was digested and appropriated by the global public, it is possible to see the ways in which its author was reconstructed as a public-historical figure. Within months of the death sentence which gave him global notoriety, a number of 'Salman Rushdies' had already come to exist in the popular imagination, and throughout the media. Some of these were undeniably dangerous. Certainly, Rushdie's fictional work has consistently sought to demonstrate the slipperiness and multiformity of history. And in practice too, his control over the ways in which he himself has come to be portrayed 'historically' has been shown to be radically limited.

Indeed, in an age in which the newspapers and cinema screens of Los Angeles and Karachi thrive equally (and hugely) on dramatising the power-struggle between fanatical, murderous Islam and the free West – or between heroic Islam and the corrupt, murderous West – Rushdie has provided an easy target for caricature. In a matter of a few years, both the author and his work were appropriated into a vast popular-historical drama which extended way beyond his professional orbit as a middle-class writer working out of Britain and the United States. Speaking to the film-maker David Cronenberg in 1995, Rushdie provides a symptomatic example:

> I had the strange experience of becoming a subject of a movie – this appalling movie made in Pakistan called *International Guerrillas*. It's about the freedom fighters of Islam searching for me, trying to kill me. I'm the villain of the movie. There is a character called my name who is the author of *The Satanic Verses* who wears a series of appalling safari suits. And every time this guy arrives on camera there's a sort of satanic 'dahh dahh.' And the cameraman always looks to his feet. And there's a slow 'pan' up . . . this guy, me, lives in what appears to be an island in the Philippines, protected by what appears to be the Israeli army. And various members of these Islamic radicals were arrested by these Jewish soldiers and are brought to the 'me' character who tortures them, has them tied up and cut about with swords. And at the end of the film I actually get killed by the Holy Book itself. The Koran appears in the sky above me and fries me with lightning.
>
> This dreadful film is so badly made that it's actually difficult to take it too seriously, but it came to England and was banned. And I found myself in the strangest position. I'm fighting an anti-censorship fight and here's somebody banning a film which is brought about by me. It ended up with me writing to the censors here, guaranteeing that I would not take legal action against them. And telling them that I do not wish to be protected in this way.
>
> (Cronenberg, 1995, p. 6)

In Britain, Salman Rushdie was reconstructed in different ways. One tabloid Rushdie has his own private pimping service, provided by high-profile friends. Another likes to call himself 'Simon Rushton', in an effort to deny his Indian origins and fit in as a white Englishman (Rushdie, 1991, p. 405). According to Umar Elahi Azam's *Rushdie's Satanic Verses* (1990), differently again, Salman Rushdie is a malicious conspirator with 'the accursed Jews' (p. 8) who 'should have kept his poisonous and loathsome perversions and fantasies in his own sick mind' (p. 5). With this grotesque caricature in mind, it is Azam's recommendation that 'Any Muslim should be glad to kill Rushdie' (p. 7).

These various popular-historical Rushdies are not completely unrelated. Indeed, as he argues in his essay 'In Good Faith', the concerted attack on Rushdie and his writing has been greatly assisted by the creation of this false self. 'Simon Rushton' has featured in several Muslim portrayals of my debased, deracinated personality. My 'greed' fits well into the conspiracy theory, that I sold my soul to the West . . . in return for pots of money. 'Disloyalty' is useful in this context, too. Jorge Luis Borges, Graham Greene and other writers have written about their sense of an Other who goes about the world bearing their name. There are moments when I worry that my Other may succeed in obliterating me.

(Rushdie, 1991, pp. 405–6)

The rewriting of Rushdie as a historical figure in the wake of the *Satanic Verses* affair, then, provides a further insight into the way history-making happens, in the late twentieth and early twenty-first centuries.

In her essay 'The Site of Memory' (1990), Toni Morrison refers to the historical novel in terms of the need to reclaim lost ground, to fill silences. For Rushdie, the relationship between fiction and the past is seen in quite different terms. History is conceived as an overwhelming superabundance of experience, a tumult of competing voices. Thus, discussing his influences in writing *Midnight's Children* (1981), Rushdie describes his work as an attempt to salvage control and form out of the excess and anti-form of culture:

> The shape of the book more or less arose out of an attempt to control this huge flood of material. The first version of the book was almost twice the length and I felt I was being drowned by the stuff: I didn't feel in control of it. The shape the book gradually adopted was the shape of the attempt to impose shape on what seemed formless, which is why the book sort of has the meat on the inside and the skeleton on the outside, because the skeleton was gradually imposed on the book.
>
> (Chaudhuri, 1990, p. 1)

As a result of this, the text of *Midnight's Children* contains a crucial opposition. On the one hand, the novel continually demonstrates the excess and the multiplicity of history. Yet on the other hand it conveys equally clearly the sense of a focused historical *argument* running through all this cacophony.

In *The Moor's Last Sigh* (1995), too, there is a balance between the novel's ultimate 'direction' and its quality of freewheeling superabundance. 'This time I was absolutely certain of the final note, which was very freeing because it meant I could fool around as much as I wanted and compose this great long arc of a novel as long as I never lost sight of the fact that I had to go *there*' (Rushdie, 1999, p. 2). This is true of the general experience of reading

Rushdie's fiction. His range of vocabulary and image is partly designed to overwhelm the reader. His range of allusion like Joyce's is deliberately, formidably enormous. Some critics have seen it as their job to pin down and identify as many of the references and images in Rushdie's texts as possible. But, as with Joyce's work, it is dangerous to approach Rushdie's texts too much as one would an encyclopaedia. It is easy not to see the wood for the trees. Informed reading and the ability to trace references is obviously a basic requirement. But at the same time it is necessary to recognise excess and readerly overload as a feature of Rushdie's aesthetic. Even on the level of vocabulary, as he says, 'it's fun to read things when you don't know all the words' (p. 2).

As a writer, Rushdie is often admired for the vividness of his portrayals, most memorably of Bombay and of the cities of India and Pakistan. The rich intermingling of colours, tastes and smells, the turmoil of the metropolis, the fabulousness, saturation and immediacy of his historical descriptions earned him, early in his career, a reputation as the Indian who had finally wrested the pen from the grip of Kipling and Forster. Yet Rushdie cannot simply be considered as an Indian writer *per se*. When we look more closely at his work, a critical and imaginative distance from the subcontinent and its history quite clearly emerges.

For example, *The Moor's Last Sigh* is certainly a celebration of cosmopolitan Bombay. From the faeces-filled Bombay Central lock-up to the sparkling Cashondeliveri Tower, however, Rushdie's is a Bombay of the imagination, not a real but a magic realist city. In the post-historical novel *Midnight's Children* too, the land to which he returns is not an actual but an imaginary homeland:

> It may be that writers in my position, exiles or emigrants or expatriates, are haunted by some sense of loss, some urge to reclaim, to look back, even at the risk of being mutated into pillars of salt. But if we do look back, we must do so in the knowledge – which gives rise to profound uncertainties – that our physical alienation from India almost inevitably means that we will not be capable of reclaiming precisely the thing that was lost; that we will, in short, create fictions, not actual cities or villages, but invisible ones, imaginary homelands, Indias of the mind.
>
> (Rushdie, 1991, p. 10)

In the same way, as we will see, *Shame* (1983) is a novel which provocatively claims to be 'not quite' (p. 29) about Pakistan. Like Maxine Hong Kingston and Toni Morrison, Rushdie's technique is to insert his imagination into the cracks and faultlines of historical orthodoxy. Unlike them, though, his eye is the eye of an expatriate. Even as his texts (with amazing vividness) recreate the flavour of Kerala spices, Rushdie's analytic gaze remains that of a sophisticated Western metropolitan intellectual.

This distinction, between the notion of a writer working in and out of India itself, and the notion of the (Cambridge, London, New York) intellectual who 'looks back' on India through the lens of metropolitan postmodernism, is a crucial one. Indeed, it is probably the key to understanding the success with which Rushdie has been able to 're-describe' the East to the West. The cultural range of his work is undeniable, and it certainly does show a profound imaginative attachment to Bombay and the Malabar Coast, Karachi and Kashmir. His texts are saturated with the historical struggles of the subcontinent, and not least with their mythologisation in Hindi and Islamic literature and film. The way Rushdie appropriates all of these elements, however, is typically through the form of postmodern pastiche, through semi-serious, semi-ironic quotation.

The Western and metropolitan sensibility which I'm identifying here in Rushdie's work can at times be problematic. In an interview with Christopher Hitchens (1997), for example, he has great words for those Indian writers who, by choosing English as their literary language, have as he sees it 'managed to break through into world literature'. But as for contemporary literature in the sixteen other major languages of the subcontinent, his attitude is unmistakably scathing and dismissive:

> The besetting sin of the vernacular language is parochialism. It's as if the twentieth century hasn't arrived in many of these languages and the range of subjects and the manner of the treatment of them is depressingly familiar: village life is hard, women are badly treated and often commit suicide, landowners are corrupt, peasants are heroic and sometimes feckless, disillusioned, and defeated. The language is a kind of Indian equivalent of what, in the Soviet Union, was called 'Tractor Art.' When attempts are made to take notice of some of the developments in the rest of the world, the clumsiness is sometimes embarrassing.

To present this as the sum total of Rushdie's perception of Indian or Hindi or Islamic literature would obviously be a gross distortion. Indeed the parables and stories of Hinduism, Islam and (to a lesser extent) Buddhism and Christianity are at least as crucial an influence on his work as canonical writers of English-language literature like Daniel Defoe and James Joyce. His portrayal of postcolonial Englishness in *The Satanic Verses* is as scathing as anything you are likely to read in contemporary fiction. But Rushdie is a writer whose work is informed centrally by a left-liberal European politics. It is from this position that he has both celebrated and critiqued the histories of India, Pakistan and the Middle East.

Unlike that of Morrison or Kingston, Rushdie's work does not hinge particularly on silence or concealment. Nor can his texts be considered to any great extent as an attempt to reclaim history for the marginalised and dispossessed. For him, as we have already seen, the problem of history lies instead in its omnipresence and bewildering multiplicity. Like literature and culture, for Rushdie, history is something that is shifting and multiple. Thus, unlike novelists working in the realist tradition as well, his writing doesn't seek to represent the social past as a knowable totality. At their best, rather, his novels are magnificently cacophonous. As the narrator of *Midnight's Children* famously warns:

> There are so many stories to tell, too many, such an excess of inter-twined lives events miracles places rumours, so dense a commingling of the improbable and the mundane! I have been a swallower of lives; and to know me, just the one of me, you'll have to swallow the lot as well.
> (p. 9)

In all of Rushdie's texts, the jostling plotlines, anecdotes and images are polymorphously provocative and multi-level. And it is frequently difficult to separate in his writing the various layers of fantasy and the real. And yet *through* these qualities of multiplicity and multiformity, Rushdie's concerns in these texts are clearly historical and political to their core.

Both *Midnight's Children* and *Shame* are mesmerising works of the imagination. But they are also both strenuous attacks on powerful political regimes. *The Satanic Verses* is a novel about the workings of dreams, which also runs the gauntlet of one of the world's most formidable matrices of power, Islam. *The Moor's Last Sigh*, though (perhaps understandably) less direct in its political engagements, is still populated by real historical figures such as Jawaharlal Nehru, first premier of the free state of India. Here, Rushdie has Nehru intermingling freely with a host of fictional and even fantastical characters. On the one hand, therefore: an aesthetic of excess, multiformity, a kaleidoscopically appropriative imagination. And on the other hand: a set of hardheaded political, philosophical and historical concerns. Understanding how these apparently contradictory elements fit together is essential to reading Rushdie's fiction.

Midnight's Children

On the eve of Independence from British rule, Jawaharlal Nehru said this:

> To the people of India, whose representatives we are, we make an appeal to join us with faith and confidence in this great adventure. This is no

time for petty and destructive criticism, no time for ill-will or blaming others. We have to build the noble mansion of free India where all her children may dwell.

(Rushdie and West, 1997, p. 2)

Both in the decades before Independence and in the seventeen years of his premiership, Nehru's politics could certainly be read in terms of the broad principle of inclusiveness. In his conception of a secular state, in his attempt at even-handed relations between the Cold War superpowers, in his resistance to Muslim and Sikh separatism, in his attacks on the divisiveness of the Hindu caste system – in all of this, the tendency towards liberal inclusiveness can easily be framed as a defining theme.

To compare this kind of ideological positioning with the politics of Rushdie's writing is certainly illuminating. Twenty years after Nehru's death, on the assassination of Indira Gandhi, Salman Rushdie wrote this:

But it is up to the new leadership to show the way. To reject the idea of getting votes by appealing to religious sectarianism. To give up using the Congress Party machine as an instrument of patronage . . . To desist from bribing and corrupting the supporters of one's political opponents in order to achieve in back-rooms what has not been achieved by the ballot box. To show that India is not in the grip of any new *Imperium*. And to *restore our faith in the India-idea*.

What, centrally, is that idea? It is based on the most obvious and apparent fact about the great subcontinent: multitude. For a nation of seven hundred millions to *make any kind of sense*, it must base itself on the concept of multiplicity, of plurality and tolerance . . . let difference reign.

(Rushdie, 1991, p. 44, italics in original)

For each of them, there is a fundamental belief in something which is simultaneously political, historical and imaginary: what Rushdie calls the 'India-idea'. For each of them, equally, if the India-idea is to survive it must be based on the accommodation of plurality and contradiction. India cannot 'make sense' simply as a land mass, as a set of imposed geographical boundaries. It cannot be characterised as a group of people with a common language and shared way of life. In the wake of multiple cultural and religious differences, rather, the idea is that it can be held together only by common subscription to a kind of Western democratic model of India as a plural, secular and tolerant society. What is required fundamentally is not pragmatic reform or even detailed political restructuring. According to Rushdie, what is required is a collective leap of the imagination.

In the sense that it can be read as an expression of this argument, *Midnight's Children* is certainly a historical novel. Its central allegory can clearly be interpreted, in these terms, as an analysis of post-Independence India. Read in that way, its subject is therefore India's *failure* to sustain the spirit of tolerance and difference, its failure to sustain that collective imaginative effort. Rushdie's midnight's children, with their diversity of backgrounds, creeds and castes and their plethora of magic powers, on one level clearly represent the vast potential of the new India that was reborn free at midnight on 14th August 1947:

> Understand what I'm saying: during the first hour of August 15th, 1947 – between midnight and one a.m. – no less than one thousand and one children were born within the frontiers of the infant sovereign state of India . . . It was as though – if you will permit me one moment of fancy in what will otherwise be, I promise, the most sober account I can manage – as though history, arriving at a point of the highest significance and promise, had chosen to sow, in that instant, the seeds of a future which would genuinely differ from anything the world had seen up to that time.
>
> (p. 195)

In using the idea of the midnight's children as an allegory for the new nation, moreover, Rushdie's text also describes a particular model of India itself. For example, his magical community of the gifted includes not a single child from Pakistan, as if, in being born, the midnight's children instantly recognise the 'naturalness' of partition. None of the children is amongst the millions who died in the violence following that hasty postcolonial compromise. At the same time, his conference of midnight Indians *does* include membership from independent Kashmir, which on 15th August had yet to be invaded by either Pakistani or Indian troops. Strategically, Rushdie's narrator also places midnight's children in the sensitive borderlands of Thar and the Sundarbans Jungle. Thus clearly, in making his magic children representative of India itself, Saleem's story also describes a political position on the question of what India is or should be. Read in the most literal terms: he accepts partition, he claims Kashmir, he is reluctant to relinquish the borders of East Pakistan/Bangladesh.

In this sense the idea of the midnight's children could certainly be read in historical terms. But in another sense, the novel also pulls away from such a reading. In the same way as it represents a commentary on India, the idea of the nation-wide children's conference also explicitly invokes India's most powerful political institution, the Indian National Congress, headed by Gopal Krishna Gokale, Mohandas (Mahatma) Gandhi, Jawaharlal Nehru and eventually by Nehru's daughter, Indira Gandhi. But again Rushdie's children's conference represents, not a reflection, but an ideal model of the Congress movement. Far from being a direct allegory of the Anglophile, Brahman-dominated Congress movement that assumed control in 1947, his children come from all castes, regions and creeds. In a kind of magic meritocracy, they are united and motivated only by their special powers and potential.

In a conventional literary-historical reading, similarly, it is easy to fix on the Widow as the destroyer of the Midnight's Children's Conference, just as Indira Gandhi broke away from Congress grandees to form her New Congress Party in the years before her authoritarian 'Emergency' period. Many critics have accepted this reading, foregrounding the penultimate chapter of the novel in which the children are rounded up and surgically sterilised. But if we read a little more closely, it becomes clear that the Widow's murderous regime is only the last nail in the coffin of a Midnight's Children's Conference that (unlike the Congress Party) has been long dead by that stage. As representatives of an enlightened, democratic model of India, their true end is not with the Emergency of 1975 but with the war with China in 1962, related in the chapter 'Drainage and the Desert':

> In the high Himalayas, Gurkhas and Rajputs fled in disarray from the Chinese army; and in the upper reaches of my mind, another army was also destroyed by things – bickerings, prejudices, boredom, selfishness – which I had believed too small, too petty to have touched them.
>
> (p. 298)

In this way, *Midnight's Children* can be read clearly as a counter-historical novel. From near the beginning of the text, it sets up a symbolic opposition between knees and nose, Shiva and Saleem, brute strength and enlightenment. As surely as Shiva begins to dominate the children's conference, using his violence to eclipse Saleem's liberal idealism – so on a historical level the novel describes not the dissolution of the Congress movement itself, but rather the dissolution of the aspirations it once seemed to represent:

> Shiva-the-destroyer, Shiva Knocknees . . . he became a sort of principle; he came to represent, in my mind, all the vengefulness and violence and simultaneous-love-and-hate-of-Things in the world; so that even now, when I hear of drowned bodies floating like balloons on the Hooghly and exploding when nudged by passing boats; or trains set on fire, or politicians killed, or riots in Orissa or Punjab, it seems to me that the hand of Shiva lies heavily over all these things, dooming us to

flounder endlessly amid murder rape greed war – that Shiva, in short, has made us who we are.

(p. 299)

In the same sequence as the narration of the Chinese war, the draining of Saleem's nose deprives him, likewise, of his midnight's gift of insight. And as if to hammer home the pivotal importance of this chapter, it even begins by repeating the words of the novel's opening 'once upon a time. No that won't do, there's no getting away from the date . . .' (p. 294). In this way the Midnight's Children's Conference can be read as a representation, not of the Congress movement or even India itself as such, but rather of the Congress movement and India as they should, or might have been.

Read as a counter-historical account, then, the novel's gradual descent into darker and darker territory reflects a clear analysis of the development of modern India, through the 1971 war over East Pakistan/Bangladesh to the crisis of the 1970s. Most specifically, as the critic Catherine Cundy (1996) shows, the novel is vitriolic in its attack on Indira Gandhi, whose 'Emergency' period from 1975 to 1977 did (not just allegedly) include some of the roundings-up and jailings, the violent slum clearances and the campaign of mass sterilisation which feature in Rushdie's novel. But again, *Midnight's Children* makes no secret of the fact that its account of Gandhi's regime is extremely partisan. Indeed the novel flaunts its disregard for balance or fairness.

For Rushdie, India's 'multitude' is the sign of its plurality and potential. For Gandhi, that same 'multitude' is the sign of population explosion, and the threat of mass starvation. But those arguments are never allowed to take place in the novel. Instead, through the voice of its 'unreliable narrator' Saleem, the text opts for gothic melodrama:

the Widow's arm is long as death its skin is green the fingernails are long and sharp and black. Between the walls the children green the walls are green the Widow's arm comes snaking down the snake is green the children scream the fingernails are black they scratch the Widow's arm is hunting . . .

(p. 208)

Midnight's Children's attack on Mrs Gandhi – at that time one of the world's most powerful women – was enough to bring a vigorous response. His depiction of the Widow with her murderous grasping black-nailed fingers became the subject of her successful lawsuit against Rushdie after the novel's first publication in 1981. To be sued by a current prime minister was no mean feat for an expatriate novelist, clearly foreshadowing the controversies to come.

Throughout the text, the possibility of partiality, even unfairness, is openly admitted. At the same time as we follow Saleem's disjointed history, we are alerted to the possibility of forging different ones. As the narrator says:

> reality is a question of perspective; the further you get from the past, the more concrete and plausible it seems – but as you approach the present, it inevitably seems more and more incredible . . . The assassination of Mahatma Gandhi occurs, in these pages, on the wrong date. But I cannot say, now, what the actual sequence of events might have been; in my India, Gandhi will continue to die at the wrong time. Does one error invalidate the whole fabric? Am I so far gone, in my desperate need for meaning, that I'm prepared to distort everything – to rewrite the whole history of my times purely in order to place myself in a central role? Today, in my confusion, I can't judge.
>
> (pp. 165–6)

In the undeclared war over Kashmir, similarly, we are given a deliberately ambiguous account of the violence. The planes flying overhead are 'real or fictional' and the bombs they drop 'actual or mythical' (p. 341) according to our particular view. As Rushdie himself has acknowledged, historical ambiguity, silence and even error are written into the narrative at every level. His essay '"Errata": Or, Unreliable Narration in *Midnight's Children*' clearly illustrates the extent to which the novel as a whole is historically awry, discussing a whole range of different kinds of errors and omissions:

> Concrete tetrapods have never been used in Bombay as part of any land reclamation scheme, but only to shore up and protect the sea wall along the Marine Drive promenade. Nor could the train that brings Picture Singh and Saleem from Delhi to Bombay possibly have passed through Kurla, which is on a different line . . . [And] let me confess that the novel does contain a few mistakes that are mine as well as Saleem's. One is to be found in the description of the Amritsar massacre, during which I have Saleem say that Dyer entered the Jallianwala Bagh compound followed by 'fifty white troops'. The truth is that there were fifty troops, but they weren't white. When I first found out my error I was upset and tried to have it corrected. Now I'm not so sure . . .
>
> (Rushdie, 1991, pp. 22–3)

Discussing the reception of *Midnight's Children* by critics and other readers, Rushdie in no way claims that the book is supposed to be some sort of definitive history of modern India. Instead his metaphor is that of the imaginative map.

One of the paradoxes that the book deals with is that India may be an ancient civilisation but it's also a new country. One of the things you have to do with new countries is to draw maps of them. That's one of the things that the book was an attempt to do. And that's one of the things that writers can do for readers, provide them with imaginary maps.

(p. 23)

Unlike the traditional academic history, Rushdie's notion of the imaginary map is far from final or definitive. Unlike the closed conventions of historical narration, moreover, it has the power to fictionalise and mythologise in pursuit of truths beyond the banality of 'what happened'. It is a mind-drawing, a partial selection of the possible landmarks, contours and details to be depicted. Reflecting on the writing of *Midnight's Children*, Rushdie says:

When I began the novel (as I've written elsewhere) my purpose was somewhat Proustian. Time and migration had placed a double filter between me and my subject, and I hoped that if I could only imagine vividly enough it might be possible to see beyond those filters, to write as if the years had not passed, as if I had never left India for the West. But as I worked I found that what interested me was the process of filtration itself. So my subject changed, was no longer a search for lost time, had become the way in which we remake the past to suit our present purposes, using memory as our tool.

. . . Thereafter, as I wrote the novel, and whenever a conflict arose between literal and remembered truth, I would favour the remembered version. This is why, even though Saleem admits that no tidal wave passed through the Sundarbans in the year of the Bangladesh War, he continues to be borne out of the jungle on the crest of that fictional wave. His truth is too important to him to allow it to be unseated by a mere weather report. It is memory's truth, he insists, and only a madman would prefer someone else's version to his own.

(pp. 23–4)

'Memory's truth', here, is of course not without its own problems. Indeed, it reveals the nostalgic nature of much of *Midnight's Children*'s imaginary map. Instead of witnessing the bloodshed of the Bangladesh war, Saleem and his young companions become lost in a magical forest. Rather than being forcibly expelled from Bangladesh, amid the diverse tragedies of a million refugees, they are excitingly washed out on the crest of some Tom-and-Jerry tidal wave. Unlike the millions who died in inter-religious violence in the years after partition, Rushdie's protagonist is free to move between India, Pakistan and Bangladesh as the historical 'action' dictates. His eye is that of one to whom the rules do not apply, who is party to the machinations of the rich and powerful, and who is detached enough, secure enough, to satirise them.

Shame

In *Midnight's Children* we see the possibility of an India different to that governed by the Congress Party under Indira Gandhi. The novel is, as we have seen, both a complex work of the imagination and a strenuous political attack. *Shame*, which focuses on Pakistan, is also a text written between the folds of history and the imagination. Even more than India at Independence, *Shame* suggests, Pakistan is a country which has had to be imagined, willed into existence. Formed in 1947 out of a political compromise with the departing British, in two land masses a thousand miles apart, and subject to a series of humiliating military defeats at the hands of its larger and wealthier rival, the novel tells the story of Pakistani nation-building.

As we would expect, Rushdie's portrait of his other homeland is far from a closed historical account. Rather, it is written counter-historically, at a tangent to Pakistan's orthodox, authorised past:

> My story's palimpsest-country has, I repeat, no name of its own. The exiled Czech writer Kundera once wrote: 'A name means continuity with the past and people without a past are people without a name.' But I am dealing with a past that refuses to be suppressed, that is daily doing battle with the present; so it is perhaps unduly harsh of me to deny my fairyland a title.
>
> There's an apocryphal story that Napier, after a successful campaign in what is now the south of Pakistan, sent back to England the guilty, one-word message, 'Peccavi'. *I have Sind.* I'm tempted to name my looking-glass Pakistan in honour of the bilingual (and fictional, because never really uttered) pun. Let it be *Peccavistan.*
>
> (p. 88)

On the most literal level, *Shame* follows the entwined careers of Zulfikar Ali Bhutto and Mohammad Zia ul-Haq, whose power struggles dominated Pakistani politics throughout the 1970s and 1980s. But at the same time, the principal subject of this text is something far less tangible. A feeling or emotion, a spectre of the imagining mind: the idea of shame itself. Each of these interlocked stories, the literal and the symbolic, provides a different kind of construction of the history of Pakistan.

Throughout Rushdie's text, the narrative voice frequently intrudes to remind us of the allegorical and symbolic nature of the stories we are reading.

Even the choices and influences that contribute to the construction of particular characters are freely discussed. Perhaps the most obvious example of this is provided by the figure of Sufiya Zinobia. As is indicated with sledgehammer subtlety by her two surnames, Shakil and Hyder, Sufiya is something of a Jekyll and Hyde character. As the narrator says, she is based partly on the story of a British Pakistani girl in the East End of London, who was killed by her father because he thought she had slept with a white boy. Shame, embarrassment, decency, propriety, dishonour are all tied up together in the ideological complex Rushdie calls *sharam*, a principle strong enough to make a man sacrifice his child. In the novel Sufiya is explicitly representative of this notion of shame.

Another of her constituents, however, is the character of a different British Asian girl (this time imagined) who, frustrated with the racism she encounters, suddenly turns on her tormentors and ferociously beats them. In a third sense, moreover, Sufiya is also representative of Pakistan itself – in its incarnation as an Islamic 'Land of the Pure'. On each level, she symbolises the dialectic of shame and violence, the union of modesty, moderation and ferocious retribution. What *Shame* tries to do through the figure of Sufiya is to allow us to imagine our way into this union of opposites. Thus we are invited to understand the turbulent history of Pakistan, not in terms of facts, but in terms of a struggle of ideas. The relations between religious belief, violence and retribution are not as simple as they appear, Rushdie's narrator suggests. Even in describing it, he says, 'I feel gleeful about this notion: it's a seductive, silky thing, this violence, yes it is' (p. 117).

In *Midnight's Children*, as we have seen, Rushdie sets up his opposition between Anglophile liberalism and sectarian violence through the twin figures of Saleem and Shiva. In *Shame*, a parallel opposition is put in place by the marriage of Sufiya Zinobia to Omar Khayyam Shakil. Whilst Sufiya has been raised to epitomise her family's shame, Shakil's three mothers educate him sternly to live a life of shamelessness. Like Pakistani Independence itself, he is conceived in a cosy meeting between upper-class Muslims and the departing British. On a crude level, then, the marriage of Sufiya and Shakil can be taken to symbolise the union of – or struggle between – unworldly piety and secular modernity in the nation of Pakistan. She is innocent, pure and slow-witted; he is debauched, Europhile and intellectual.

In the novel, however, this becomes more complicated than it seems. Crucially, it is to be remembered, what underlies Sufiya's demure surface is a vein of implacable violence. Throughout the text, this keeps resurfacing allegorically. As, on a political level, the Islamist factions of the governing class repeatedly meddle with the power balance, substituting their own alternative constitutions, so Sufiya becomes obsessed with rearranging the household furniture. Just as the nation becomes repeatedly involved in disastrous military campaigns, so she begins the habit of self-harming:

> He becomes convinced that Sufiya Zinobia is willing the damage upon herself. This is the significance of her case: it shows that even a broken mind is capable of marshalling macrophages and polymorphs; even a stunted intelligence can lead a palace revolution, a suicidal rebellion of the janissaries of the human body against the castle itself.
>
> (p. 143)

Omar Khayyam Shakil, the representative of Western-style secularism, science and education, tries to ward off the worst effects of her violence-disease by the use of immunosuppressants. At the end of the novel, however, he is ultimately powerless to prevent her from destroying them both in a spectacular nuclear blast. Underneath his urbane exterior is a core of weakness and self-doubt. Like secular modernity itself, in terms of the shaping of events, he is always a 'peripheral man' (p. 283).

This opposition of shame/violence versus shamelessness/urbanity is explicitly mapped on to the historical struggle between Bhutto and Zia through the characters of Iskander Harappa and Raza Hyder. Harappa, a city playboy, is clearly a commentary on Bhutto, and despite Rushdie's denials his daughter Arjumand 'the Virgin Ironpants' is, equally obviously, a representation of the future prime minister Benazir Bhutto. The 'target' of Rushdie's Raza Hyder, Sufiya's father, is the Islamist dictator General Zia. Considering that *Shame* was both written and published during the height of the Zia regime, Rushdie's depiction of Hyder fleeing in drag, lying in a bed full of his own excrement and dying in a horrendous death-trap of stiletto blades represents, undoubtedly, a viciously personal (and dangerous) attack on the Pakistani presidency. Clearly, it is an assassination by fiction and wishful-thinking:

> How does a dictator fall? There is an old saw which states, with absurd optimism, that it is in the nature of tyrannies to end. One might as well say that it is also in their nature to begin, to continue, to dig themselves in, and, often, to be preserved by greater powers than their own.
>
> Well, well, I mustn't forget I'm only telling a fairy-story. My dictator will be toppled by goblinish, faery means. 'Makes it pretty easy for you,' is the obvious criticism; and I agree, I agree. But add, even if it does sound a little peevish: '*You* try and get rid of a dictator some time.'
>
> (p. 257)

Amongst the other key allegorical figures in the novel, President Shaggy Dog mirrors the martial law administrator General Agha Mohammad Yahya Khan. Sheikh Bismillah (a pun on the Arabic *bi smi llaah* or 'In the name of Allah') caricatures the popular Bengali leader and first prime minister of Bangladesh, Sheikh Mujib. Thus, whilst on one level *Shame* is a playful fantasy on the theme of shame, a fairytale beginning with three daughters named Chhunni, Munnee and Bunny, it is also a risky and provocative political novel. Once again foreshadowing the *Satanic Verses* controversy, the text itself even half-jokingly suggests, 'But suppose this were a realistic novel! . . . The book would have been banned, dumped in the rubbish bin, burned' (pp. 69–70).

As well as the execution of Zulfikar Ali Bhutto, one of the novel's most important historical targets is the 1971 war over Bangladeshi Independence, which as we have seen is somewhat inadequately represented in *Midnight's Children*. In an essay on the later novel, Ashutosh Banerjee (1990) has illustrated very well how the sense of collective *sharam* in (West) Pakistan associated with the defeat in their East Wing provides a crucial part of the novel's subject matter. '*Shame* is about the impact of that war on what remained of the country, the erstwhile West Wing. That the effect had been devastating for the national *psyche* is not to be doubted.' And as Banerjee goes on to argue, 'defeat in the 1971 war had been a crushing blow to the Pakistani ego precisely because Pakistan's aristocracy had been predominantly military. Even a civilian leader like Zulfikar Ali Bhutto spoke in terms of a "thousand-year war with India"' (pp. 71–2). Banerjee's interpretation of Rushdie's novel is convincing as far as it goes. But ultimately, the postmodern radicalism of *Shame* is that it refuses to offer any *one* narrative of events as the closed, final history of Pakistan. Rather, it presents history itself as a struggle between multiple versions and accounts, all struggling for supremacy.

One such history is woven in the eighteen 'shawls of memory' created by Harappa's wife, Rani. Against the grain of public record, the shawls depict a dark underside to her husband's life, including the despotism and corruption underpinning his regime. In the mind of her daughter Arjumand (Rushdie's Benazir Bhutto), meanwhile, a diametrically different narrative of his career seeks to establish itself as history:

> Her thoughts, Arjumand's, do not dwell on the war that followed, except to note that of course the idolatrous nation positioned between the Wings backed the Eastern bastards to the hilt, for obvious, divide-and-rule reasons. A fearful war. In the West, oil-refineries, airports, the homes of God-fearing civilians bombarded by heathen explosives. The final defeat of the Western forces, which led to the reconstitution of the

East Wing as an autonomous (*that's a laugh*) nation and international basket case, was obviously engineered by outsiders: stone-washers and damn-yankees, yes. The Chairman visited the United Nations and bawled those eunuchs out: 'You won't destroy us while I'm alive.' He stormed out of the General Assembly, handsome, intemperate, great: 'My country hearkens for me! Why should I stay in this harem of trans-vestite whores?' – and returned home to take up the reins of government in what was left of the land of God . . . Arjumand at Mohenjo, replete with memories, allows her remembering mind to transmute the preserved fragments of the past into the gold of myth.

(pp. 179–81)

At many points in the text, as we have seen, political subjects are treated directly. The problem of Zia's continuing dictatorship is freely discussed, as are the infamous circumstances of Bhutto's execution at his hands. The novel's portrayal of a looking-glass country that is 'not Pakistan, or not quite' (p. 29) forms a critical dialogue with these asides. In this parallel universe, it is possible for a tyrant to be cartoonishly murdered, for a police chief to be clairvoyant (so that he can arrest and intern people before they have even committed the crimes he foresees) and for the destructive obsessionality of shame to finally go up in smoke.

As *Shame* suggests, it is possible for histories to be woven in different patterns. In the text as a whole, the past is represented as a palimpsest, a text that is written over and over from different perspectives, driven by different personal, political and religious agendas. In a nation of reversals, it takes only moments for strength to become weakness, and for triumph to turn to collapse: 'throughout the war, hourly radio bulletins described the glorious triumphs of the Western regiments in the East. On that last day, at eleven a.m., the radio announced the last and most spectacular of these feats of arms; at noon, it curtly informed its audience of the impossible: unconditional surrender, humiliation, defeat' (p. 180). At the same time as it engages with the narratives of public history, as they are created in the media and institutionalised by dominant interests, therefore, the effect of *Shame* is to debunk those very processes of history-making. This is nowhere more striking than in the commentary on the construction of Pakistan itself:

It is well known that the term 'Pakistan', an acronym, was originally thought up in England by a group of Muslim intellectuals. P for the Punjabis, A for the Afghans, K for the Kashmiris, S for Sind and the 'tan', they say, for Baluchistan . . . So it was a word born in exile that then went east, was borne-across or trans-lated, and imposed itself on history; a returning migrant, settling down on partitioned land, forming a palimpsest on the past. A palimpsest obscures what lies beneath. To build Pakistan it was necessary to cover up Indian history, to deny that Indian centuries lay just underneath the surface of Pakistani Standard Time. The past was rewritten . . . It is possible to see the subsequent history of Pakistan as a duel between two layers of time, the obscured world forcing its way through what-had-been-imposed. It is the true desire of every artist to impose his or her vision on the world; and Pakistan, the peeling, fragmenting palimpsest, may be described as a failure of the dreaming mind. Perhaps the pigments used were the wrong ones, like Leonardo's; or perhaps the place was just *insufficiently imagined*, a picture full of irreconcilable elements, midriff-baring immigrant saris versus demure, indigenous Sindhi shalwar-kurtas, Urdu versus Punjabi, now versus then: a miracle that went wrong.

As for me: I too, like all migrants, am a fantasist. I build imaginary countries and try to impose them on the ones that exist. I, too, face the problem of history: what to retain, what to dump, how to hold on to what memory insists on relinquishing, how to deal with change.

(pp. 87–8, italics in original)

In its explosive, clairvoyant conclusion, *Shame* quite appropriately remains ambiguous. Sufiya's atomic detonation may describe the final burning-out of religious violence in Pakistan, or the final burning-out of Pakistan itself. It may symbolise the exit of the nation from the world stage, Pakistan as 'a figure of dreams, or a phantom with one arm lifted in a gesture of farewell' (p. 286). Or perhaps it prophesies the final conflagration of the arms race with India. What Rushdie's counter-historical method seeks to suggest is not only the possibility of different readings of the past, but the possibility of alternative futures too, including futures different to those which seem to be defined by present political circumstances.

According to the French philosopher Jean-François Lyotard (1979), the most important characteristic of the postmodern moment is our collective scepticism towards overbearing grand narratives. In chapter 1, we explored this idea in some detail. Living in the aftermath of the atrocities of Fascism and imperialism, Lyotard and others suggest, we are reluctant to give credence to any authoritarian orthodoxy, or any historical belief-system that purports to explain everything. As we saw in chapter 1, Marxism's narrative of revolution has, in some places, been one of the casualties of this climate of ideological scepticism. And liberalism's narrative of civilised progress, too, has been amongst the most important targets for critique by contemporary thinkers and writers. In this book, from McEwan to Kingston to Winterson to Morrison to Rushdie, each of the writers we have examined so far is affected in different kinds of ways by the sense of 'incredulity' Lyotard describes. All of them attempt to use the creative resources of the novel to burrow under the surface of collective memory and established belief. All of them attempt to re-address, in an age of scepticism, the question of historical responsibility.

10 Angela Carter: Genealogies

Angela Carter's work forms one of the most interesting and provocative counter-historical projects in contemporary fiction. History, in her writing, is no longer the domain of facts. It is a self-contradictory, problematic, conglomerated inheritance of meanings. The primary focus of her texts is the figure of 'woman', and the legacy of encrusted meanings and values which come to define her contours. Carter's fiction was amongst the first of a new generation of writing, which emerged as a response to the counter-cultural revolutions of the late 1960s. As she says in her 1983 essay 'Notes From the Front Line':

> I can date to that time and to some of those debates and to that sense of heightened awareness of the society around me in the summer of 1968, my own questioning of the nature of my reality as a *woman*. How that social fiction of my 'femininity' was created, by means outside my control, and palmed off on me as the real thing.
>
> (Carter, 1998, p. 38)

Her work approaches gender and sex as historical constructs to be examined, played with and dismantled. In so doing, it produces some of the most unorthodox and enjoyable texts of the era.

Since her death from cancer in 1992, there has been an explosion of interest in Carter's writing. In that year, famously, the British Academy received more applications to study her work than they did for the entire eighteenth century. This in itself came as something of a revelation in critical circles, where Carter's reputation as the 'high priestess of postgraduate porn' (Sebestyen, 1987, p. 38) had been rather uneven. Paradoxically, one of the realisations that Carter's death brought with it, however, was the extent to which her texts had been misunderstood. One obituary, from *The Times* newspaper, quoted by Joseph Bristow and Trev Lynn Broughton in their collection *The Infernal Desires of Angela Carter* (1997) stands out in particular:

Angela Carter was an unashamed fantasist, a fabulist of daemonic energy. She dwelt naturally in the world of myth, dream and fairy tale. Above all, in writing about sex she confronted the question of whether a woman can realistically cross the barrier between her natural maso-chism to inhabit the sadistic terrain of the male, with a seriousness which is wholly absent from novels of her contemporaries. She squarely faced the possibility that sex is ultimately a violent business and that women can acquiesce in that.

Considering the wide range of interpretations to which a set of texts like Carter's can be subjected, it seems a perverse kind of achievement to be this *wrong*. As a way of dispelling a few misconceptions about Carter's work, nevertheless, the passage provides a good place to start.

Far from perpetuating myths and fairytales, first of all, Carter frames her work quite explicitly in terms of *de*mythologising. Digging through the legacies of culture, she is concerned to lay bare the origins and operations of controlling myths about women. As Carter (1979) says in her examina-tion of one such myth-maker, the Marquis de Sade:

All the mythic versions of women, from the myth of the redeeming purity of the virgin to that of the healing, reconciling mother, are consolatory nonsenses; and consolatory nonsense seems to me a fair definition of myth, anyway.

(p. 5)

Equally, it is an important misinterpretation to read Carter's work as reinforcing a view of sex as 'naturally' characterised by violence, especially violence against women. Certainly, texts like *Shadow Dance* (1966) and *The Passion of New Eve* (1977) contain themes of exploitation and sexual violence. But these are deployed as part of a strategy of subversion. Carter's rewritings of familiar stories such as 'Little Red Riding Hood' and 'Bluebeard' in *The Bloody Chamber*, similarly, need to be understood as efforts to reveal the ways in which patriarchal and misogynistic representations of femininity are perpetuated. The vehicle in this case is the long-established tradition of 'improving' folktale that is part of the bedtime diet of little girls. In later works such as *Nights at the Circus* (1984), similarly, such 'timeless' patriarchal myths as that of the angelic virgin are amusingly subverted and reworked. *Wise Children* (1991) takes the cliché of the actress/whore. In each case, Carter's texts play around with inherited representations of femininity, always looking for the possibilities of transformation.

Carter's writings, then, are fundamentally intertextual. That is, they are constantly engaged in the quotation, appropriation and subversion of other texts. As well as folk and fairytale sources, her work engages with a wide range of other texts and references. Like Salman Rushdie, she makes good use of eighteenth-century forms, especially the picaresque and the gothic. Her texts are patterned with iconic references to the history of European art, from the ancient Winged Victory of Samothrace to the modernist nudes of Toulouse Lautrec. In texts like *The Passion of New Eve*, *Nights at the Circus* and *Wise Children*, there are all sorts of witty references to popular songs, film iconography, variety and music hall. And at the same time, there are frequent drawings from critical philosophy, ranging from the Marxist Louis Althusser, in the early work, to the psychoanalyst Jacques Lacan later on.

In terms of Carter's political and philosophical analysis, moreover, it is useful again to note the influence of Michel Foucault, whose work is largely contemporary with Carter's own. In the work of each, we can see a common disrespect for traditional verities. In each, a provocative tendency to wash dirty linen in public. Looking at specific texts it is, certainly, possible to trace direct Foucauldian influences in Carter's work, for example in her use of the Panopticon prison in *Nights at the Circus*, which draws on his study of the penal system, *Discipline and Punish* (1975). But in more general terms, it is helpful to think about Carter's work in relation to the wider project of genealogy.

In chapter 1, I outlined the ways genealogies set out to trace the inter-relationships between power, discourse and the body. Even in the very earliest of Carter's texts, we see an interest in the dispersal of power in discourse, especially in powerful systems of iconography and conventions of narration. Whilst all of her texts play with figures of authoritarian control – Uncle Philip in *The Magic Toyshop*, Zero in *The Passion of New Eve*, the Grand Duke in *Nights at the Circus* – what they are much more centrally concerned with is the way particular kinds of gender representations become institutionalised, and how it might be possible to subvert those represen-tations. In texts like *The Bloody Chamber* (1979), we see an investigation of the way patriarchal myths are encoded into the popular fairytale tradition. The collection then offers a set of witty narrative interventions which set the fairy tales off in more emancipatory directions.

Equally, there is a detailed consideration of the way power inscribes itself on the body itself. *Shadow Dance* and *The Passion of New Eve* are perhaps the novels in which this idea is developed in the most literal way. Throughout Carter's *œuvre*, however, we can see all sorts of experimental efforts to play around with bodies and to investigate the ways they are regulated within culture. At the same time, there is a constant attempt to populate our field of vision with representations of the marginal, the freakish, the disqualified, and a constant dissection and subversion of social and sexual orthodoxies.

At the level of character, certainly, it is possible to see the effects this approach brings with it. In the older liberal humanist conventions of historical writing, the individual is habitually identified as the prime agent of history. Likewise, in the political principles of liberal democracy, there is a stress on the fundamental rights, the rationality and the conscience of the individual in society. The democratic mandate of rulers and governments is theorised as an expression of the collective will, the pooled sovereignty of individuals. And in the established humanist traditions of fiction as well there is a corresponding focus on individual consciousness and conscience. It is easy to see how, in this tradition, the presentation of the 'fully rounded' protagonist becomes the ideal, exemplified in such iconic characters as Jane Austen's Elizabeth Bennet or Emma Woodhouse.

In the post-humanist tradition of which Carter and Foucault are both a part, this philosophical focus changes quite dramatically. We become much more interested in the construction and regulation of the subject through regimes of power/knowledge. In an effort to explore and expose such complex mechanisms of 'subjectification', it is no surprise, then, to find that Carter has dispensed with the model of the 'fully rounded' character in favour of figures who appear constructed or even pantomimic, characters for which the operation of power is written on to the very surface and form of the body. It is no surprise, either, to encounter protagonists, such as Evelyn/ Eve or Fevvers, who test and transgress the boundaries of the 'normal/ healthy' and the 'deviant/perverse'.

One of the obvious consequences of this is that Carter's texts need to be read quite differently from those of humanist and realist writers. To return to the *Times* obituary with which we started, her writing is certainly concerned with collective fantasies, myths and representations, as well as with the imbrication of sex with violence and power. But those explorations should definitely not be understood as some kind of escapism, or as an abdication of the responsibilities of the novel. Rather, they need to be recognised as philosophically and politically grounded strategies, clearly located in a tradition of resistance.

Shadow Dance

Certainly, the presentation of Carter's first novel, *Shadow Dance* (1966), is neither liberal nor realist. Far from 'fully rounded' characters, the text is populated from the start by grotesque bodily representations, and saturated with the sense of deviancy. In its opening confrontation between the creepy and ineffectual 'hero', Morris, and his former lover, Ghislaine, moreover, there is a violent reversal of the conventions of romance fiction:

The scar drew her whole face sideways, and even in profile, with the hideous thing turned away, her face was horribly lop-sided, skin, features and all dragged away from the bone.

She was a beautiful girl, a white and golden girl, like moonlight on daisies, a month ago. So he stared at her shattered beauty.

(p. 3)

Before the narrative opens, its pretty, delicate heroine has already been slashed and disfigured. Initially, we are invited to speculate about Morris's involvement in the attack. Though he did not wield the knife himself, perhaps he incited the violence of his friend Honeybuzzard. This is no Victorian detective fiction, however, in which rationality and justice are going to prevail. Rather, as the narrative proceeds, we move further and further into darkness, as the text becomes more and more enmeshed in the misogynistic fantasies of its male characters.

At first Morris disfigures pornographic photographs of the victim with exaggerated facsimiles of her knife-wound. He dreams of cutting her with broken glass to the applause of gathered onlookers. Gradually these dreams begin to become both more ritualised and more homely:

He dreamed he was cutting Ghislaine's face with a kitchen knife. The knife was blunt and kept slipping. Her head came off in his hands, after a while, and he cut her into a turnip lantern, put a candle inside and lit it through her freshly carved mouth. She burned away with a greenish light.

(pp. 39–40)

Like his own subservient wife, Edna, the idea of Ghislaine has to be cut down in Morris's fantasy to a role of utility and decoration. And the novel goes out on a limb to entertain that metaphor of cutting and to frame it in the terms of ritualised violence. Set against other writers of the late 1960s, then, what we are clearly dealing with is a writer using a set of strategies quite different from those of her major contemporaries.

In the mainstream of the period, the works of morally committed figures such as William Golding or Iris Murdoch have established a canonical status. It is not so much against these texts, however, but against the background of such influential feminist works as Doris Lessing's novel *The Golden Notebook* (1962) and Betty Friedan's popular study *The Feminine Mystique* (1963), that the radicalism of *Shadow Dance* comes into focus. Lessing's book explores the relation between political and sexual-political struggle for women in the early Cold War period. Friedan critically examines the revival of domestic ideology in the United States. As the feminist critic Susan

Watkins (2001) argues, both books struck important chords amongst women of Carter's generation. The re-emergence of an ideal of domesticity described by Friedan was seen as representing, for many, a radical step back from the 'assertive, career-oriented image of the "new woman" of the early decades of the twentieth century' (p. 34). For a radical writer working in the wake of these texts, the strategies of *Shadow Dance* are in one sense, then, extraordinarily surprising. By glaring contrast to contemporary feminist orthodoxies, Carter has her female characters in *Shadow Dance* almost completely contained within the patriarchal and misogynistic imaginations of Morris and Honeybuzzard. Most obviously, the carving of Ghislaine's face comes more and more strongly to stand as a metaphor for the carving of her identity into the contours of patriarchal subordination.

Morris's wife, Edna, similarly, in her very domestic sphere, is disturbingly subservient to the patriarchal *status quo*:

> She was a Victorian girl; a girl of the days when men were hard and top-hatted and masculine and ruthless and girls were gentle and meek and did a great deal of sewing and looked after the poor and laid their tender napes beneath a husband's booted foot . . .
>
> (p. 45)

And in the scene in which Morris and Honeybuzzard break into the home of an elderly café waitress, this third woman's reaction to the image of a male attacker is even more redolent of violent subjection and powerlessness:

> She gaped up baffled, wondering; like the Virgin in Florentine pictures meeting the beautiful, terrible Angel of the Annunciation, she all heaped upon the ground, her slack mouth opening and closing soundlessly . . . At last, from the oblong hole of her mouth, came a wild, animal shriek, taking up and fearfully intensifying his own cry; and her withered grey hands clutched at the air and she pitched forward on her face, twitching, convulsive.
>
> (p. 136)

In a strong strand of feminist critical work in the 1970s, articulated for example in Arlyn Diamond and Lee Edwards' collection *The Authority of Experience* (1977) the designated role for women writers is to repair the damage done by 'inauthentic' or reductive portrayals of women in male-authored texts, to produce work that is true to women's experience, and to provide positive representations of women and their roles in modern society. Clearly, what we see in *Shadow Dance* is, once again, the opposite of this kind of feminist strategy. Instead of women's liberation, what we see is an examination of masculinist fantasies pushed to their extremes. Rather than offering us a set of feisty, resistant female characters, Carter's novel is saturated in misogynistic representations.

Clearly, this needs some explanation. In his study *Angela Carter* (1998), Linden Peach notes the influence on Carter of Leslie Fiedler, and especially his analysis of American Gothic. As Peach says, 'The Gothic mode is essentially a form of parody, a way of assailing clichés to the limit of grotesqueness' (p. 27). In Britain, though it draws on motifs from medieval art and architecture, Gothic fiction is a genre which emerged in the late eighteenth century, with writers like Horace Walpole and Ann Radcliffe. During the nineteenth century, it is possible to see how Gothic conventions percolate into the work of women writers like Mary Shelley and the Brontës, into sensation fiction and melodrama. And in the twentieth century, too, Gothic undoubtedly survives as a powerful form, for example in science fiction and horror writing and film.

In terms of sexual politics, the Gothic conventionally functions as an extreme articulation of domestic ideology – in which 'virtuous' femininity involves passivity, dependency and innocence, and in which unbridled sexual desire is associated with madness and death. Importantly, though, because these sexual-political conventions are so firmly to the fore in Gothic writing, it is also a canonical feature that they are open to manipulation and subversion. The Gothic is a mode, in other words, which often uses extreme representations of gender and sexual identity as a kind of symbolic vocabulary with which to explore the constitution of gender and sexuality themselves.

In *Shadow Dance*, the very clichéd quality of Carter's characters self-consciously follows this set of conventions. Thus in the novel, it is possible to see how figures are used as much for symbolic or allegorical impact as for 'psychological depth' or realism. Not by accident, the figure of the distressed woman, above, takes the exact form of the terrified Virgin in religious iconography. Like the 'Bride of Frankenstein' (p. 4) Ghislaine, too, bears plainly on her face the sign of her enthralment. Through the mouth of Honeybuzzard, we have already been told 'all the clichés fitted her' (p. 3). Until the end of the narrative, Edna's self-sacrificial faithfulness to the sanctity of marriage is, similarly, too sickly pure, too anti-naturalistic to be swallowed. Even the villain, Honeybuzzard, is kitted out with the melodramatic paraphernalia of the wolf – pointed ears, an 'inexpressibly carnivorous' mouth, and fangs, 'brilliantly white, sharp, like wounding little chips of milk glass' (p. 56).

The strategy we see in the novel, then, is twofold. Firstly, Carter traces back to the gender conventions of the Gothic mode in the eighteenth and nineteenth centuries, transplanting them into a contemporary setting.

Secondly, she sets out to push those representations to their sickening and violent conclusions. When Honeybuzzard ultimately enacts his fantasies of rape and murder on Ghislaine's body mounted upon a crucifix, we are clearly very near that point. Slightly later, when Morris gazes at the body and fantasises about his friend being executed, the text underlines his equal complicity: 'Honey, as bright as Lucifer before his fall, gasping to death at the end of a rope . . . For doing what Morris had always wanted' (p. 177).

Throughout *Shadow Dance*, moreover, it is notable that the cultural legacy of Gothic which the novel seeks to strip bare is closely associated with the rotting Victorian architecture of post-war Britain. Via Morris and Honeybuzzard, the novel gives us a guided tour of the crumbling suburbs and abandoned houses, whose jumbled contents seem nothing but archaic curiosities. And there is only a kind of generalised sorrow for the wrecked lives that lie all around. As Honeybuzzard says to Morris: 'They are all shadows. How can you be sorry for shadows.' Like himself: 'Morris could only see the shadowed profile of his soft-fruit face' (p. 86). In this junkshop of cultural remains, we see a world in which an oppressive regime of sexual exchange is about to burn itself out.

The time has come, in the late 1960s, for Edna to jettison the burden of history, and the domestic ideology that comes with it. Morris, a 'poor shivering wretch', is no longer equipped to be a romantic lead: 'I cannot make an adequate job, even, of squeezing a pimple' (p. 42). When he finds his wife in bed with a rival, he does not demand some duel with him to the death. At the end of the novel, it is left to the demure and self-determined Emily to call up, by telephone, some prospect of modernity. With her final act, crouching on the pavement, 'vomiting as if she would bring her heart up', it is as if she has purged herself of the whole misogynistic diet of an earlier era. What lies ahead for her and for the rapist's child she is carrying, however, remains uncertain.

The Magic Toyshop

In *The Magic Toyshop* (1967), Carter's project is considerably more complex than in *Shadow Dance*, in the sense that the novel juggles with not one but several historical traditions of gender representation. Elements of Gothic certainly remain, but these take their place in a much more divided theatre of representation, encompassing modernist art, classical mythology and fairytale. Unlike *Shadow Dance* as well, the novel offers a more naturalistic protagonist, Melanie, set in the context of semi-surrealistic surroundings. One of the key events in the novel is the transplanting of Melanie from the bourgeois propriety of her country home to the London toyshop owned by her forbidding Uncle Philip, an environment in which the patriarchal power relations are graphically literalised. In a narrative strategy that is very characteristic of Carter's work, Melanie's cultural transplantation forces her to address and to defend her idea of herself, and it is through this that the novel explores the processes of her reconstitution.

At the opening of the novel, there is already a struggle going on for the styling of Melanie's body. As she traces the outlines of her flesh, her finger is already that of the colonialist, 'a physiological Cortez, da Gama or Mungo Park' (p. 1), her body that of a soon-to-be-conquered Mexico, India or West Africa. Her opening words, 'O, my America, my new found land' (p. 1), taken from John Donne's 'To His Mistress Going to Bed' (1633), adopt the avaricious, objectifying voice of a male seducer. And we see how the hatted and gloved image of bourgeois femininity provided by her mother is being supplanted, in Melanie's bedroom mirror, by a set of sexual representations defined by a canon of male artists and writers. Thus, the catalogue of body styles with which she experiments is structured completely by the male gaze:

> A la Toulouse Lautrec, she dragged her hair sluttishly across her face and sat down in a chair with her legs apart and a bowl of water and a towel at her feet . . . She was too thin for a Titian or a Renoir but she contrived a pale, smug Cranach Venus with a bit of net curtain wound round her head and the necklace of cultured pearls they gave her when she was confirmed at her throat. After she read *Lady Chatterley's Lover*, she secretly picked forget-me-nots and stuck them in her pubic hair.
>
> (pp. 1–2)

Beginning with a situation in which her heroine has already 'gift-wrapped herself for a phantom bridegroom', (p. 2) Carter returns to the founding myth of the Fall to précis the destruction of her closeted femininity. Within a few pages, Melanie finds herself in an Eden-like garden, clothed in the garment of patriarchal virginity (her mother's wedding dress). Predictably, she meets her downfall in the branches of an apple tree. The wedding dress is sullied and torn, and the security of her closed world is symbolically shattered. A telegram arrives (she already knows its contents) breaking the news of her parents' death. Like the heroine of 'The Tiger Bride' in *The Bloody Chamber*, at a stroke her old world, and the security of the bourgeois femininity that came with it, are erased, and she has nothing but herself and her wits to fall back on.

On one level, then, what *The Magic Toyshop* seems to do is to pose various sets of institutionalised, patriarchal gender representations against each other. Looking back over this episode in the narrative more carefully, however, we can see how, between these contesting images, the text opens up a possibility of autonomy. Importantly, the pivotal scene in the garden, in which the traditional white dress and constant emphasis on virginity condition us to expect a 'fall from grace' and a defloration, turns out instead to be a kind of self-birthing: 'Since she was thirteen, when her periods began, she had felt she was pregnant with herself, bearing the slowly ripening embryo of Melanie-grown-up . . .' (p. 20). Shedding the dress, Melanie climbs the apple tree naked, and, after the intense focus on her newly sexualised flesh, it is notable that this birthing is also imagined as a shedding of the body itself, 'as if she had taken even her own skin off and now stood clothed in nothing' (p. 21). Before she has even opened the telegram confirming her parents' demise, Melanie has already wrecked her room, the scene of her girlhood development. And the mirror that, only a few pages before, framed the disciplining of her body within a masculine economy of desire, is smashed. 'She met herself in the mirror, white face, black hair. The girl who killed her mother. She picked up the hairbrush and flung it at her reflected face. The mirror shattered' (p. 24). Recalling the body-without-a-past in Jeanette Winterson's fiction, then, the whole first chapter of *The Magic Toyshop* can be read as, not a fall, but an awakening.

In Melanie's orphaned state, the physical transition to the new world of London is again symbolically represented as a rite of passage: 'The train was a kind of purgatory, a waiting time, between the known and completed past and the unguessable future which had not yet begun' (p. 22). The world of Uncle Philip into which she and her brother and sister are thrown is, on one level, a mythological world, in which the power relations between the various characters which populate it appear to be immediately intelligible. Uncle Philip's authoritarian control, in particular, is overblown to the point of being pantomimic.

In one sense, though, this transition represents a step forward for Melanie. From a position in which she is completely complicit in her own subjection, the text moves its protagonist to a position in which her enthralment within a patriarchal system is recognisable and self-evident to her. Thus, far from being a step back into oppression from the apparent freedom of her middle-class life, the transition to the toyshop can be read as a necessary stage of understanding which Melanie's character needs to go through, in her journey towards self-liberation.

Philip's world, she recognises immediately, is one of control, in which the bodies of puppets and people alike are choreographed according to the patriarchal will. His wife, Margaret, like some fairytale damsel, has been struck dumb on her wedding day. And, like the toys in *The Nutcracker*, the brothers Finn and Francie only emerge from their tightly defined roles when the house has gone to sleep.

In Carter's narrative, however, we are some way from the happily-ever-after domesticity of Peter Tchaikovsky's ballet. Indeed, the dark undertones of the text are closer to E. T. A. Hoffmann's original story, 'The Nutcracker and the Mouse King' (1816). In the climactic rape scene in Philip's puppet theatre, however, the text literalises the power relations of Uncle Philip's regime in terms of a much older mythological blueprint. Using Melanie as the heroine, Philip stages a reproduction of *Leda and the Swan*, the classical Greek myth in which the god Zeus, in the form of a swan, rapes and impregnates a young girl. In Homeric mythology, the Leda story invokes a whole history of heroism and patriarchal conflict – because rivalry over the product of the rape, Helen of Troy, is the instigator of the epic Trojan War. In order to position himself in the ultimate patriarchal position of Zeus, Philip needs Melanie to be positioned in the canonical role of female sexual subordination. Importantly, by this stage Melanie is able to recognise this as the inherited role within which she was previously enthralled: 'Melanie would be a nymph crowned with daisies once again; he saw her as once she had seen herself' (p. 141). At first she is dismissive of Philip's home-made model of wood, rubber and feathers, a pathetic parody of the 'wild, phallic bird of her imaginings' (p. 165). But as she rapidly discovers, power and violence still remain in the ancient narrative it represents.

As in this episode, when Philip encourages Finn to rape Melanie in actuality, the agenda is certainly not sexual desire, but once again male rivalry and power. Sexuality, and particularly the prospect of pregnancy, is a weapon in a class and family war: 'He's pulled our strings as if we were his puppets, and there I was, all ready to touch you up just as he wanted . . . You represent the enemy to him, who use toilet paper and fish knives . . . And so I should do you because you shave under your armpits and maybe you would have a baby and that would spite your father' (pp. 152–3). Finn's refusal to deploy his sexuality to further Philip's designs, of course, is just one of the instances in the text where we see the subversion of the absolutist regime in the house.

In his reeking, magnetic maleness, Finn already represents an alternative paradigm of masculinity to that of his uncle. In gender terms, of course, this is not in itself necessarily subversive. If we compare the novel with the autobiography *Soul on Ice* (1968), published a year after *The Magic Toyshop* by the African American activist Eldridge Cleaver, it is possible to see why. In the book, Cleaver describes what he sees as an age-old battle for masculine supremacy between what he terms the 'supermasculine menial' and the 'omnipotent administrator'. In this battle, of course, the sexual possession of both white and black women becomes simply a means for men to assert themselves over each other. In Carter's text, we appear to see a recapitulation of this canonical rivalry, between the Irishman Finn, 'a tawny lion poised for the kill' (p. 45), and the black-suited 'immense, overwhelming figure of a man' (p. 69) that is Uncle Philip. In terms of its romantic trajectory, then, clearly one of the problems for Carter's text is to deal with the conventional assumption that, as the 'hero', it will be Finn's role to fight Uncle Philip for possession of Melanie. And certainly, the narrative does play around with that idea. Arguably, though, its solution is to try to present Finn as the inverse of patriarchal control, a 'Lord of misrule' (p. 183), who wants to bury his brother-in-law's authority (in the figure of the swan) but not to usurp it.

Indeed, as Sarah Gamble argues in her study *Angela Carter* (1997), the deconstruction of patriarchy in *The Magic Toyshop* is achieved not by the substitution of an alternative phallic figure to Uncle Philip, but through the constant undermining and erosion of his regime of control. As the text gradually reveals, first in a glimpse through a keyhole and later in full view, there is always a space of carnivalesque subversion at the bottom of the house, maintained by Margaret, Francie and Finn. In opposition to Philip's contrived and violent performances, we see Finn's dextrous and eloquent dancing. In defiance of Philip's arid and orderly domination, we feel the tender and sinuous strokes of Francie's violin bow. Breaking the silence of her patriarchal dumbness, we hear the tune of Margaret's ebony flute. And of course, the final mocking subversion of Philip's phallic authority is provided by Margaret and Francie's incestuous and adulterous enjoyment of each other.

At the end of the novel, as the house burns to destruction, Finn and Melanie finally turn to each other 'in a wild surmise' (p. 200), Keats' description of Cortez as he first faced the open Pacific. In a gesture which, like the conclusion of *Shadow Dance*, is very characteristic of the late 1960s, we are left with a sense of jubilation at the collapse of the old order, whilst the future is left as an undefined space of newness and possibility. Arguably, the conclusion of the novel raises as many questions as it answers, particularly in its surprising recapitulation of the colonial theme. We start with the ripe-for-exploitation 'new found land' of Melanie's body, and conclude with something similar in the re-invocation of Cortez. Moreover, the clear expectation we are left with – that Melanie will now go on to marry and bear children for Finn – seems similarly problematic. Although it is not bourgeois respectability, neither is it the celebration of deviancy we are offered with Francie and Margaret. Thus in one reading, the novel's conclusion seem to run counter to some of its more deconstructive suggestions.

As we can see in the discussion of Carter's work so far, the political engagement in her texts by no means demands adherence to realist techniques and perspectives. Indeed, in a 1982 paper 'Fools Are My Theme', she suggests the reverse. Here, she argues that realistic representation can often get in the way of fiction's primary job of work, which is to facilitate the play of ideas. For her:

one of the functions of fiction is to ask questions that can't be asked in any other way . . . through constructing imaginary worlds in which ideas can be discussed. And speculations about the nature of our experience on this planet [should be able to] be conducted without crap about the imitation of life getting in the way.

(Carter, 1998, p. 35)

In texts such as *Heroes and Villains* (1969), exactly this blend of anti-realism and politics is clearly in evidence. Its focus, as in Foucault's work, is very much on the way social identities are constituted within particular regimes of power/knowledge, and how those regimes might be contested. This particular novel presents an imagined (perhaps post-revolutionary) world in which the social and intellectual lines are deliberately simplified. The horizon of the novel encompasses just two rival communities, the 'professors' and the 'barbarians'. There are no alternative social positions, and between the two, we see only wandering 'outcasts' who have 'forfeited their social personalities' (p. 8).

Again, the novel features the transplantation of its adolescent girl protagonist from the security of her home environment into one where all her assumptions will be questioned. Escaping from the professors' compound with a barbarian prisoner, Marianne's initial motivations are boredom and the desire for a rendezvous with some imagined romantic savage. What she finds in the barbarians' tribe, however, is a reversal of her liberal imaginings, a world stinking with vermin, excrement and disease. Far from being a site of social and intellectual freedom, the barbarians' community is held within an even cruder ideological framework than that of the professors, through the operation of a cult religion. The priest/guru Donnally is absolutely explicit about his methods of institutional control when he confides patronisingly to Marianne:

It seemed to me that the collapse of civilisation in the form that intellectuals such as ourselves understood it might be as good a time as any for crafting a new religion . . . Religion is a device for instituting the sense of a privileged group, you understand.

(p. 63)

In the revisionary collection *The Bloody Chamber* (1979), as we have already seen, Carter again focuses on the processes of subject formation, and especially the formation of gender and sexual identities. But here the narratives she examines are those of the folk and fairytale traditions. The reasons for this again, as the writer makes clear in 'Notes From the Front Line', are solidly rooted in sexual politics: 'It turned out to be easier to deal with the shifting structures of reality and sexuality by using shifting structures derived from orally transmitted traditional tales' (p. 38). The major methods deployed in this book, as in the earlier work, are an archaeological investigation of gender representation, coupled with a set of creative attempts at subversion. In *The Passion of New Eve* (1977) we see a similar strategy. The difference with this far more substantial novel, however, is that the range of reference Carter uses is very much wider, drawing not just on traditional tales but on a whole economy of popular cultural representations.

The Passion of New Eve

In 'Notes From the Front Line', Carter emphasises the feminist commitments that run to the heart of her writing, which need not necessarily equate to a subscription to the mainstreams of the feminist movement. Alongside this, in all of her work it is important to recognise the influence of a socialism, inflected by structuralism, which she embraced in the late 1960s along with many other writers and intellectuals. In a way that chimes with many leftist revisionaries of the period, what this means is that for Carter, the problems and questions of politics are recognised as *simultaneously* real and ideological:

> This investigation of the social fictions that regulate our lives – what Blake called the 'mind forg'd manacles' – is what I've concerned myself with consciously since that time . . . I'm in the demythologising business. I'm interested in myths – though I'm much more interested in folklore – just because they *are* extraordinary lies designed to make people unfree.
>
> (p. 38)

Writing *The Passion of New Eve*, Carter's excavation of the structures of myth becomes both more careful and more systematic than in the earlier works. At the same time, following in the wake of works like Roland Barthes' 1957 study *Mythologies*, the range of popular reference with which the novel engages is far wider than we see in earlier texts. In Barthes' hands, not just literary texts but film iconography, striptease and a whole range of other practices had been opened up to critical analysis. In *The Passion of New Eve*, this kind of analytic focus on the inherited forms of popular culture is, similarly, deployed to great effect.

Indeed, all of the novel's main characters are deliberately composed out of passed-down imagery and mythology. Tristessa, the beautiful screen heroine, is an assemblage of iconic images of Hollywood stars like Greta Garbo, Marlene Dietrich and Louise Brooks, held together only by 'the phenomenon of persistence of vision' (p. 5). The fact that she turns out to be a celluloid illusion enacted by a drag artiste functions to foreground this very quality of constructedness. The novel's main character, Eve, is created from a male prototype, Evelyn, in a different way, via a sex change and wholesale bodily remodelling based on 'a consensus agreement on the physical nature of the ideal woman drawn up from a protracted study of the media' (p. 78). Surgically formed to match up to the '*Playboy* center fold' (p. 75), Eve's consciousness is also reconstituted in well-established popular cultural traditions. S/he is schooled in the nature of womanliness by the study of Hollywood movies (including those of Tristessa) and by a forced diet of gender-laden, sickly-sweet nature films.

The seductress/victim Leilah, whom Evelyn encounters in New York at the beginning of the novel, is, we find later, nothing more than a masquerade, a deliberate personification of Evelyn's misogynistic fantasies, designed to snare him for the purposes of gender reassignment. And Mother, the fantastic many-breasted fertility goddess-cum-women's guerrilla leader, who surgically transforms Evelyn into Eve, turns out to be a construct too – firstly of her own scalpel, and ultimately of the collective imagination itself. Both phallic and feminine, Mother is the 'apotheosis of Tiresias' (p. 186), the intersexual figure of Greek mythology. At the end of the text, when Eve journeys symbolically back to Mother's womb, what s/he finds in there is not some originary, essential site of femininity, but the reverse. As s/he finally realises, the idea of 'Mother' has no more substance than any other construction of the sexed and gendered body: 'I'm not so scared as once I would have been . . . for I know, now, that Mother is a figure of speech' (p. 184).

In Foucault's well-known genealogies, as we saw in chapter 1, the major focus is on knowledges such as medicine, psychiatry and penology. In *The Passion of New Eve*, the focus is on a realm of discourse that is at once more dispersed and more pervasive. In the novel we see a very concentrated focus on the formation and styling of the body within the social institution of femininity. As Foucault says in *Power/Knowledge*:

> Let us ask . . . how things work at the level of on-going subjugation, at the level of those continuous processes which subject our bodies, govern our gestures, dictate our behaviours . . . we should try to discover how it is that subjects are gradually, progressively, really and materially *constituted*.
>
> (p. 9, my italics)

In her 1990 study *Gender Trouble*, Judith Butler builds and develops this approach. Like Carter, her work seeks to interrogate the relationship between gender roles, body styles and the idea of 'natural' sex. Butler's work has, also, already been mentioned in the discussion of genders and bodies in chapter 3, and in relation to Jeanette Winterson in chapter 7. In *Gender Trouble*, she asks us to suspend the habitual belief in the 'natural' binary of male/female sex, and to think instead about body styles and representations as *effects* of power/knowledge:

> Consider that a sedimentation of gender norms produces the peculiar phenomenon of a 'natural sex' or a 'real woman' or any number of prevalent and compelling social fictions, and that this is a sedimentation that over time has produced a set of corporeal styles which, in reified form, appear as the natural configurations of bodies into natural sexes existing in a binary relation to one another. If these styles are enacted, and if they produce the coherent gendered subjects who pose as their originators, what kind of performance might reveal this ostensible 'cause' to be an 'effect'?
>
> (p. 140)

In *The Passion of New Eve*, Carter experiments with really extreme restylings of bodies, and uses them to interrogate inherited models of femininity, from the masturbatory fantasy of the dumb blonde, to the screen heroine (defined by fragility and loss), to the nurturing Earth Mother. Obviously, one of the text's key strategies here is the mismatching of bodies with genders. In the narrative, it is particularly notable that Carter has Mother *refuse* to operate on Tristessa, uniting his/her 'perfect' performance of self-sacrificial femininity with a 'perfect' hetero-desirable corporeal form. Instead the scalpel is taken to the arrogant and misogynist Evelyn.

Thus, around both of these differently trans-gendered figures, there is a crucial, in-written ambivalence. In neither of their cases is femininity allowed to reach completion and closure, because for both of them, the masculinist fantasies they represent can only imperfectly map on to their reformulated bodies. When Eve and Tristessa finally come together in an ecstatic embrace, the text figures this epiphany in a way that is the opposite of canonical representations of sex by writers such as D. H. Lawrence. Rather than 'discovering themselves' as real men/women in the nakedness of sexual passion, we see a radical breakdown of that binary:

> Turn and turn about, now docile, now virile – when you lay below me all that white hair shifted from side to side over Old Glory, your hair dragged your head impetuously with it, this way and that way; I beat down upon you mercilessly, with atavistic relish, but the glass woman I saw beneath me smashed under my passion and the splinters scattered and recomposed themselves into a man who overwhelmed me . . .

Masculine and Feminine are correlatives which involve one another. I am sure of that – the quality and its negation are locked in necessity. But what the nature of masculine and the nature of feminine might be, whether they involve male and female, if they have anything to do with Tristessa's so long neglected apparatus or my own factory fresh incision and engine-turned breasts, that I do not know.

(pp. 149–50)

From his/her bodily transformation onwards, the novel tracks Eve in his/her search for a match between the corporeal form s/he sees in the mirror, and some notion of an 'authentic' womanliness. Whilst Tristessa comes into being on the silver screen, the surface on which Eve tries to inscribe his/her femininity is that of the mirror. When Eve first sees his/her reflection, the experience is one of disjunction: 'I was the object of all the unfocussed desires that had ever existed in my own head. I had become my own masturbatory fantasy. And – how can I put it – the cock in my head, still, twitched at the sight of myself' (p. 75).

Later, as an apprentice in sexual subordination with Zero, Eve is constantly apprehensive that his/her 'inauthenticity' will be exposed. At the point of rape, the feminine position becomes intolerable, and Eve's only place of escape is back into the masculine gaze itself: 'when he mounted me . . . I felt myself to be, not myself but he . . . When he entered me, the act seemed to me one of seppuku, a ritual disembowelment I committed upon myself' (pp. 101–2). Similarly, when the earlier abuse of Leilah is turned full circle, and Eve is made to perform a pornographic dance for Zero's titillation, the male fantasy reflected by the mirror becomes, in its very 'otherness', his/her only escape: 'I would remember watching Leilah watch herself in the mirror and now I sensed all the lure of that narcissistic loss of being, when the face leaks into the looking-glass like water into sand' (p. 103).

In the second half of the book, Eve is constantly digging for an authentic, whole, psycho-physiological experience of femininity. It isn't to be found in any of the canonical places – not in female orgasm, nor in the prospect of maternity that follows. In his/her entry to the cave that is both the living womb of Mother and the 'pages of a gigantic book' (p. 180) s/he once again searches for a final answer, but finds only ambiguous images. When s/he looks into the mirror once more, 'the glass was broken, cracked right across many times so it reflected nothing, was a bewilderment of splinters and I could not see myself nor any portion of myself in it' (p. 181).

If in *Shadow Dance* and *The Magic Toyshop* we see an archaeology of inherited gender roles, then, in this novel we see a more radical interrogation of the age-old myth of sex itself. From the very naming of the novel and that of its protagonist, we have long expected a return to the Judaeo-Christian creation story, the myth of Eden. When it happens, predictably enough, what we are offered is not a confirmation but a problematisation of the originary Adam/Eve binary. In place of that hetero-normative coupling, the text takes us back to a single 'miraculous, seminal, intermediate being' (p. 185), the archaeopteryx. Immediately afterwards, in a rush of amniotic fluid, we see the birth of a different kind of seminal and intermediate figure, already pregnant with its own 'tribute to evolution' (p. 186), the protagonist him/herself. Thus, in place of the biblical Eve, with her narcissism, weakness and duplicity, the text concludes by offering a figure that is, as the title says, fundamentally 'new'.

Nights at the Circus

In *Nights at the Circus* (1984), we can see a reflection of many of the concerns of Carter's earlier fiction. Compared with the sharp sexual-political edge of texts like *The Passion of New Eve*, however, the novel is far more carnival-esque and celebratory in style. Together with *Wise Children* (1991), *Nights at the Circus* is often seen as a product of Carter's 'maturity'. Certainly, it retains Carter's trademark concern with the polymorphousness of the body, and with the oppressive and reductive effects of orthodox gender represen-tations. But Carter's handling of these established themes is inflected here with an even greater writerly unruliness, wit and irreverence.

Unlike *The Passion of New Eve*, *Nights at the Circus* makes use of a particular, dated moment, the last year of the nineteenth century. Rather than offering a closed historical account, however, the novel plays with many aspects of the sexual representations of the period. The text centres on the character of Fevvers, a winged trapeze artist. A figure of trans-formation, one of her central functions in the first part of Carter's text is to explore the patriarchal culture of London, 'at the fag-end, the smouldering cigar-butt, of a nineteenth century which is just about to be ground out in the ashtray of history' (p. 11). Throughout the text she is constantly beset by the lascivious intentions of various powerful and authoritarian men, and key episodes in the narrative are devoted to her escapes from them. At the same time, Fevvers is used to explore the turning twentieth century as a moment of possibility, heralding 'the New Age in which no women will be bound down to the ground' (p. 25). Appropriately enough, it is the 'whirling air' itself that becomes her first lover: 'Yes! I must be the bride of that wild, sightless, fleshless rover, or else could not exist, sir' (p. 33). But Fevvers is also a problematic figure, like Melanie in *The Magic Toyshop*, who is partially caught up in the culture she seeks to transcend. At the end of the second part of the novel, we see the breakdown of the feminine masquerade with which she has braved the Victorian era. As the narrative unfolds, then, it becomes clear that Fevvers is not a simple figure with any single allegorical meaning.

Like Eve/Evelyn and Tristessa in *The Passion of New Eve*, she is a vehicle used not to define, but rather to problematise the various canons of representation which hold a subjugated femininity in place. Growing up in a house of whores, for example, Fevvers offers herself as an angelic virgin. A grotesque giantess, she is also the 'Helen of the high wire' (p. 7), the epitome of classical beauty. She starts her career as Cupid, the cheeky Roman god of love, and vacations as a cockney Venus. In her final incarnation, mounting her startled lover in a smothering apotheosis of passion and feathers, she recapitulates and reverses the ravishing of Melanie by the Swan in *The Magic Toyshop*. By implication, here, her final incarnation is of Zeus, the rapacious father of the gods. But at the same time, the all-embracing and subversive laughter with which she finally fills the novel is the inverse of patriarchal authority:

> The spiralling tornado of Fevvers' laughter began to twist and shudder across the entire globe, as if a spontaneous response to the giant comedy that endlessly unfolded beneath it, until everything that lived and breathed, everywhere, was laughing. Or so it seemed to the deceived husband, who found himself laughing too, even if he was not quite sure whether or not he might be the butt of the joke.
>
> (p. 295)

In Fevvers' construction out of a history of representations, one of the most important is that of the winged victory, an iconic figure in European art and mythology. Here Carter draws her reference from the celebrated second-century BC 'Winged Victory of Samothrace', which occupies one of the most privileged positions in the Paris Louvre. This figure is a representation of Nike, the Greek goddess of victory, whose image has been recycled in countless iconographies and, latterly, marketing campaigns. On the Rolls-Royce, she is synonymous with power and wealth. On the feet of millions of children, Nike's single stylised wing speaks a different kind of respect and social arrival. In different guises, she is everywhere.

One of the compelling features of the iconic, headless and armless Samothrace figure is its multiplicity of association and suggestion. Whilst Carter's character is clearly far more present and capable, she too is a figure of irreducible ambiguity. Of course Fevvers' wings themselves are the most literal index of this undecidability. Are they fact or fiction? Are they freakish or fraudulent? In the narrative of her girlhood, the emergent buds between her shoulder blades are inextricably linked with puberty. And frequently they become a metaphor for insatiable desire. As the fanatical

Mr Rozencreutz proclaims to a simultaneously alarmed-yet-nonchalant
Fevvers:

> Queen of ambiguities, goddess of in-between states, being on the
> borderline of species . . . creature half of earth and half of air, virgin and
> whore, reconciler of fundament and firmament, reconciler of opposing
> states through the mediation of your ambivalent body, reconciler of the
> grand opposites of death and life, you who come to me neither naked
> nor clothed, wait with me for the hour when it is neither dark nor light,
> that of dawn before daybreak, when you shall give yourself to me but I
> shall not possess you.

> (p. 81)

Like *The Passion of New Eve*, in terms of form *Nights at the Circus* borrows
from the eighteenth-century picaresque, with Fevvers herself taking the dual
role of heroine and adventuring rogue. In his book *Angela Carter* (1998),
indeed, Aidan Day quotes Carter's own comments on her use of this format:

> the idea behind *Nights at the Circus* was very much to entertain and
> instruct, and I purposely used a certain eighteenth century fictional
> device – the picaresque, where people have adventures in order to find
> themselves in places where they can discuss philosophical concepts
> without distractions.

> (p. 169)

Accordingly, the text's central strategy is to carry us, by means of a
continuous adventure narrative, through a series of different environments,
structured by contrasting regimes of power/knowledge.

In Ma Nelson's whorehouse in London, the power relations implicit
in Victorian sexual exchange are made explicit. Titian's *Leda and the
Swan*, depicting the rape of a virgin, hangs on the wall like a talisman, a
gift from a client attracted by Nelson's own shaved, infantilised sex.
Respectability and patriarchal convention, encoded in her leather armchairs
and ironed copies of *The Times*, provide the frame for the house's gentlemanly exploitation. In this regime, of course, Fevvers' role as a living statue
is precisely that of the 'angel in the house', the winged virgin who provides
the traditional counterpoint to her sisters' prostitution. Obviously, the novel
plays with, and reworks this scenario, so that Fevvers' experiments with
her new wings are modelled not on Leda but on the imperious swan. What
we then see is a repeated re-visioning of Fevvers' body, from angel to
'Winged Victory' to the *Victory* itself, the hundred-gun battleship of another
Nelson.

Beginning with these transformations, from Nelson's whorehouse to Rosencreutz's mock-Gothic mansion, to her representation in the sceptical reporter Walser's notebook itself, the entire focus of the novel's first part is on a series of efforts to contain and police Fevvers' metamorphosing body in various different kinds of patriarchal regimes. Voiced largely through Fevvers' own mouth, the narrative follows her own varying strategies to escape and resist literal or metaphoric incarceration, and to preserve her own self-determination.

In part two of the novel, in which we leave London for Colonel Kearney's Grand Imperial Tour, the perspective changes. Here, our focus moves to masquerade itself. At first, this seems like liberation. When Walser looks into the mirror and sees the face of a clown, this is precisely what he senses:

> As he contemplated the stranger peering interrogatively back at him out of the glass, he felt the beginnings of a vertiginous sense of freedom . . . the freedom that lies behind the mask, within dissimulation, the freedom to juggle with being, and, indeed, with the language which is vital to our being.
>
> (p. 103)

And for Fevvers too, the performance of a masquerade (the 'flying' trapeze artist), and her refusal of 'authentic' self-presentation are precisely what keep her in control, guarding against her objectification as a 'freak'. As the narrative unfolds, however, the inherited codes of the circus masquerade begin, themselves, to become imprisoning. The circus is not a carnivalesque free-for-all, by any means. It is a regime in which identities are self-consciously stylised – but within fixed and traditional forms. Rather than 'protecting' some originary identity, the rubric of expression and gesture defined by the mask irresistibly comes to constitute identity itself. Thus, for the celebrated chief clown Buffo, the donning of the face is a moment of becoming, but also of self-deconstruction:

> 'The code of the circus permits of no copying, no change. However much the face of Buffo may appear identical to Grik's face, or to Grok's face . . . it is, all the same, a fingerprint of authentic dissimilarity, a genuine expression of my own autonomy. And so my face eclipses me. I have become this face which is not mine, and yet I chose it freely.'
>
> (p. 122)

Towards the end of the 'Petersburg' section, too, we begin to see the limits and dangers of Fevvers' masquerade, and particularly the way it is constituted within the virgin/whore terms of Victorian patriarchal discourse. When

Fevvers is tempted to dine at the Grand Duke's house by the promise of a diamond necklace, her thinking remains framed very much within the terms of traditional seduction. Using her celebrated virginity as the bait, she looks forward to a very traditional, material kind of return. As the episode unfolds, moreover, we begin to see the potential violence that underlies this regime of desire. Amongst the Grand Duke's collections of 'marvellous and unnatural artefacts' (p. 187), and trapped by her own masquerade of seducee, Fevvers soon begins to lose confidence in her own autonomy. With it, the boundaries of reality and appearance also start to dissolve.

In this magic realist domain, the protagonist is quickly knocked off balance. When the Grand Duke shows her the tiny gilded cage he has had made, she confronts her own mistake: 'Fevvers did not shrink; but was at once aware of the hideous possibility she might do so. She said goodbye to the diamond necklace . . . and contemplated life as a toy' (p. 192). As the magnificent diamond-clad ice sculpture of the Winged Victory collapses among the dinner things, we see the collapse, too, of her Victorian masquerade. Fevvers' escape from the rape-scenario whilst the excited Grand Duke is ejaculating is abrupt and self-consciously unconvincing. And for the first time in the novel we see the underside of the Leda/swan mythology on which she has been trading, a girl 'raddled with tears, hair coming down, again, gypsy dress ripped and clotted with semen, trying as best she could to cover her bare breasts with a filthy but incontrovertible tangle of pin feathers' (p. 193).

In the final part of the novel, we see neither the patriarchal regime of late Victorian London, nor the masquerade of the circus, but instead a new and blank landscape. In these Siberian wastes, correspondingly, the text explores an idea of identity as a *tabula rasa* or clean slate. Repeatedly, in this last part, it plays on the erasure and rewriting of subjectivity. In Walser's sojourn with the Siberian Woodsman, for example, this erasure is treated literally. His former identity is suspended, and he enters the inverted dream-world of the forest dwellers, to train as a shaman in a 'permanent state of sanctified delirium' (p. 254).

In the asylum of Countess P., we are introduced to a very much more rationalistic regime. But again it is organised around the remodelling of identity. Here, Carter borrows the motif of the Panopticon from Foucault's discussion of eighteenth-century prison reform in *Discipline and Punish*. By direct contrast to the imperious power of the Grand Duke at the end of part two, based on personal strength and charismatic authority, the regime of Countess P. is one of faceless discipline. With her personal collection of female murderesses, her interest is not in the punishment of crimes. Rather, the Panopticon's intricate system of surveillance, regulation and sensory deprivation is designed to remould the inmates' bodies and minds into figures of repentance. Like Tristessa in *The Passion of New Eve*, its goal is the production of a femininity out of 'a perfected variety of the bitterest loneliness', silence and loss (p. 213). The Panopticon is a house not of retribution, but of correction, in which the attitudes and functions of the body are regulated with tireless scientific precision. It is a penitentiary in the most literal sense, 'a machine designed to promote penitence' (p. 212), or as the Countess conceives it to herself, a 'laboratory for the manufacture of souls' (p. 214).

In Foucault's work, the idea of panopticism is not limited to the prison, but becomes a metaphor for the regulatory and coercive methods of modern society at large. What is perhaps surprising about Carter's text, from this perspective, is that it *does not* place the character of Fevvers inside the Panopticon (as she is placed inside the whorehouse, inside the circus, and so on). And neither does the final part of the novel extend the Panopticon's regime of regulation and surveillance to fill the Siberian landscape – despite its infamous associations with the *gulag* system of 'corrective labour colonies'. One possible reason for the fact that Carter's text refuses or neglects to pursue this obvious narrative possibility is because the analysis of disciplinary society presented by Foucault seems to foreclose too radically on the possibility of personal autonomy. Certainly, it virtually precludes the kinds of transformative possibilities that Fevvers represents. Thus to represent the emerging twentieth century in the image of Panoptic surveillance and discipline would be to risk fatally compromising the novel's emancipatory theme.

One of the major criticisms from feminist critics directed towards Foucault and some of the postmodernists who have been influenced by him, indeed, is that their work seems to leave less and less room for principled resistance to the *status quo*. If we as subjects are largely constituted and regulated by dominant regimes of power/knowledge, then the idea of emancipation is a much less easy thing to think about. Obviously, this kind of argument implies quite a negative reading of Foucault, who is, arguably, highly concerned with the disruptive effects of subjugated, deviant knowledges and identities. Carter's work, whilst it explores the power relations implicit in dominant systems of representation, is clearly concerned to hold on to these kinds of subversive possibilities.

It is not Fevvers who breaks open the Panopticon. But the totalising regime of Countess P. is able to be subverted nonetheless – by an invisible language of desire: private signs, touches and gestures which eventually lead to a mutiny. It is the Countess herself who ends up the red-eyed personification of her own disciplinary obsession. Similarly, throughout *Nights at the Circus*, all attempts to imprison the protagonist within the terms of dominant oppositions – freak/fraud, virgin/whore and so on – are foiled by her inventive and varying masquerade, even if her escapes are sometimes narrow ones. Fevvers' resistance to the objectifying gaze of lovers and punters is precisely a refusal of disciplinary surveillance. Even after her own final seduction of a rejuvenated Walser, the text offers no closure to her character. Instead, her laughter over the whole age-old con of virginity gives voice to an exuberant refusal of containment.

With the protagonist of *Nights at the Circus*, then, we can see the culmination of a development that takes us some way from the strategies of early texts such as *Shadow Dance*. Where Ghislaine, in that novel, is disturbingly enthralled within the Gothically exaggerated conventions of male desire, in Fevvers we see a character of spectacular irreducibility. In each of the texts we have looked at, there is a continuing process of excavation, exposing the construction and regulation of femininity within a variety of inherited regimes of representation. Across the spread of Carter's *œuvre*, too, there is a commitment to exploring the possibilities for imaginative resistance to the gendered legacies of culture.

Carter's fictions from *Shadow Dance* onwards deploy a number of genealogical strategies. But at the same time, in tune with many feminists who have seen the need to critique and revise the terms of the Foucauldian project, her texts keep a weather eye on the eventuality of sexual-political emancipation. In *The Magic Toyshop*, with the burning of Uncle Philip's house, we see the 'wild surmise' (p. 200) of a new world for Finn and Melanie. In *The Passion of New Eve*, our final image is of the open ocean that will bear the protagonist to a different 'place of birth' (p. 191). In *Nights at the Circus*, we are left with Fevvers copulating and laughing in the open landscape of Siberia.

Certainly it is very significant that, in each case, this promise of liberation is presented against the backdrop of a symbolically blank horizon. And thus in this sense, the only 'solution' these texts seem to offer to the problem of emancipation is, ultimately, to position their characters *outside* of society and history. In Toni Morrison's fiction, we have already explored the potential dangers of such wilful amnesia in an African American context. And as we see in Maxine Hong Kingston's work too, escapes from history often have costs as well as benefits. What the costs of such a move might be in Carter's feminist project, however, is open to question.

11 After 'race': Hanif Kureishi's writing

In chapter 4, I examined the spectre of 'race', referring to a number of contemporary writers who engage with its problematic legacy. In a British context, Hanif Kureishi is amongst the most important. Growing up in Bromley, South London, he began his career as a dramatist. Drawing on his own experiences of discrimination as an English boy with a Pakistani father, his professional reputation was built upon his subtle presentations of hard-hitting issues like racism, in texts such as the 1981 play *Outskirts*. That said, however, his texts are far too playful, irreverent and counter-cultural to fit into any orthodox political agenda.

Even in these early texts there is a clear willingness to break the mould. In *Outskirts* he approaches racism not from the point of view of the victim, but from the inside, in terms of the lives and frustrations of its adherents. Other plays like *The King and Me* (1980) are even more unorthodox, mixing 'serious' issues like class and unemployment with unexpected themes like Elvis impersonation. At the age of twenty-eight Kureishi became writer-in-residence at the progressive Royal Court Theatre in London, and it was here that he produced the first of his major screenplays, *My Beautiful Laundrette* (1985).

The significance of this background for reading Kureishi's prose fiction is considerable. Perhaps because both the theatre and film are fundamentally interactive and collaborative media, they tend to produce a method of working quite different from that of the novel. So in a sense it is unsurprising that in Kureishi's work there is never a sense of authorship as a process of God-like control. Even in the role of screenwriter, he never seeks to create the aura of the genius *auteur*. Instead what we see in his work is a process of reworking and renegotiation, a vision of writing as craft rather than art, of high-level intellectual labour coupled with fun, experimentation, collaboration.

Discussing the making of *My Beautiful Laundrette*, for example, Kureishi shows the profound effects that this method of working has on the form of his texts. *Laundrette* started out with the massive dimensions of an Attenborough or Scorsese epic. Only in the process of planning did it become focused into the more gritty and contemporary piece of work we see on screen, or in the pages of the screenplay. Indeed, reading the whole range of Kureishi's texts, the biographer Kenneth Kaleta (1998) shows that processes of drafting and collaborative negotiation have been, from the start, a hallmark of Kureishi's writing practice. In the case of My *Beautiful Laundrette*, it is possible to see how apparently fundamental questions of scale and style are, in practice, secondary to the development of key questions and ideas. As Kureishi (1996) makes clear, scale, tone and even genre are seen as part of the detail to be filled in once the thematic framework of the text has been decided:

> The film started off as an epic. It was to be like *The Godfather*, opening in the past with the arrival of an immigrant family in England and showing their progress to the present. There were to be many scenes set in the 1950s; people would eat bread and dripping and get off boats a lot; there would be scenes of Johnny and Omar as children and large-scale set pieces of racist marches with scenes of mass violence.
>
> We soon decided it was impossible to make a film of such scale. That film is still to be made. Instead I set the film in the present, though references to the past remain.
>
> It was shot in six weeks in February and March in 1985 on a low budget and 16mm film. For this I was glad . . . We decided the film was to have gangster and thriller elements, since the gangster film is the form which corresponds most closely to the city, with its gangs and violence. And the film was to be an amusement, despite its references to racism, unemployment and Thatcherism. Irony is the modern mode, a way of commenting on bleakness and cruelty without falling into dourness and didacticism.
>
> (Kureishi, 1996, pp. 4–5)

In Kureishi's later fiction, we can see a carry-over from the habits and approaches of his dramatic writing. Typically, his settings are fairly spare, with relatively short individual scenes, frequently based upon dramatic confrontations and individual interactions. Similarly, there is a continuing interest in visual effect, in fashion and particularly in music. As a literary chronicler of British society from the 1970s onwards, Kureishi shows better than almost any other writer the importance of youth culture in this period, a culture whose influence – he argues – far exceeded that of art or poetry in the formation of a contemporary sensibility:

It is well known that at different times, in different cities, certain arts are primary or central, and at this time it was pop, with London being as important as anywhere in the USA. Britain's cornucopia of music prevented the country from becoming a third-rate cultural outpost, the complete victim of US cultural power. Britain couldn't be entirely Americanised while it continued to generate its own identity through music and fashion and the political culture and activism of its youth.

(Kureishi, 1992, p. xii)

All of these things work to sustain and fill out his texts in relation to their contemporary milieu, and are a crucial part of the way his texts manufacture their patina of 'authenticity'.

Where Kureishi's writing dramatises the issues of racism and of ethnic affiliation, it is very much through this attention to the cultural specificity of a particular place and a particular moment. In *My Beautiful Laundrette* his presentation of ethnic tensions strenuously avoids the temptation to simplify the relationships it examines, along lines of 'racial' stereotype. Genghis, the closest we have to a racist character, provides a good example of this. Our first image of him in *My Beautiful Laundrette* is of a shivering, sickly white boy being evicted by his Pakistani landlord. But even the graffiti which adorns the squat he and Johnny share, 'we will defeat the running wogs of capitalism' (p. 9), serves to illustrate the confusing mix of classist and racist resentments that underpin their hostility and aggression.

As they see Omar walking down the street, out of unemployment and towards his new job at the garage, there is an unmistakable wistfulness in Johnny's comment: 'That kid. We were like that' (p. 13). But Genghis, too, implicitly acknowledges where the source of his anger lies. That is, in the progressive realignments of power and wealth in Thatcher's Britain: 'I'm angry. I don't like to see one of our men grovelling to Pakis. They came here to work for us. That's why we brought them over. OK?' (p. 38). In Kureishi's screenplay, a response to his sentiments is forthcoming immediately, as seconds later we cut to an image of Johnny kissing Omar. Between them, the pull of friendship and sexual attraction cut through the ideological obsessions of Genghis and his fascist companions. Their adherence to pre-war delusions of Empire are seen to do nothing except ensure their increasing marginalisation.

It is not only for the white British, however, that ethnic identifications are having to be realigned. Omar, the son of a white British woman and an influential Bombay journalist (now the derelict 'Papa'), is adopted by Nasser with little question that the boy will become the heir to his patriarchal domain. But it is ultimately with 'disgust' (p. 49) that Omar responds to this prospect. By the end of the text both of the older men are left impotent as we watch the younger generation, Johnny, Omar and Tania, embarking on a life of relative freedom from family and traditional mores. The only promise of continuity we have is in the partnership of the two young men, as they laugh and splash each other (the final image) in a prelude to sex. Problems of class, gender, sexuality and ethnicity certainly remain as the credits roll, but the relationships between them are changing fast.

In his essay 'The Rainbow Sign' (1986) Kureishi discusses the issues of 'race' and ethnic identification in a particular way, describing his own troubling experience as a teenager, of 'passing' as a white fascist. Together with a skinhead friend who later became the model for 'Johnny' in *My Beautiful Laundrette*, he met with racist lads down at the football ground, where they 'congregated to hunt down Pakistanis and beat them' (p. 75). As a British teenager in the 1950s, the writer describes his reaction to this encounter with 'race' as one of self-abhorrence:

> I was desperately embarrassed and afraid of being identified with these loathed aliens. I found it almost impossible to answer questions about where I came from. The word 'Pakistani' had been made into an insult. I was a word I didn't want used about myself. I couldn't tolerate being myself.

> (Kureishi, 1996, p. 76)

In his mature writing, Hanif Kureishi acknowledges this attitude in order to definitively reject it. Indeed, throughout his work there is a continual resistance to 'racial' separatism. In 'The Rainbow Sign' he attacks the way that, in the 1950s and 1960s, black activists like Malcolm X and Eldridge Cleaver seemed to combine the turn to Islam and Africa with a form of anti-white racism. For Kureishi, each of the proffered alternatives of separatism or meek assimilation represents an equal failure to grasp the nettle of 'a digested political commitment to a different kind of whole society'. For Kureishi, 'a society that is racist is a society that cannot accept itself, that hates part of itself so deeply that it cannot see, does not want to see – because of its spiritual and political nullity and inanition – how much people have in common with each other' (p. 95).

The Buddha of Suburbia

What emerges here is the democratic liberalism that underlies Kureishi's writing, and the way it strenuously seeks to avoid ghettoisation. Texts like *The Buddha of Suburbia* (1990) certainly do have a political content and are not shy of dealing with issues like sex, race or class antagonism. At least as importantly, though, *The Buddha of Suburbia* is a novel addressed to the mainstream, a comedy about music, fashion, teenage sexuality and the experience of growing up in the centre of London youth culture in the late 1970s.

In this sense, one of the novel's most striking features is the way in which it explores the birth of a new kind of metropolitan consciousness. Notably, Kureishi co-opts the old imperialist language of 'race' to talk about a different kind of transition within British culture, marked not in terms of skin colour but in terms of a rejection of conformism and consumerism:

> Charlie stirred restlessly as he leaned there. He hugged himself in self-pity as we took in this alien race dressed with an originality we'd never imagined possible. I began to understand what London meant and what class of outrage we had to deal with . . .
>
> When the shambolic group finally started up, the music was thrashed out. It was more aggressive than anything I'd heard since early Who. This was no peace and love; here there were no drum solos or effeminate synthesisers. Not a squeeze of anything 'progressive' or 'experimental' came from these pallid, vicious little council estate kids with hedgehog hair, howling about anarchy and hatred.
>
> (pp. 129–30)

Here and throughout the text, the culture shocks sustained by a particular city in a particular period are described with a vivid sense of immediacy. Ethnic disjunctions are an important piece of the jigsaw, but certainly not the whole.

The Buddha of Suburbia, then, can be read in one sense as a text which lays the groundwork for a move beyond the politics of 'race'. In its treatment of racism it is witty and dismissive, deploying weapons of ridicule and derision. A prime example of this is the depiction of 'Hairy Back' with his vocabulary of 'blackies', 'wogs' and 'coons'. Within the comedy of the text, we are presented with Hairy Back as an anachronistic buffoon, and we are invited to laugh him off the page. The pleasure of the text, in other words, is completely invested here in the reader's willingness to participate in the text's anti-fascist critique.

In terms of the analysis of Kureishi's text, moreover, it is useful to consider the way in which that laughter is generated. In one particular scene, for example, Karim uses Hairy Back's car to transport his Indian immigrant friend from the airport:

> Helen and I got in front. This was a delicious moment of revenge for me, because the Rover belonged to Helen's dad, Hairy Back. Had he known that four Pakis were resting their dark arses on his deep leather

> seats, ready to be driven by his daughter, who had only recently been
> fucked by one of them, he wouldn't have been a contented man.
>
> (p. 78)

The comic effectiveness of scenes like this depends on our willingness to
participate in a kind of ironic 'post-racism'. Coming full circle, we are required
to recognise the word 'Paki' as the name of a laughable stereotype, a racist
imaginary existing nowhere but in the minds of bigots.

In a sense this is a high-risk strategy. Whilst racism remains a violent
reality, as witnessed by events like the killing of Stephen Lawrence in 1993
and the Brixton nail bombing in 1999, it is reasonable at least to question
whether it is appropriate to approach the problem of 'race' through farce.
The subsequent neo-Nazi attack on Changez is another case in point:

> It was a typical South London winter evening – silent, dark, cold, foggy,
> damp – when this gang jumped out on Changez and called him a Paki,
> not realising he was Indian. They planted their feet all over him and
> started to carve the initials of the National Front into his stomach with
> a razor blade. They fled because Changez let off the siren of his Muslim
> warrior's call, which could be heard in Buenos Aires.
>
> (p. 224)

Whilst humour is generated here through the comic stereotyping of Changez
himself, the racists themselves are allowed to disappear back into the
shadows of Kureishi's text. The charge Kureishi risks here is clearly that his
text is effectively sugar-coating race hatred with humour. What the novel
certainly does do is to skate on the edge of political orthodoxy.

On one level, then, it is possible to see how *The Buddha of Suburbia* works
by playing around with ethnic stereotypes in a deliberately provocative way.
Turning to the text's treatment of the more subtle forms of middle-class
racism, however, we can see a different kind of technique in play. In the
case of the director Shadwell, for example, the text forces us to consider a
less readily identifiable form of covert racism. Where Hairy Back's bigotry
was farcical, Shadwell's is more subtle and perfidious. Most importantly, it
functions by appropriating Karim's own body, gesture and voice, enlisting
Karim's own naïvety in the representation of a racist fantasy.

In Shadwell's adaptation of *The Jungle Book* (subversively renamed *The
Jungle Bunny* by its cast), Karim finds himself transformed into a Mowgli
figure, swinging from tree to tree in an imaginary India. Despite the leftist
rhetoric which saturates the world of 1970s alternative theatre, Shadwell's
directorial role allows him the power to replace Karim's London voice with
what he deems an 'authentic' accent and animal noises, and his clothes and

skin with 'a loin cloth and brown make-up, so that I resembled a turd in a bikini-bottom' (p. 146). Karim is eager to accept his first break as an actor from this established director, but the price he has to pay on stage is a personal and political one.

In this respect *The Buddha of Suburbia* illustrates, extremely deftly, the ideological process that Edward Said names 'orientalism'. According to Said, a crucial part of the way imperialist ideology operates is by generating fictional images of the 'Orient' and of 'Orientals', whose purpose is to illustrate various kinds of moral and mental inferiority, and thereby to form a justification for the 'Orient's' colonial subordination. In the work of Gobineau and others, as we saw in chapter 4, it is possible to identify exactly how racism operates similarly by creating stereotypical images of 'the black race' or (for example) 'the Arabs' or 'the Jews' which work to sustain particular exclusionary/exploitative perspectives. The significance of Said's orientalism as a theory, then, is the way it shows the crucial role of *representation* in the operation of imperialist and racist ideology.

What is particularly interesting about *The Buddha of Suburbia* from this point of view is that it explores not only Hairy Back's or Shadwell's or Pyke's but Karim's own complicity in sustaining an orientalist construction of himself. After Karim's performance in *The Jungle Book*, Kureishi sets up a dramatic confrontation with Jamila to bring this complicity to the fore:

> 'You looked wonderful,' she said, as if she were speaking to a ten-year-old after a school play. 'So innocent and young, showing off your pretty body, so thin and perfectly formed. But no doubt about it, the play is completely neo-fascist –'
> 'Jammie –'
> 'And clichés about Indians. And the accent – my God, how could you do it? I expect you're ashamed, aren't you?'
> 'I am, actually.'
>
> (p. 157)

Throughout the text, Karim is repeatedly placed in relationships – with Eva, with Eleanor, with Shadwell, with Pyke – in which 'advancement' in one form or another comes at the cost of trading on his 'exoticness'. In Pyke's staggeringly pretentious performance group, for example, where 'two of us were officially "black" (though truly I was more beige than anything)' (p. 167), Karim's minority status fits perfectly into the director's 'radical' professional and sexual agenda.

In *The Buddha of Suburbia*, therefore, it is not only through white bourgeois and petit-bourgeois characters that Kureishi explores the problem of 'race'. At least as importantly, his text explores the grey area where race-thinking shades into the manufacture and exploitation of 'oriental' ethnicities. Haroon, for example, is a comic character precisely because of the way he exploits his appearance to fulfil the stereotypical guru-image of the Buddha. Similarly, when it suits his brother Anwar's interests to have his daughter obey him, Anwar is more than willing to mix-and-match amongst subcontinental traditions in his Pakistani appropriation of the 'Gandhi-diet'. As Karim says, 'It was certainly bizarre . . . I'd never known him believe in anything before, so it was an amazing novelty to find him literally staking his life on the principle of absolute patriarchal authority' (p. 64).

It is through the text's presentation of characters like Changez that we come to recognise the orientalism and even potential racism implicit in Karim's own gaze as 'an Englishman born and bred, almost' (p. 3). Perhaps the clearest example of this emerges through Karim's portrayal of Changez as an immigrant in Pyke's play, in which he draws the audience's laughter by pastiching 'the sexual ambition and humiliation of an Indian in England' (p. 220).

Throughout the text, Karim is a fallible narrator, whose negotiation of the pitfalls of prejudice and opportunity raises as many problems as it solves. Sometimes, he is obtuse and self-deluding. But at other times Kureishi uses him as the mouthpiece for a more self-conscious critique, both of the prejudicial construction of 'blackness' in England, and of the complex way in which, at the same time, difference becomes fetishised and even eroticised. In this regard, Karim's meditation on the loss of Eleanor provides a particularly interesting example:

> It was over, then, my first real love affair. There would be others. She preferred Pyke. Sweet Gene, her black lover, killed himself because every day, by a look, a remark, an attitude, the English told him they hated him; they never let him forget they thought him a nigger, a slave, a lower being. And we pursued English roses as we pursued England; by possessing these prizes, this kindness and beauty, we stared defiantly into the eye of the Empire and all its self-regard – into the eye of Hairy Back, into the eye of the Great Fucking Dane. We became part of England and yet proudly stood outside it. But to be truly free we had to free ourselves of all bitterness and resentment, too. How was this possible when bitterness and resentment were generated afresh every day?
>
> (p. 227)

Here, the sexual possession of the quintessentially white 'English rose' becomes both a revenge and a defence against the racism and imperialism of England. But equally, it does little to deconstruct the assumptions of imperialist and racist discourse. What does the fetishisation of white

Englishness amount to other than an inversion of Karim's own exoticisation as an 'oriental'? As Karim already begins to recognise, this is far from being a solution to the problem of race-thinking.

The Black Album

In *The Black Album* (1995) Kureishi adopts a different narrative approach in order to take these questions further. Firstly, the text is much less of a comic novel, signalling the shift away from 'entertainment' that is apparent in much of his later work. Secondly, the kind of focus on racism that *The Black Album* offers has moved on significantly. In *My Beautiful Laundrette* racism is reasonably clearly attributed to fascist skinheads, and in *The Buddha of Suburbia* it seems to be apportioned between suburbia and the self-satisfied environs of middle-class theatre. In *The Black Album*, however, racism is more disturbingly dispersed – a few young children here, a young mother there:

> 'You wanna find someone who hates another race?' Strapper stopped scratching himself long enough to motion at Southern England. 'Just knock on any door.'

> (p. 143)

In a parallel way, in *My Beautiful Laundrette* and to a lesser extent in *The Buddha of Suburbia*, pop culture and especially sexual freedom seem to be set up as an alternative to outdated racist and classist antagonisms that belong to the past. In these texts it sometimes feels as if racism itself might simply be passed over as a 'generation' thing. And yes, in the early sections of *The Black Album* too, it appears that the peace/love/equality ethos of Acid House might be a possible solution to the disharmonies of the past. At the parties to which the main character, Shahid, goes with his teacher/lover Deedee Osgood, it seems that all ethnicities, genders and sexualities might intertwine in a hallucinatory spiral of pleasure. But even in those early sections the viability of pop/drug culture as an escape from ethnic, political and religious affiliations is already in question. And at the end of the novel when we see Shahid at the seaside with his white bohemian lover, we are never invited to believe that his escape can be anything other than a holiday from the questions that still need to be answered.

The Black Album centres on precisely these oppositions. Throughout the novel, Shahid is placed in a succession of scenarios in which he is torn between the lures of mainstream youth culture, with its drugs, sex and espousal of personal freedoms, and the influence of young British Asians who, by the late 1980s, have become less accepting than their parents of the continued hostility of British society.

More than racism *per se*, then, the primary focus of *The Black Album* is on the militant response to racism offered by one particular segment of society. In 'The Flesh Made Word' (1997) Kureishi argues (in a perhaps over-simplified way) that the rejuvenation of Islam amongst the young in contemporary Britain can be directly related to the effects of white racism. More specifically, here, he suggests that the peculiarly exclusionary and condemnatory character of so-called Islamic 'fundamentalism' adopted by a segment of British young people can be identified as a reciprocal response to the attitudes of exclusion and discrimination that characterise popular views of 'Great British-ness'. From the point of view of the excluded, he argues, one can't put up for ever with the effects of 'being made to feel inferior in your own country'.

For Kureishi, then, what is most understandable about this Islamic revival in Britain is the way it functions to insulate its adherents from racist attack. But what is far less intelligible is the way it simultaneously debars young people from what he regards as the privileges of contemporary British culture. Understanding 'fundamentalism' as an assertion of ethnic pride and as a response to racism is the easy part of the question Kureishi raises in *The Black Album*. Making sense of its hostility to literature, to critical thought and to pleasure is, as he sees it, much the more difficult part.

In both *The Black Album* and his later short story and film *My Son the Fanatic*, Kureishi presents a particular image of young British Muslims, whose parents are no longer necessarily observant of Islamic orthodoxy, but in whose lives the promises of harmonious ethnic 'integration' have failed to be delivered. For this group, a return to certain forms of Islamic orthodoxy is seen as representing a source of purpose, pride and self-worth – expressed partly through modesty and self-denial. In Kureishi's texts, this leads to a very particular set of questions: 'Why was it important that this group kept pleasure at a distance? Why did they wish to maintain such a tantalising relation to their own enjoyment, keeping it so fervently in mind, only to deny it?' (Kureishi, 1997).

In *The Black Album* the figure of Chad dramatises his question very clearly. Far from simply being a matter of religious adherence, Chad's espousal of the most self-flagellatory denial of literature, music and all corporeal pleasures save that of violence, provides an important foil for the protagonist Shahid's own internal struggle. In Kureishi's portrayal faith does not seem to be enough for Chad, but only faith in its most austerely puritanical form, faith in the form of a militancy so uncompromising that finally, literally, it ends up burning his face.

At first, the novel seems to suggest a parallel between the intensity of experience offered by literature, drugs and religion: all high-grade 'kicks' from which Shahid is invited to choose in his quest for adventure and meaning. Initially, at points of crisis it is with a book or pen and paper that Shahid seeks to discover and reorientate himself. Increasingly, though, the unshakeable belief of Riaz, Chad and their companions exercises a powerful pull on his imagination. As the critic Bart Moore-Gilbert argues in his study *Hanif Kureishi* (2001), in the novel as a whole, we see many progressive aspects of Islam: 'its desire for social justice, its hostility to the unrestrained capitalism of the Thatcher era, the second chance in life it offers characters as diverse as Chad and Strapper' (p. 135). At the same time, however, Kureishi's protagonist is always kept at a critical distance from faith itself. At the house party, on the other hand, Shahid's experience of the drug ecstasy seems to offer a different, direct route to higher insight: 'He had been let into a dangerous secret; once it had been revealed, much of life, regarded from this high vantage point, could seem quite small' (p. 63). In Kureishi's narrative, of the three it is religion which fails to deliver the vertiginous experience of envelopment and understanding Shahid craves.

In his non-fictional writing, Kureishi has certainly been critical of Islam: 'Open the Quran on almost every page, and there is a threat' (Kureishi, 1997). Whilst *The Black Album* itself offers no such 'stock' conclusions, its liberal drift is certainly in the same direction. This emerges most clearly in relation to the novel's central event, the burning of Salman Rushdie's book *The Satanic Verses*.

Some of the contexts of the 'Rushdie affair' were explored in chapter 9. Kureishi's portrayal of the backlash against Rushdie's work by no means overplays the history of 1989, in which twenty thousand people were involved in violent demonstrations in London, and which in April saw the bombing of bookstores which stocked the offending novel. Rather than dealing with the *fatwa* and the campaign to have *The Satanic Verses* banned in isolation, however, *The Black Album* operates by setting up a parallel between these events and another historical happening of 1989. That is, the discovery by a Leicester family of the Arabic inscription 'God is everywhere' in the flesh of an eggplant.

In effect, Kureishi's text invites us to consider the contrast between the spectacle of a vegetable which people flock to read, and a literary work which they seek to ban without knowing its contents. The political agenda implicit in this parallel is clearly a contentious one. Within the text its clear function is to begin to align Islam in the protagonist's mind with ignorance and superstition.

According to this reading, arguably, Kureishi's text again risks pandering to prejudice, and specifically to the agenda of the right-wing media, which sought in 1989 to establish a derogatory impression of British Muslims, by exactly the same means. Within Kureishi's narrative, of course, the book burning also functions to reveal the hypocrisy and, perhaps, confusion of the leftist-libertarian Deedee and her Marxist husband, Brownlow. But both of these taken together fit easily with what I am suggesting is the fundamentally liberal agenda of *The Black Album*.

In this context, it is not difficult to understand the text's apparent espousal of literary 'greatness' over the claims of faith-based ethnic allegiance. Clearly *The Black Album* is written as a text against racism, which shows both racism's casual violence and the conditions of ignorance and material resentment out of which it arises. But it is also a weighing-up and rejection of the primary – and perhaps most powerful – response to racism amongst young British Muslims.

When it comes to a choice between the values of Islam and the values of Western liberalism, Kureishi's work quite clearly locates itself in terms of the latter. Certainly, in 'The Flesh Made Word' his presentation of the function of writing is very much a liberal humanist view, emphasising the values of creativity, humanity and individual freedom. For Kureishi, speaking of the importance of literature over religion: 'This creativity, the making of something which didn't exist before, the vigour and stretch of a living imagination, is a human affirmation of a different kind, and a necessary and important form of self-examination. Without it, our humanity is diminished.'

As a text, *The Black Album* in particular can be read as an argument, in these terms, on literature's behalf. In defence of a particular conception of personal and intellectual freedom, it opens up a space of opposition not only to the obscenities of race-thinking, but also to those manifestations of religious faith which, in seeking to create a pure and positive mind-set, end up by needing to outlaw and embargo imaginative creativity.

In this sense, the broad orientation of Kureishi's work seems to be increasingly geared towards occupying the liberal mainstream in British culture. Indeed, in some of the later texts such as *Intimacy* (1998) and the collection *Midnight All Day* (1999), even issues of ethnicity are deeply submerged amongst other concerns, such as class identity, sexuality and desire. In the struggle against race-thinking, certainly, the strategies of Kureishi's writing cannot be totalised in terms of the old opposition of separatism versus integration. More usefully, perhaps, his work can be thought of as a play for the imaginative centre ground.

12 Rewriting ethnicity in Buchi Emecheta's fiction

Hanif Kureishi and Buchi Emecheta are frequently grouped together under the umbrella 'Black British Writers'. What these easy words are apt to obscure, however, are two very distinct sets of influences. In terms of biographical background, certainly, there is a significant contrast. Whilst Kureishi grew up in south-east England, Emecheta's childhood was spent in south-eastern Nigeria. Kureishi's mother was a white middle-class English housewife. Emecheta's mother escaped life as an Igbo slave. In her autobiography, *Head Above Water* (1986), Emecheta pays tribute to her mother, in a way that, through its very extremity, highlights the potential importance of this cultural background in considering the writer's work:

> My mother, Alice Ogbanje Ojebeta Emecheta, that laughing, loud-voiced, six-foot-tall, black glossy slave girl, who as a child suckled the breasts of her dead mother; my mother who lost her parents when the nerve gas exploded in Europe, a gas that killed thousands of innocent Africans who knew nothing about the Western First World War; my laughing mother, who forgave a brother that sold her to a relative in Onitsha so that he could use the money to buy *ichafo siliki* – silk head ties for his coming-of-age dance. My mother, who probably loved me in her own way, but never expressed it; my mother, that slave girl who had the courage to free herself and return to her people in Ibusa, and still stooped and allowed the culture of her people to re-enslave her, and then permitted Christianity to tighten the knot of enslavement.

> (p. 3)

Buchi Emecheta describes in her autobiography how, when she herself was a baby girl, it was decided by an aunt that she should be fed nothing but water, and in effect be left to die. The writer attributes her survival only to the intervention of nurses at the colonial hospital. In the text, her relationship to her family is presented as a difficult one, and as a young girl she went behind their backs to compete for a scholarship to a missionary school. There, she was the recipient of a virulently anglophile Christian education. Throughout her childhood, the autobiography recounts, Emecheta harboured deep-seated ambitions to go to the United Kingdom, and this early strand of anglophilia forms an important theme of her fiction. In both the autobiographical novel *Second Class Citizen* (1974) and in *Head Above Water*, Emecheta critically reflects on this extraordinarily idealised view of the United Kingdom, as seen from the distance of colonial West Africa. The UK is conceived as a kind of heaven, a place of prosperity, manners and education, and racism is something that never enters consideration. With the benefit of detailed first-hand experience as an immigrant, therefore, one of the most important themes of Emecheta's early writing is to expose and debunk that colonial myth.

In the Ditch *and* Second Class Citizen

In Emecheta's first novel, which was burned by her husband before it could reach a publisher, a lot of the idealism and sentimentality which she describes here seems to have survived. The first of her works to reach publication, *In the Ditch* (1972) and *Second Class Citizen*, however, are far from being similarly romanticised. Based on her own experiences as a 'Black Briton' in the 1960s, these texts deploy a quite different, documentary realist style. Both texts work to interrogate the alleged 'advancement' of British civilisation as it is manifested in a highly specific historical period, that of the Macmillan and Wilson governments.

Calling Emecheta a realist in these early works is not to suggest that her texts exhaustively record every detail of her subjects and the period. Rather, her texts seek to portray a range of representative situations and characters in a gritty and unsentimentalised way. Thus, the roach-and-rat infestation of a single bedsit, the racist prohibitions of a few lodging houses, the xenophobia of a particular council officer are made to represent a particular segment of London life at a particular historical moment. Proceeding through example rather than theoretical generalisation, her texts are uncompromising in their presentation of the climate of deprivation and hostility that dominated the experience of immigration in Britain during the last period of its decline as an imperial power.

Early in both novels, the notions of English 'freedom' and 'civilisation', previously so crucial to colonial ideology, are set up for reappraisal. *In the Ditch* opens with an almost unquestioning sense of faith in English 'freedom' and 'rationality', which the heroine, Adah, compares with the corruption and 'juju' practised by her Nigerian landlord. But the novel soon turns to a scathing critique of the colonial centre, and the way it works to reconstitute an educated, industrious Nigerian woman into a 'problem person', dependent on the state and debarred from the privileges of mainstream society.

In *Second Class Citizen*, the prequel to *In the Ditch*, education and advancement are at first, again, unquestioningly equated with the United Kingdom and its values. It is only later that the potential of education begins to be reconsidered as a way out of subjection and into independence. Throughout Emecheta's novels, we are frequently given insights into the poverty and the elitism that exist at the twin extremes of Nigerian society. What *In the Ditch* and *Second Class Citizen* do is to illustrate how the British welfare state works to establish and entrench those same inequalities in the 'enlightened' UK and to sustain its traditional, exclusionary *status quo*.

Both novels centre on Emecheta's presentation of the poverty trap in Britain. Adah, a single mother, is again used as a representative case. As a claimant, she cannot work without forfeiting her benefits. And as a single mother responsible for children, there is no work on offer which could pay well enough to make her benefit-independent. Thus, by means of a well-recognised socio-economic mechanism, she is forced to remain on the poverty line. The effect of this 'civilised' arrangement on Adah is to drive her to desperation. Back in Nigeria, Adah looks with detachment, even distaste, on the complex family and support networks of Igbo society. But once entrenched in her London isolation, she begins to see them in a different light.

In Emecheta's early fiction there is clearly an attempt, then, to debunk the post-war rhetoric of the British welfare state as the measure of its 'civilisation'. Her texts' exposure of the poverty trap mark the beginning of this critique but not its limits. Beyond that, they seek to represent the complex processes by which Adah's self-determination and autonomy as an immigrant to Britain are comprehensively broken down by the very institutions which purport to protect and support her. Necessary concessions, like the retention of her children at the local nursery, become dependent on her ability to style herself as a 'problem' mother. And the delivery of social services itself is administered less often in the spirit of civil entitlement than in the spirit of charity and patronage.

In parallel with this critique, there is a necessary reappraisal of the cultural relations between Britain and West Africa, which begins in these semi-autobiographical texts. In *In the Ditch*, Emecheta seeks to establish an explicit analogy between Adah's condition of subjection and that of post-colonial Nigeria. In the same moment that she struggles for autonomy, she finds herself manoeuvred into a position of complex dependence. In trying to break free from the British state, she finds herself affected by a disabling ambivalence.

> She had been spoonfed for so long that she could not cut off from Carol
> and the Children's Department just like that. The position she was in
> reminded her of young nations seeking independence. When they got
> their independence, they found that it was a dangerous toy.
>
> (p. 95)

Like Kureishi's, Emecheta's texts are stridently critical of British racism
and of imperialist attitudes. But at the same time, this early writing is
particularly interesting for the way it attempts to deal with the vestiges of
colonial nostalgia. In *Second Class Citizen*, she makes common cause with
other Nigerian writers who heap scorn on the English-educated politicians
of Nigerian independence. But her critique is a double-edged one. It is not
simply that she is critical of middle-class Nigerian men in that era for their
unquestioning attitude towards the imperial 'centre'. Her scorn is also
focused (paradoxically) on their failure to live up to the ideal model of
English education. Thus the early novel *Second Class Citizen* seems in a sense
both to uphold and to critique imperialist assumptions simultaneously:

> These groups of men calculated that with independence would come
> prosperity, the opportunity for self-rule, posh vacant jobs, and more
> money, plenty of it. One had to be eligible for these jobs, though,
> thought these men. The only way to secure this eligibility, this passport
> to prosperity, was England. They must come to England, get a quick
> degree in Law and go back to rule their country. What could be more
> suitable? . . . Most of the first generation of Nigerian politicians, who
> sprang up from everywhere after independence, just like mushrooms,
> were from among these men. Some of them actually made it; they
> came back to Nigeria, equipped with law degrees, and a great talent for
> oratorical glibness. They had mastered enough political terms to turn
> the basic proposition of having enough food for everybody into beautiful
> jargon, which left their listeners lost in the middle of long, jaw-breaking
> words. Some of these listeners sometimes wondered whether they were
> not better off with the white master, who would at least take the trouble
> to learn the pidgin English which they could understand.
>
> (pp. 81–2)

Here, the notion of the United Kingdom as the gold standard of civilisation
and education is resisted on one level, only to be reaffirmed on another.

In his influential *Culture and Imperialism* (1993) the Palestinian intellectual Edward Said illustrates the complexity of combating racist and
imperialist assumptions in the postcolonial period. His study draws attention
to the character of many postcolonial regimes by way of evidence. In support
of Said, it is not difficult to construct an argument to suggest that the leaders

of independence movements, in particular, have often had strong ties with the colonial centre. Jawaharlal Nehru in India, like Mohandas Gandhi, gained his legal and political education at the London Inns of Court, as did the first president of Pakistan, Mohammed Ali Jinnah. Nabib Bourguiba, who led Tunisia out of French control, went to the Sorbonne in Paris. And likewise, the British-sponsored (though soon eliminated) first president of independent Nigeria, Abubakar Balewa, was a student at London University.

These kinds of connections of privilege and education between post-colonial leaderships and the old imperial centre are, in fact, far from being demonstrable in every case. But Said's argument is a general rather than a particular one. It is that thoroughgoing liberation from the ideological assumptions of racism and imperialism is often a gradual and staged process. It is not sufficient, he suggests, for a successor regime to simply displace a colonial administration, retaining its methods and privileges, without adequately deconstructing the cultural frameworks and assumptions that constituted and supported imperialism. In Emecheta's later works, this theme of ambivalence is explored in a detailed and interesting way.

Destination Biafra

In Emecheta's study of the Nigerian civil war, *Destination Biafra* (1982), the complex cultural relation between Britain and Nigeria is addressed in a different context to the early novels. As a historical event, the 'Biafran' war has been a huge influence on West African writing since the 1970s. Texts like Chinua Achebe's *Girls at War* are well known for their attempts to attack the destructive self-satisfaction and arrogance of the political elites during the Biafran conflict, and their role in perpetuating the suffering and degradation of ordinary people. Similarly, novels such as Festus Iyayi's *Heroes* (1986) are vociferous in their presentation of the corruption and futility of the war, and Emecheta's *Destination Biafra* dwells on similar themes.

Both Iyayi and Emecheta use protagonists who are outsiders, who bring a partially detached and critical gaze to the conflict. In *Heroes*, the journalist Osime Iyere presents a class analysis of the war, in which it is the ordinary soldiers and civilians who pay the price with their lives for the greed and ambition of the politicians and army elites. Most of Iyayi's narrative takes place in cities under martial law, at army checkpoints or in military barracks. And throughout the text, we are continually referred to what is missing from the scene, Osime's nostalgia for a simpler, traditional Nigerian way of life, connected to the land, beyond nationalisms and ethnic rivalries:

> Members of the working class never bothered about boundaries, about countries until the ruling class thought them up and imposed them. The

ruling class need their little kingdoms. The kingdom of the working
class is the earth itself . . . But the generals run from one little place to
another because no place is really theirs. They are the vagabonds of the
earth, the bastards of the earth.

(p. 133)

The leaders at whom Iyayi's attack is levelled are certainly not entirely
imaginary. They include men such as the commander (and later president)
Olusegun Obasanjo, whose autobiographical account, *My Command* (1980),
was published at the end of his own spell of military rule (1976–9). In a way
that fully bears out Iyayi's critique, Obasanjo uses this text in an extraordinarily blatant way to establish himself in history as the 'hero' of
the Nigerian struggle, the man who virtually single-handedly restored the
nation's 'self confidence and pride'.

Emecheta's text, like Iyayi's, presents itself as a fictionalisation of the war.
At the same time, however, it is undoubtedly a political analysis, caricaturing
some clearly recognisable public figures. Her 'Sardauna' is a closely referenced
portrayal of the Sardauna of Sokoto, the hereditary ruler of northern Nigeria
who was gunned down in his garden, early in the conflict. Emecheta's
'raw' northerner, Saka Momoh, mirrors the wartime leader of the Nigerian
Federation, Yakubu Gowon. And similarly, the 'gentlemanly' Oxford-
educated Chijioke Abosi has to be read as a representation of the Biafran
leader, Odumegwu Ojukwu. Just as we saw in the case of Salman Rushdie's
Shame, this strategy of re-framing recognisable public figures through
fictional doubles allows for a critical, counter-historical perspective on the
period Emecheta examines, resisting the demand for 'authentic' historical
representation. In a further parallel with *Shame*, in *Destination Biafra* these
quasi-historical figures interact in the text with fictional characters who
serve to represent particular ethnic and class positions. Examples of these
are the British ex-colonial administrator, Alan Grey, and the anglophile
upper-class Nigerian, Debbie Ogedembe.

In this way Emecheta's text seeks to critically reconstruct the complex
transition in Nigeria from independence to civil war, focusing on the
persecution of Igbos in the period up to and including the attempted
secession of the south-east as the 'Republic of Biafra' in 1967. It concludes
with the flight of Abosi/Ojukwu in 1970, which signals the defeat of the
Biafran cause at the hands of British- (and Soviet-) sponsored Federal
troops.

Ostensibly *Destination Biafra* is the memoir of a privileged, Oxford-
educated young Nigerian woman. In terms of class, Debbie Ogedembe is
firmly located within the elite. She enjoys personal friendships with both
the Biafran and Federal leaders, and has contacts and friends in England.

She is also the lover of the most senior British representative left in Nigeria, Alan Grey. By positioning her narrator as a woman who is an insider, then, what *Destination Biafra* brings to Nigerian civil war writing is a distinctive perspective on the British colonial connection within the conflict.

Certainly, Emecheta's text is highly critical of the British involvement in its former colony, in terms of its political manipulation of the post-independence settlement, in terms of its dubious pursuit of Nigerian oil interests, and also in terms of its role in arms trading during the Biafran war. The novel begins with the patronising and racist assumptions of the departing colonial regime, and ends with those same attitudes recapitulated by Grey as he flees the civil war. By dramatising their manipulation of Momoh/Gowon and others in order to secure lucrative oil rights over the north and east, moreover, Emecheta uses her novel to implicate the British governing class as one of the parties most responsible for independent Nigeria's collapse into war.

For the protagonist, Debbie Ogedembe, importantly, the course of the war is itself a metaphor for Nigeria's postcolonial struggle to free itself from British influence. In this sense, *Destination Biafra* is far more theoretical in orientation than *In the Ditch* and *Second Class Citizen*. Stylistically, the novel does make gestures towards documentary realism once again. Debbie's account of rape and death on the roads of the south is by no means abstracted in its narrative effects. Certainly, the novel goes to considerable lengths to detail aspects of Nigerian politics and culture – and Emecheta pays tribute in the text to close relatives of hers who were killed in the war. But for all this, Debbie's portrait of the conflict as a whole is so deliberately subjective in tone as to force a space of critical distance, and thereby to complicate our response to her account.

In Debbie's eyes, for example, the Islamic Hausa militias are nothing short of bestial, carelessly slaughtering the respectable Kano middle classes: 'They carried clubs and machetes, tore down from their own areas into the Sabon Garri shouting, "Death to the Kaferi infidels!" At the Barclays Bank, they hacked humans to death and those who tried to escape were clubbed and battered to death' (p. 82). When Debbie is on the road travelling east, similarly, the Yoruba Federal troops she encounters are quick to disregard her status and set about the gang-rape of herself, her mother and their pregnant companion.

Meanwhile, both of these groups contrast sharply with her portrayal of the Biafrans: '"Come out, all of you, come out," said the gentle voice of an Igbo soldier. "Where are your husbands? How come you are travelling with no men to protect you?"' (p. 178). Despite the fact that she professes a 'neutral Itsekiri' (p. 228) perspective, there is little doubt as to the ideological drift of Debbie's narrative. It is a celebration of the doomed vision of Biafran freedom, represented in the figure of a newly born child, and the post-colonial betrayal which cost its life.

As a political novel, of course, the significance of *Destination Biafra* lies also in its insistence on a gendered reading of the Nigerian civil war. Throughout, the novel emphasises the suffering and the courage of women, both in the military and in the civilian population. Compared with the portrayal of Achebe's young woman soldier in *Girls at War*, indeed, *Destination Biafra* makes an important stand in refusing to recapitulate the canonical images of passive womanhood associated with Biafran war writing.

Even in its analysis of the sexual politics of the conflict, however, the text has provoked strong expressions of dissent. According to the critic Abioseh Porter (1996), Emecheta is guilty of offering a 'cartoon-like portrayal of the atrocities and consequences of the war itself (where we often see her biases leading her to create some highly implausible, idealised, and even preposterous situations and characters)' (pp. 314–15). What Porter conspicuously fails to do in making this judgement is to recognise the critical distance between the author, Emecheta, and her narrator, Debbie. As I have already suggested, the way the novel operates politically is to set up Debbie very consciously as a fallible narrator. But Debbie's fallibility is a function not of her femininity, but rather of her class position and her ideological relation to the former imperial centre. Her struggle as a representative of the elite is certainly to challenge the way she is positioned within the patriarchal assumptions of the military and wider Nigerian society. But at least as importantly, that struggle is also to re-evaluate the anglophile mindset she herself has inherited.

In important ways, the Biafran war is a struggle along ethnic lines. In the war zone, it is language, accent and dialect which distinguish Hausa from Yoruba from Igbo, what licenses rape or killing in this case and friendship or self-sacrifice in that. Continually, in the backs of trucks or hiding with others in the bush, Debbie is compelled to disguise the anglo-inflected 'been-to' accent that betrays her as one of the privileged, whose power games are at the heart of the war. Notwithstanding her rape and humiliation, still, her voice defines her as one with the means to escape from Nigeria altogether, should she so wish, and the connections to demand the attention of all the most powerful figures in the land. In order for Debbie to free herself as a Nigerian woman – the reader understands long before she herself does – it is first necessary for her to recognise the oppressive nature of these privileges.

Destination Biafra is an attempt to imagine a move beyond the divisive postcolonial legacy in Nigeria, and at the same time to mount a critique of the sexual exploitation and gender inequality within Nigerian society. As a fictional memoir, it documents the slow change in Debbie's understanding of, and attitude to her national and gender identity. As she reflects on the defeat of the Biafran leadership, it is only at the end of the novel that she comes to finally, fully recognise the need to move intellectually and emotionally beyond the mind-set of subordination: 'I see now that Abosi and his like are still colonized. They need to be decolonized. I am not like him, a black white man; I am a woman and a woman of Africa' (p. 245).

Kehinde

In *Kehinde* (1994), Emecheta returns once again to the problems of ethnic and gender identity in the context of contemporary Britain. As a novel *Kehinde* presents itself highly consciously in terms of tensions and contradictions. The text opens, for example, with what is in a sense a very English scene, a London mother serving beans on toast to her kids, before she herself settles down to a bowl of ground rice and egusi soup. Kehinde works for Barclays, a bank boycotted by her country of birth (and many liberal Europeans) because of its connection with South African apartheid. And the narrative concludes as the heroine drinks down a sweet cup of tea, the archetypal drink of Englishness and of colonialism: 'At length she put the cup to her lips. She felt the sweet liquid running through her inside, warming every part' (p. 141).

Kehinde is frequently read as a novel about a British Nigerian who returns to her country of birth, only to find the culture alien and (in sexual-political terms) degrading. It is in England, according to this reading, that she finds most opportunity for autonomy and self-respect. This interpretation of the novel is an over-easy one which, on closer examination of the text, proves to be quite problematic. Perhaps most importantly, it does nothing to avoid the imperialist tendency to equate 'Africa' with intransigent traditionalism and 'England' with freedom, enlightenment and education, themes which are constantly at issue from Emecheta's early novels onwards.

In fact, in this novel Emecheta shows Nigeria as a nation where formal education, etiquette and civil intercourse are held paramount, and indeed where motherhood is quite compatible with high professional status. England, meanwhile, is presented as a place in which choices and aspirations are almost stereotypically governed by ethnicity:

> They all had their dreams. Prahbu's was to own big grocery stores and newsagent's shops. Mike dealt in stocks and shares and had many contacts through his synagogue. John and the others dreamt of holiday villas in Spain or Madeira, where they could live in retirement. Albert's dream was to be made a chief in his homeland, but while the others could talk about their dreams, Albert felt shy. He was afraid Prahbu would ask, 'Are you sure you're doing the right thing, going back to

Africa?' Albert knew that their images of African chiefs were gathered from old Tarzan films and *Sanders of the River*.

(p. 16)

With the character of Kehinde, Emecheta avoids offering a simple opposition of 'Nigerian-ness' and 'English-ness' or 'British-ness' between which her protagonist might choose. Instead ethnicity is presented as much more complex than that. In its representation of her childhood, the text does not position Kehinde simply as a south-eastern Nigerian Igbo girl. Instead, she is located as a mid-westerner who is exiled to Lagos because of the circumstances of her birth. In *Things Fall Apart* (1958), readers of Nigerian fiction will be familiar with Chinua Achebe's depiction of the abandonment of twins in traditional Igbo culture, because of their association with bad fortune. In *Kehinde*, Emecheta returns to the same theme in quite a different way. Kehinde, whose name means 'second twin', is indeed cast out by her Igbo family. But it is not to the forest that she is banished, but to Yoruba land, where twins are traditionally celebrated as the epitome of luck. Amongst the Yoruba, nevertheless, she is metaphorically exiled again – by the silence and secrecy about her origins. Her destination is Catholicism, the imperialist faith to which her foster mother, Aunt Nnebogo, is an adherent.

Thus at the age of eleven Kehinde is already positioned on the borderlines of ethnicities, her identity defined by hybridity: 'I was still confused. I did not see why Aunt Nnebogo should have taken me away from my brothers and sisters, whether they were half or full. I wanted to protest, to say that when I grow up, I am going to be like the white people. I will look after my own only' (p. 80). As an adult in England, accordingly, Kehinde's feelings about 'home' are ambivalent and confused. With Albert she adopts the outward role of a proud Igbo wife. But her inner consciousness is defined by the dialogue with Taiwo (the first twin) who, in a spirit of Yoruba rebellion, refuses to stay dead and buried.

Kehinde is set in the mid-1980s, soon after Muhammed Buhari's military coup of December 1983. As a woman of forty, Kehinde has lived away from Nigeria throughout its formative phase as an independent nation state, throughout the violent ethnic rivalries of the civil war, the transition in and out of 'one Nigeria' civilian democracy, and the complex politics of the 1970s oil boom. The Nigeria to which both she and Albert look back in different ways is now no more than a nostalgic projection. As we have seen, moreover, Emecheta positions her heroine from the very beginning as a woman distanced and uprooted from traditional Igbo culture. But *Kehinde* is not a novel about a woman in search of a single cultural identity. In London, for example, we are given no suggestion that she is interested in doing more than cherry-picking the elements of English culture she finds amenable. Rather, it is because of London's lack of structure and because of its very hybridity that it becomes a place where Kehinde's aspirations and identities can be renegotiated.

> Joshua looked at her in amazement. He had expected her to be the ideal Ibusa village mother, but she lived in London, not the village. Then he said abruptly, 'I saw you in bed with him.'
>
> 'Oh, is that what this drama is all about? I'm sorry, we weren't sure it was you. You weren't meant to, believe me, but it's not a crime to love. Your dad has taken two other wives in Nigeria, and I'm not complaining. That's one of the beauties of polygamy, it gives you freedom. I'm still his wife, if I want to be, and I'm still your mother. It doesn't change anything.' Kehinde laughed, as Taiwo, the spirit of her rebellious sister, took over.
>
> (p. 138)

In a different way from the political analysis of *Destination Biafra*, *Kehinde* shows the complexity of cultural relations between Britain and Nigeria, and the distorted, mythologised position each has in the culture of the other. As a young woman, Kehinde leaves Nigeria explicitly to escape from polygamy, and from what her Catholic education tells her are the 'superstitions' of Igbo culture. Yet the novel concludes in London, with Kehinde establishing herself with a second man and taking strength from a dialogue with the spirit of a dead sister. In Britain she is frustrated at the low regard in which motherhood is held, and its incompatibility with professional success. Yet it is in Nigeria that her feelings and position as a woman, a wife and a mother are most comprehensively frustrated.

When placed against that of writers like Iyayi, as I have already suggested, Emecheta's work is most often celebrated because of its insertion of a sexual-political dimension to the fictional representation of Nigeria. Certainly, works like *Second Class Citizen* and *Destination Biafra* must be recognised, in their different projects, for the ways in which they insist on the necessity of a feminist analysis in anglophone West African writing. As we can see in *Kehinde*, and in her early writing too, it is necessary to read Emecheta as a writer working to renegotiate reductive ideas about the boundaries of both ethnic and gender identification.

Speaking to Susheila Nasta (1988) before the writing of *Kehinde*, Emecheta speaks of her desire to use her work for the benefit of a new generation, to explore and articulate the notion of an inclusive Black Britishness that moves beyond questions of geographic origins, and beyond the patriarchal assumptions of traditional British and Nigerian culture. In

The New Tribe (2000) too, she shows the redundancy of 'racial' categories for articulating a comfortable sense of Black Britishness, and for explaining its radical difference from older notions of an 'essential' Black or African identity. *Kehinde* can certainly be related to that project. What it shows above all is the complexity of ethnic identification in Britain and Nigeria alike.

Certainly, the analysis developed in the texts of Hanif Kureishi and Buchi Emecheta does not necessarily lead to the same conclusions. Each of them does display a measure of ambivalence towards the notion of Britishness, coupled with a variously articulated demand for Britishness to change and move with the times. But as we have seen, this is a demand which can be articulated in a variety of different ways, and from a variety of different perspectives. Clearly, there can and should be no single account that can encompass the complexity of change in the postcolonial period. For that reason, as I suggested in chapter 4, it is clear just how little nineteenth-century notions of 'race' can contribute to the serious understanding of cultural difference. Manifested as racism, it is something that needs to be coped with, critiqued and deconstructed, in fiction and elsewhere. In its place a very much more developed vocabulary is required to understand the transitions of contemporary culture, and their consequences in lived experience. In the next chapter I turn to a writer who addresses this demand from a different location, and with a different kind of boldness and creativity.

13 Writing as activism: Alice Walker

In chapter 4, I briefly referred to the Civil Rights movement and Black Nationalism in the United States, and their relation to 'race' and resistance. Clearly, there is no unified African American position in relation to either of these ideas. And historically too, the picture is quite a complex one.

In the language of Marcus Garvey's 'Universal Negro Improvement Association' in the 1920s, for example, 'race' is used quite freely. In that decade a variety of responses to 'race' thinking are played out in the writing of the Harlem Renaissance, ranging from the poetry of Langston Hughes, through the fiction of Nella Larson to the groundbreaking anthology edited by Alain Locke, *The New Negro* (1925). The debate between the opposed objectives of separatism and integration in the early part of the century is again played out in exchanges between iconic figures like Malcolm X and Martin Luther King Jr in the 1950s and 1960s. Arguably, by the end of this period there is an agreement between these two men on the need to critique racist ideology, and to promote ethnic solidarity in its place. But this in itself contrasts significantly with the 'racial' rhetoric of other contemporary black leaders such as Elijah Muhammad.

During the decades that follow the deaths of Malcolm X and King, there is a proliferation of positions, ranging from the withdrawal from politics of a new black middle class, through the radical non-participationist philosophy of Louis Farrakhan, to the liberal 'rainbow' politics of Jesse Jackson. In literature, further crucial divides entrench themselves, between urban and rural-focused, northern and southern black writing. And at the same time, we see the crucial intervention of a new generation of black feminist writers like Toni Morrison, Maya Angelou and Alice Walker.

In the 1975 essay that opens her collection *In Search of Our Mother's Gardens* (1984), Alice Walker seeks to respond to the diversity of African American writing by characterising it overall as a tradition of activism. The aim of her paper is to trace the key influences that have shaped her work as a black writer, and the figures she highlights – Zora Neale Hurston and Jean

Toomer – are by no means the most orthodox. There is at least one feature
that their work does have in common with a wide variety of other black
American writing from the slave narratives onwards, however. That is, their
common concern with moral and physical struggle.

If we imagine a kind of patriarchal canon running from the abolitionist
writings of Frederick Douglass to (perhaps) the political fiction of Richard
Wright, an element of activism certainly can be traced through the heart of
African American letters. Walker's work undoubtedly draws on this
tradition. At the same time, though, it is obvious that African American
writing cannot simply be constituted as protest work, and often exists in an
uncomfortable relation to it. Jean Toomer, who produced one of the most
influential modernist treatments of the rural and urban black experience in
Cane (1923), is a case in point. In a sense Toomer is one of the embarrass-
ments of the Harlem Renaissance, disappearing from the black literary scene
after the text's publication, to spend most of the next four decades passing
as a white American.

Alice Walker's writing, too, is especially interesting for its political
unorthodoxy and ambivalence. Her work is saturated by the notion of
writing as a form of struggle, but hers is not an activism which fits easily into
the rhetoric of the black political mainstreams. Even in her civil rights novel
Meridian (1976), the major emphasis is on her protagonist's search for
alternative, less phallocentric forms of struggle than those proposed by the
male figureheads of the early 1970s.

A common response to this political alternativism, especially in Walker's
later work, is to see it as an effective abdication of political responsibility.
In my view this is a fundamental misreading. Rather, I argue in this chapter
that it is political aspiration which links all of her work together – on black
education programmes, on voter registration, on grass-roots campaigning
and consciousness raising, on feminist film-making, on promoting black
women writers, and in the writing of her own fiction and poetry.

Necessarily, then, the relation of writing itself to political activism is one
of the key questions which Walker's texts encounter. In *Meridian*, the semi-
autobiographical protagonist burns most of her work soon after it is written.
The Color Purple (1983) consists of a series of letters, of which many never
reach a recipient. In *The Temple of My Familiar* (1989) the diary of the
adventurer/activist Eleanora is crumbling and worm-eaten. In *Possessing the
Secret of Joy* (1992) the key text that Tashi needs to unlock is not even
written down, but takes the form of a dream.

In all of her work, there is a sense of writing's provisionality. Walker's
texts do not simply presume their own validity. Rather, her work seems
always self-consciously concerned to justify itself in creative, moral and
political terms. Perhaps the most obvious example of this is Walker's study

of female circumcision, *Possessing the Secret of Joy*. Not only are this novel's imaginative resources remorselessly focused on the means and effects of female genital mutilation, but much of its financial proceeds too are, as we shall see, committed to the furtherance of the text's feminist goals. As is true in this example, Walker's political commitments have frequently attracted hostility from the critical establishment. Like that of both Kureishi and Emecheta, her work is profoundly self-directing, pursuing themes which are well outside the mainstream of both black and white liberal opinion.

A brief outline of Walker's work from *The Color Purple* onwards illustrates this tendency very well. It was with this text, which won the Pulitzer Prize and became a global film success in collaboration with Steven Spielberg, that Walker first achieved wide public acclaim. On the back of this popularity, we may ask then, which of the themes explored in *The Color Purple* did Walker choose to pursue in her later texts? In the novel's sequel, *The Temple of My Familiar*, her decision to focus on the themes of animist spirituality and reincarnation seemed almost calculated to militate against secular critical sensibilities. The final novel of the trilogy, *Possessing the Secret of Joy*, on the other hand, pursued the theme of female genital mutilation. It hardly needs to be said that highlighting this deeply problematic aspect of traditional African culture represented an unwelcome challenge to the romanticisation of 'roots' by contemporary African American writers and critics. Focusing on a tradition of institutionalised sexual violence largely endemic to Africa, Asia and the Middle East, likewise, produced a connected ideological dilemma for liberal feminist supporters of Walker's work, who were forced by the novel into a deeply uncomfortable confrontation with the principle of respect for cultural difference. Meanwhile, *By the Light of My Father's Smile* (1998) offered a challenge of another order, with its radical figuration of sexuality within the black Christian nuclear family.

Walker's work, then, is almost synonymous with unorthodoxy. In each of these cases, it is possible to see how the political and ideological concerns of her texts seem to override pragmatic considerations of popularity and readerly expectations. Looking at her profile as a whole, it is almost certainly true that Walker's pursuit of writerly autonomy has been to the detriment of wider critical recognition. Ironically, that may be one of the costs of working on the boundaries of ideological acceptability.

Meridian

Meridian is a novel written in what Alice Walker terms the 'lull' in the civil rights struggle which followed the assassination of Martin Luther King Jr in 1968. As a student, Walker was deeply involved in the pursuit of civil rights through non-violent protest. In Georgia, where she grew up, formal segregation was a facet of everyday life. For black children, there was still a colour bar on many facilities like ice-cream parlours and public swimming pools. And it is not controversial to say that in Georgia in the post-war period, both institutionalised and covert racist practices were ubiquitous. In the 1960s the student political activities of which she was a part were highly practical and directed, focusing on the 'testing' and occupation of segregated facilities like restaurants, beaches and public transport, as well as more traditional forms of popular protest like the massive March on Washington of August 1963. In her literary and critical writing Walker frequently returns to specific instances, like the denial of food relief to her mother by a bigoted white administrator, and seeks to place them within a wider social and ideological context.

After 1968, there was a significant fragmentation of both strategy and leadership amongst the various militant and non-violent arms of the black movement. *Meridian* can be located within the context of those later debates. The novel is a timely working through of the goals and means of struggle, and centres on an ultimate question, whether or not we should be willing to kill in defence of black civil rights. Within the novel, these issues are primarily explored through the personal and ideological struggle of the protagonist, Meridian:

> 'I don't trust revolutionaries enough to let them choose who should be killed. *I* would probably end up on the wrong side of the firing squad, myself . . . I think that all of us who want the black and poor to have equal opportunities and goods in life will have to ask ourselves how we stand on killing, even if no one else ever does. Otherwise we will never know – in advance of our fighting, – how much we are willing to give up.'
>
> 'Suppose you found out, without a doubt, that you could murder people in a just cause, what would you do? Would you set about murdering them?'
>
> 'Never alone,' said Meridian. 'Besides, revolution would not begin, do you think, with an act of murder – wars might begin that way – but with teaching.'
>
> 'Oh yes, *teach*ing,' said Truman, scornfully.
>
> (p. 192)

Throughout the novel, Meridian's position is very much one of ambivalence, or more precisely of adjacency to revolutionism. Like Walker herself (arguably) she is unwilling to let go of the example of Martin Luther King, and – less and less fashionable though it may be – unwilling to let go of the philosophy of non-violence. In the aftermath of the student civil rights protests of the 1960s, she reads a hypocrisy in the revolutionary rhetoric of her companions, as they become progressively divorced from effective political engagement. Ultimately, Meridian herself gives up everything to pursue a life of direct action with the Southern poor, and within the frame of Walker's text it is difficult to see what her more 'radical' friends like Anne-Marion have achieved by comparison, apart from consciousness-raising amongst their own small circle. In the case of her sometime lover, Truman, the deflowering of young white girls becomes a compensatory alternative to pursuing the struggle against racism and civil inequality. It is by direct contrast to their examples that Walker's heroine pursues her search for meaningful, efficacious struggle.

In this sense, the novel as a whole can be read as an attempt to *continue to take seriously* King's call for a claiming of ownership. In her 1973 essay 'Choosing to Stay at Home' Walker outlines what she sees as the radicalism of King's engagement with the problems of the South. For years, the established pattern had been for virtually all young educated and mobile blacks to be driven North by the racist economic divides of the South, its lack of opportunity, and its entrenched practices of discrimination. Across the black movement, a whole range of leaders had certainly responded to this, focusing on the importance of black economic power, and the possibility of using it to challenge the segregationist practices of public and private corporations. More radically, Black Nationalists from Marcus Garvey to Malcolm X had been calling for the establishment of an autonomous black state. King's call for the reclamation of homelands, however, was of a different order from these. It was at once more immediate and more homely. As Walker says:

> no black person I knew had ever encouraged anybody to 'Go back to Mississippi . . .' and I knew if this challenge were taken up by the millions of blacks who normally left the South for better fortunes in the North, a change couldn't help but come.
>
> This may not seem like much to other Americans, who constantly move about the country with nothing but restlessness and greed to prod them, but to the Southern black person brought up expecting to be run away from home – because of the lack of jobs, money, power and respect – it was a notion that took root in willing soil. We would fight to stay where we were born and raised and destroy the forces that sought to disinherit us. We would proceed with the revolution from our own homes.
>
> (Walker, 1984, p. 161)

In *Meridian*, then, we can see a working-through of established ideological debates, as well as a sense of struggles unfinished and work remaining to be done. One of the most important ways in which the novel mounts a critique of the mainstreams of black political struggle in the period is by focusing on its 'narrowing' tendency. The novel reflects the historical shift in the mid-1960s – including the Student Non-violent Co-ordinating Committee with which Walker was involved – towards the exclusion of white activists from the struggle for social change. At the time when she was writing the novel, Walker was herself going through the break-up of a marriage to a white civil rights lawyer, Mel Leventhal, and so from a biographical point of view it is quite enlightening to see the way in which questions of sexual and political segregation are played out in the text. In fact, the novel deals with black/white sexual relations with extraordinary boldness. As in many of her other texts, from *The Third Life of Grange Copeland* (1970) onwards, African American masculinity is subjected to a ferocious interrogation.

Amongst the first of the approaches *Meridian* makes to this examination of gender relations is the way it highlights the tendency within black politics towards the subordination of black women to secondary and supporting roles. As Walker has shown in her non-fictional writings, even high-profile women activists like Coretta King found themselves delimited within the rights struggle by the patriarchal assumptions of the male leadership. *Meridian's* experience as a female volunteer in the novel reflects this.

Far more damaging than this, however, is the text's handling of the relationships between Meridian, Truman, Tommy Odds and the white woman, Lynne. Although Walker's politics are clearly at a distance from those of a Black Nationalist like Eldridge Cleaver, her text nevertheless echoes his analysis of the battle for 'sexual sovereignty' between black and white American men. In particular, Tommy and Truman's presentation is centrally framed around anxieties about potency, adequacy and respect. Truman's serial betrayal of Meridian is explicitly framed in terms of a kind of 'racial' neurosis in which the gift of the white woman's virginity is the sign of his 'arrival' as a man. Moreover, when Walker's novel has the white woman Lynne raped by the black activist Tommy Odds, the idea of an equation between white racism and black sexual oppression is strengthened still further.

On each side of this equation, the black woman is relegated to a position of subordination and marginality. Clearly, Walker's writing as a whole seeks to contest that position, and conversely to celebrate the resources of black women. In *Meridian* we see the way she seeks to frame that project ideologically. Meridian's redemptive self-discovery is imagined specifically *in relation to* the patriarchal neurosis and the sexual exploitation of black men:

> At times she thought of herself as an adventurer. It thrilled her to think she belonged to the people who produced Harriet Tubman, the only American woman who'd led troops in battle.

But Truman, alas, did not want a general beside him. He did not want a woman who tried, however encumbered by guilts and fears and remorse, to claim her own life. She knew Truman would have liked her better as she had been as Eddie's wife, for all that he admired the flash of her face across a picket line – an attractive woman, but asleep.

(pp. 106–7)

Even the black professor, Mr Raymond, who lectures Meridian about the rape of black women by white men, is sexually exploitative at every opportunity he gets. In the cases of both Truman (the closest Walker offers to a 'hero') and Tommy Odds, the chosen route to a secure masculinity is through the sexual possession of white women. By this means it is imagined that they can 'even the score' with white men. In each of these instances, it is very clear that where *Meridian* has the opportunity to mount positive portrayals of African American masculinity (the activist, the intellectual) it side-steps them, focusing instead on the barriers put up, even by politically progressive men, to the liberation of black women.

Certainly, the novel does seek to understand the pathologies of African American masculinity in terms of the very real experience of social subordination. Tommy Odds' degeneration to revenge-rapist and Lynne's own descent into bitterness and racism are presented as the direct result of his physical humiliation at the hands of white supremacists. Walker's treatment of the amputation of his (only slightly wounded) arm by white doctors is an instance of just how hard-hitting her fiction can be in its representation of racism and resistance. Her development of the narrative up to and including the attack on Lynne, however, is hard to handle in a different way. Tommy Odds' rape of the white woman is an utterly desolate attempt to salvage 'racial' pride by 'get[ting] off on a piece of their goods' (p. 163). By forcing this uncomfortable linkage between racist and sexist oppression in the novel, therefore, it is possible to see clearly how Walker broadens the notion of struggle in her text beyond the limits of Black Nationalist orthodoxy.

In *Meridian*, then, it is possible to see how Walker's treatment of sexuality runs the gauntlet of mainstream critical opinion. At least as importantly, however, the novel is notable for the way in which it pathologises African American motherhood as well. As an imagined institution, it is worth bearing in mind the way in which the black American woman has been held up/down within both the white and black American family, as a kind of archetypal mother figure and as a guardian of Christian moral responsibility.

In Walker's novel, this canonical image is first assaulted by the portrayal of Meridian's mother, who raises her children in resentment and out of a spirit of pious self-destruction. Meridian herself, meanwhile, is almost an anti-mother. Of the children she touches in the narrative, all but one are killed. The survivor, her son Eddie Jr, only lives because Meridian gives him away for adoption, precisely because she cannot avoid the temptation to take his life. The older children, Wile Chile and Anne, meet with violent ends almost the moment Meridian attempts to assume a quasi-maternal role. By the end of the novel, Meridian's model of moral commitment plus personal freedom is not only a political stance but a sexual-political one as well. This problematisation of the axiomatic status of maternity as the destination of the black woman signals one of the key concerns of Walker's fiction. That is, the (re)constitution of black American femininity in relation to the family, to political struggle and to Christianity.

It is difficult to dispute that Christianity was, in a broad historical sense, a religion foisted on American slaves as a tool of subordination by plantation owners in the Caribbean and the American South. One canonical response to this, offered by Black Nationalists like Malcolm X and others, is conversion to more or less orthodox forms of Islam. Islam is constructed as an ideological antidote to Christianity's colonial legacy, in a gesture of political (but often not sexual-political) liberation. Against this position, it can of course be argued that across much of Africa, the history of the spread of Islam is also a history of the marginalisation of traditional beliefs. And as we see in *Possessing the Secret of Joy*, Islam has also been dubiously appropriated in order to justify oppressive practices against women, such as female circumcision. Whether for this reason or not, what Walker's texts do is to refuse Islam as a means of spiritual, sexual and political liberation for black women. Instead she moves towards the creation of a 'womanist' ethic, which is an amalgamation of contemporary feminist concerns with certain reappropriated aspects of traditional African spirituality.

In this process, the critique of Christianity is crucial. In the essay 'In Search of Our Mother's Gardens' Walker famously celebrates the spiritual strength of black American mothers and grandmothers, for whom the black Christian church was a profoundly affirmative cultural resource. In *The Color Purple* and *The Temple of My Familiar*, however, there is a very clear move away from a Christianised model of redemption. *Meridian* is the novel which lays the groundwork for this shift. Most importantly, the novel interrogates the model of struggle as *martyrdom*, and attempts to articulate an idea of black feminine agency that is not built on the premise of ultimate self-sacrifice.

Meridian's rejection of her own mother's ethic of respectable but self-sacrificial maternity represents the first stage of this ideological transition. It does not constitute its end point, however. Many times during the novel, we are explicitly alerted to the ultimate implications of Meridian's own self-martyring trajectory. The mysterious, debilitating illness she suffers each time she mounts an act of political struggle, is only the most obvious, metaphorical sign of this problem. It is her more orthodoxly militant friend who articulates Meridian's physical decline as a symptom of her limiting self-conception as an activist. As Anne-Marion finally says, 'Meridian, I cannot afford to love you. Like the idea of Suffering itself, you are obsolete' (p. 124).

In an important self-reflexive turn in the novel, nevertheless, it is Meridian who most clearly articulates the need to rewrite the narrative trajectory of her character:

> 'The only new thing now,' she had said to herself, mumbling it aloud, so that people turned to stare at her, 'would be the refusal of Christ to accept crucifixion. King,' she had said, turning down a muddy lane, 'should have refused. Malcolm, too, should have refused. All those characters in all those novels that require death to end the book should refuse. All saints should walk away.'
>
> (pp. 150–1)

Seen in this context, it is easy to argue that within the frame of the text, the description of Meridian's final healing is a deliberately utopian gesture. She finds her grail of moral and political equilibrium, and an ideologically renewed Truman is the first to cast off his worldly concerns and follow where she leads. Of course what we are being offered is a projected ideal, and this is a closing strategy that returns in later texts.

The Color Purple

As Donna Haisty Winchell notes in her book *Alice Walker* (1992), *The Color Purple* is in part an autobiographical text. Raped by her stepfather, Walker's heroine, Celie, follows the model of the author's own great-great-grandmother, who was impregnated by her master at the age of eleven. Separated by a gap of five generations, Walker herself is the genetic product of that union. By the same token, the novel also reflects certain key literary influences. The sexually and ideologically rebellious character of Shug is modelled on the writer Zora Neale Hurston, whose work Walker has campaigned with great success to rescue from disuse.

The novel is set in a poor rural black community after the First World War, and describes the flowering of a lesbian relationship between the wife and the lover of a traditional patriarchal black American man, known for much of the novel as 'Mr _____'. As Walker writes in *In Search of Our Mother's Gardens*, the text was completed in a year, whilst living in silence and isolation with her (male) lover in rural north California. Published in 1983, it was her breakthrough novel, in terms of both popularity and critical reputation.

In *The Color Purple* some of the key themes explored in *Meridian* are taken further. Perhaps most importantly, the novel continues to develop Walker's unorthodox approach to the twin notions of oppression and of struggle. Considering its setting in the deep South, in a period of racism and violent segregationist activity, one of the text's most unexpected features in this respect is that racist discrimination is not its foremost focus.

By sharp contrast to the texts of male forebears like Richard Wright and Ralph Ellison, as well as those of contemporaries such as Ishmael Reed, *The Color Purple* mounts a powerful attack on the oppressive sexual politics of the traditional African American family. Following on from *Meridian*, at its centre is a re-appraisal of the Christianised model of suffering so prominent in the constitution of Southern African American female subjectivity.

One of the principal reasons that *The Color Purple* has met with a fair amount of critical resistance is this apparent concentration on the worst facets of African American masculinity, rather than on the forms and effects of white oppression. It is important, however, to recognise that the almost total exclusion of white people from the frame of *The Color Purple* is a crucial part of its emancipatory project. Painful though much of its subject matter may be, especially in the early sections, *The Color Purple*, like Toomer's *Cane*, is a celebration of blackness. As Henry Louis Gates Jr points out in his study *The Signifying Monkey* (1988) even the colour purple is, in Toomer's work, emblematic of black skin itself. Illustrating his argument elegantly from the novel *Cane*, Gates quotes Toomer's poem 'Song of the Son':

> O Negro Slaves, dark purple ripened plums
> Squeezed, and bursting in the pine-wood air,
> Passing, before they stripped the old tree bare
> One plum was saved for me, one seed becomes
>
> An everlasting song, a singing tree
> Caroling softing souls of slavery . . .

In Walker's novel, as Gates goes on to say, 'Nettie's discovery of the near-purple (i.e. "blue-black") skin of the Africans in *The Color Purple* tips off a further meaning of "the color purple" for Walker, as well as Toomer: "The colored people"' (p. 120). Far from being in flight from the oppressive mythology of 'race', Walker's text offers a different strategy. That is, to disallow 'race' from setting the agenda, and thus to frustrate its colonising tendency.

Though *The Color Purple* concentrates primarily on the lives of black American people and especially black American women, it would obviously be wrong to suggest that the novel does not acknowledge the existence of racism at all. Sofia is imprisoned for talking back to the white mayor's wife; Celie's biological father is lynched for running a successful business. Clearly too, the novel does deal with the issue of colonialism, exploring the demise of (fictional) Olinka through the Americanised eyes of Nettie, who travels to Africa as a missionary.

Indeed, the novel offers a direct connection between African colonialism and the exploitation of blacks in the United States. The text sets up an obvious parallelism between, on the one hand, the razing of Olinka land and the destruction of their lives and livelihoods, and on the other hand, the burning down of Nettie and Celie's father's store, and the lynching of him and his brothers. And similarly, the text advertises the analogy between the fatal trauma suffered by the Olinkan Tashi near the end of the text and that suffered by Celie's mother at the beginning.

Partly as a result of the text's epistolary form, however, neither the colonisation of Olinka nor the lynching of Celie and Nettie's father is presented directly as a dramatic scene. Rather, the novel's consistent focus is on the psychological development and enlightenment of the key black women characters. By the same token, although the arrogance of the white mayor and his wife is a crucial component of Sofia's story, their actual place in the narrative is an extremely small one. In order to understand the brutality of Sofia's reining-in, it is Sofia and her peers we need to focus on. To adapt Shug's formulation, in order to see black clearly, the first thing we need to do is to 'get white off our eyeball'.

The first emancipatory gesture of *The Color Purple*, then, is the exclusion of white from the palette. Its second emancipatory gesture is the rejection of the patriarchal reading of God so crucial to the Western Christian tradition. Guided as she is by Shug, the ideological journey made by Celie 'from the religious back to the spiritual' is, according to Walker in her tenth anniversary preface, the central theme of the novel. The spirituality embraced by Shug and ultimately by Celie is not simply some kind of generic New Age '-ism'. More definitely than that, it is a feminist reworking of core elements of pre-colonial African spiritual culture.

Key moments in Celie's transition to 'spirituality' include the move from a white male personified notion of God to a notion of an omnipresent spirituality. They include the rediscovery of her aesthetic pleasure in the natural landscape of the South, which is of course (as we have seen in *Meridian*) a part of her claiming of ownership. And above all they include the reclamation of female sexual pleasure from its place of 'dirty' abjection within the Christian imagination:

> Oh, she say. God love all them feelings. That's some of the best stuff God did. And when you know God loves 'em you enjoys 'em a lot more.

You can just relax, go with everything that's going, and praise God by liking what you like.

God don't think it dirty? I ast.

Naw, she say. God made it. Listen, God love everything you love – and a mess of stuff you don't. But more than anything else, God love admiration.

You saying God vain? I ast.

Naw, she say. Not vain, just wanting to share a good thing. I think it pisses God off if you walk by the color purple in a field somewhere and don't notice it.

What it do when it pissed off? I ast.

Oh, it make something else. People think pleasing God is all God care about. But any fool living in the world can see it always trying to please us back . . .

. . . Well, us talk and talk about God, but I'm still adrift. Trying to chase that old white man out of my head. I been so busy thinking bout him I never truly notice nothing God make. Not a blade of corn (how it do that?) not the color purple (where it come from?). Not the little wildflowers. Nothing.

(pp. 167–8)

This transition from 'religion to spirituality' in *The Color Purple* is, then, the rubric Walker uses to describe her ideological remodelling of African American femininity. As we have seen, spirituality has been historically crucial to the survival of black women in the South, usually within the framework of the black church. What both *The Color Purple* and *The Temple of My Familiar* attempt to do is to recast this spirituality in a non-Christian/colonialist, non-patriarchal form.

Womanism, as defined in Walker's critical writing, then, is more than a liberal feminism tweaked for black or for lesbian women. It is a feminism which seeks to incorporate and celebrate women's sexual pleasure and women's spirituality together. And it is a feminism whose conception of the aesthetic is founded on forms such as cooking and sewing and gardening which, for generations, constituted the major creative media of black women.

Opening her collection *In Search of Our Mother's Gardens* Walker offers the definition 'Womanist is to feminist as purple is to lavender'. In her study *Womanist and Feminist Aesthetics* (1995) Tuzyline Jita Allan interprets this metaphor as 'a visual illustration of the ideological gap between womanism and feminism. The shade of difference is a matter of depth or intensity' (p. 92). Womanism (purple) is of a deeper and more intense hue than feminism (lavender). Despite the explicit stress Walker places on natural spirituality in her tenth anniversary preface, in 'In Search of Our

Mother's Gardens' and across a range of her critical writing, despite also the intense concentration on spiritual exploration in its sequel *The Temple of My Familiar*, it is quite clear that Allan is reluctant to accept the ideological importance of the spiritual in Walker's writing. As we can see from Celie's meditation above on the wonder of the colour purple and of the wild flower, however, a different kind of reading of Walker's womanist metaphor is possible. It is something like this: 'if feminism is a wild flower (lavender), then womanism is the sign of its life-force (purple)'. Read in this way, the relationship between the notions of womanism and feminism changes in an interesting way. Womanism is not just an intensification. More radically, womanism becomes the animating spark of feminist liberation. On one level, what this seems to propose is that a sense of life-affirming autonomy and creativity is a prerequisite for a developed feminist consciousness. On a second level, it facilitates an acknowledgement of the debt that con-temporary writers like Walker owe to the ideological and creative traditions of their mothers and grandmothers. And as importantly, on a third level, it therefore implies a rejection of the idea that self-consciously academic theorising is necessary for the development of a liberatory womanist con-sciousness. In *The Temple of My Familiar* it is certainly possible to see how Walker attempts (perhaps paradoxically) to elaborate on this thread of feminist anti-academicism.

In 'In Search of Our Mother's Gardens', Walker speaks of the way in which it was by searching for the source of her mother's creativity that she ultimately found her own. In Shug Avery she reanimates the spirit of a different fore-mother, Zora Neale Hurston, as another kind of necessary precursor to her work. In the novel, it is through Shug's guidance towards a womanist amalgamation of spirituality/creativity that the protagonist Celie is able to come to a developed sense of her own worth.

As in *Meridian*, what we see in *The Color Purple*, then, is a move away from the Christian definition of virtuous femininity as meekness and self-sacrifice, and towards the womanist idea. In the character of Celie we see a slow but complete transition away from the Christian ethic of martyrdom, in the sense of redemption through passive suffering. For much of the novel, the reader grinds her teeth at the continuing spectacle of Celie's self-sacrificial capacity to bear oppression. After the unpalatable realism of these sections, the 'happy ending' of *The Color Purple* comes as a redemptive rush. In the later texts *The Temple of My Familiar* and *Possessing the Secret of Joy* the utopian, even fairytale-like scenario with which the novel closes is elaborated even further. Shug and Celie become a pair of archetypal mother/lover figures, living exemplars of the womanist paradigm.

Neither is it only women who are redeemed by the transition to womanist spirituality, self-love and creativity. Challenged alike by Shug and Celie,

Albert too manages ultimately to escape his patriarchal straitjacket as Mr
_____. Punished and abandoned by his wife and lover, it is his son Harpo
who ultimately nurses him from the point of self-destruction, thereby
achieving his own reconciliation with Sofia. Relinquishing the domineering
patriarchal role does not ultimately debilitate the masculinity of either, but
rather the reverse. As Albert admits – rediscovering his enjoyment of
gossiping and sewing – 'Celie, I'm satisfied this the first time I ever lived on
Earth as a natural man. It feel like a new experience' (p. 221). Together with
the final family reunion of Celie, Shug, Nettie and Samuel, the narrative
closure Walker negotiates here is again plainly utopian in intent. And given
that fact, it is reasonable to question what kind of a politics the text
ultimately lays out.

In her critical analysis of Walker's novel, 'Writing the Subject: Reading
The Color Purple', bel hooks (1989) offers one kind of answer to that
question. She notes the unorthodox sexual politics of the text, in which
misogyny and sexism are rife but homophobia never enters the frame, and
in which the Christian ethic of monogamy is disregarded with little question.
Taken as a whole, for hooks the sexual politics of *The Color Purple* remain
problematic. Crucially, she argues that whilst Celie's passivity in the face of
her oppression is rewarded in the novel, the spirit of lively self-defence
expressed by Sofia is seriously punished:

> Unlike Celie or Shug, she is regarded as a serious threat to the social
> order and is violently attacked, brutalised, and subdued. Always a
> revolutionary, Sofia has never been victimised or complicit in her own
> oppression. Tortured and persecuted by the State, treated as though she
> is a political prisoner, Sofia's spirit is systematically crushed. Unlike
> Celie, she cannot easily escape and there is no love strong enough to
> engender her self-recovery. Her suffering cannot be easily mitigated, as
> it would require radical transformation of society. Given all the
> spectacular changes in *The Color Purple*, it is not without grave and
> serious import that the character who most radically challenges sexism
> and racism is a tragic figure who is only partially rescued – restored only
> to a semblance of sanity.
>
> (p. 222)

Certainly, hooks' arguments are damaging ones for a feminist (or
womanist) reading of *The Color Purple*. And as in *Meridian*, it is true that
Walker seems unable to conceive of a path to liberation along the traditional
lines of resistance. Instead, both novels opt to develop a model of liberation
from within. Accordingly, the whole trajectory of *The Color Purple* is not
towards the virtues of political struggle in its received forms, but towards a

recognition of the emancipatory possibilities of black women's spirituality and creativity. Within the framework of the novel, arguably, it is essential for Celie to start off as a Christianised martyr-figure, in order for her liberatory, womanist transformation to have the appropriate impact. Where this leaves a more traditional revolutionary figure like Sofia, as hooks suggests, is a difficult question for which neither *The Color Purple* nor *The Temple of My Familiar* offers a very palatable answer.

By the end of *The Color Purple*, then, we have already travelled a long way from the philosophy of challenge and protest espoused by either the Student Non-violent Co-ordinating Committee of Walker's student days, or contemporary Black Nationalism. Certainly, *The Color Purple* was received by critics and other readers as a novel of protest. Notably, however, this was often at the expense of missing (or skilfully ignoring) its core ideological/spiritual drift. In the context of this kind of reception, it is easy to envisage the kind of pragmatic choice with which Walker was confronted by the mid-1980s. On the one hand, she could develop those more conventionally feminist and political aspects of her work which had been so well received by the arbiters of international critical opinion. Or alternatively she could develop and pursue the distinct project of womanism to its ultimate literary and ideological conclusions. The tepid critical response to Walker's most unorthodox and challenging novel, *The Temple of My Familiar*, provides some indication of her response to that choice.

The Temple of My Familiar

The Temple of My Familiar offers a radical extension of the alternative paradigm explored in *The Color Purple*. In particular, it makes far more reference to traditional African notions of a spirit-infused universe, often referred to as 'animism'. Whilst the ideas of ancestor-worship and reincarnation are hardly developed at all in *The Color Purple*, these aspects of pre-colonial African spirituality are pursued substantially in the later novel. As a whole, the text represents a further rejection of the hegemonic status of patriarchal Christianity, whilst continuing to salvage from that tradition the spiritual, creative and sexual resources of black women.

The Temple of My Familiar was initially published in serial form, in various magazines ranging from *New Woman* to *Ms*, on which Walker spent many years as an editor. Perhaps as a result of that publication history, its narrative dynamic is episodic rather than linear. The text follows three heterosexual couples and their movement towards a womanist ideal. However, it is only in the later sections of the novel that their stories become substantially intertwined. So for much of the text, our experience of reading is quite fragmentary. Certainly, the text's segmentation and multiformity frustrates the possibility of readerly 'mastery', and a sense of readerly frustration is certainly reflected in many of the critical responses to the book. The critic Lillie Howard (1993), for example, finds the text 'maddening'. In her study of Alice Walker and Zora Neale Hurston, Howard's reading of the novel is appended almost with embarrassment, under the subtitle 'A Few Words About *The Temple* . . .' and the disclaimer that all she can offer the reader is an account of her 'own experiences' as a reader. Amongst other critics, Donna Haisty Winchell (1992) is typical in prefacing her remarks with a warning about the text's 'difficulty'.

In *The Color Purple*, as we have seen, the spiritual is a key axis along which Walker develops a sense of ideological resistance to racist and sexist oppression, in the face of more orthodox perspectives. In *The Temple of My Familiar* this strategy is pursued much further. Through the characters of Zedé and Lissie, a notion of genetic memory/reincarnation takes the place of empirical history, giving the text a kind of vast, mythological impression of time. It is through their alternative conceptions of the historical that the novel begins to map out its vast emancipatory horizon.

Certainly, the 'critique' of Islam is fairly peremptory. I have already noted the importance of Islam within Black Nationalism, from the 1930s onwards. It is significant, then, that through the eyes of Zedé in *The Temple of My Familiar*, Islam is depicted as a colonialist force. Far from representing a route to freedom from the domination of the white slave-holders, it is summarily condemned by her for its complicity in the slave trade. The African Muslims we see are as callous as they are avaricious: 'to see a mother sold into slavery . . . did not turn a hair on Mohametan's head' (p. 78).

What happens to Christianity in the novel, again notably, is slightly different. In *The Color Purple*, as we have seen, Christianity is something that Celie needs to escape in her progress towards sexual and personal liberation. In *The Temple of My Familiar*, by contrast, the figure of Jesus is not rejected, but reappropriated quite radically as an erotic figure:

> If there is any spirit I find truly erotic it is that one. *Aiiee!* Jesús was such a priest I used to feel as if the trees fell before him to be blessed . . . His eyes spoke. My womb leaped . . . They could not watch us every minute. During an hour they could not witness and will never own, I made love to him.

> (p. 89)

As a renegade spiritualist, the Jesus of *The Temple of My Familiar* is still fundamentally self-sacrificial. But it is significant that in Zedé's vision the central motif of crucifixion is recast as a rape and castration. In a similar way, through Lissie, the novel revisits the Genesis story and re-mythologises it as an account of the emergence of the white man. Like Eden, the forest is depicted as a kind of garden, containing its iconic trio of man, woman and serpent. Canonically, too, the 'fall' of man is linked to the loss of his virginity, as a result of which he first comes to realise his nakedness/whiteness. What the novel then does is to take the white man as a Cain figure, whose violence and resentment are concomitant to his status as an outcast. Clothing himself in the hides of animals, the white man becomes synonymous with the smell of death, and his pathologisation is complete.

Walker's representation of 'reincarnated' knowledge in the novel, moreover, is not only significant in terms of the rewriting of these iconic religious narratives. Its representation of the distant and even pre-historic past also necessarily involves a critique of the assumptions of empirical, academic historiography. In this sense Walker's work accords well with the strategies of Toni Morrison's fiction, and especially of *Beloved*, which I discussed in chapter 6. In Walker's novel, Lissie's reincarnated memories of the slave ships are explicitly set up as an 'embarrassment' to the discipline of history, such that Lissie has to constantly resist the attempts to 'academicise' her by the white woman history professor who comes to hear her speak. In *The Color Purple* the portrait of young 'Bill Duboyce' (clearly W.E.B. Du Bois) is already an acerbic and intellectually aggressive figure. By *The Temple of My Familiar*, the figure of the young African American scholar has become 'zombie-like'. As the history teacher, Suwelo, gradually comes to realise, black figures seem at best only to fit 'into the gaps' of established history. For any project of black self-emancipation, the novel strongly suggests, it is therefore necessary to get beyond the whole limiting horizon of the academic gaze.

Like other writers, such as Toni Morrison and Maxine Hong Kingston, then, Walker uses the novel to explore radically alternate possibilities of historical memory. In their writing, this revisionary effort involves a breaking down of the barriers between memory, imagination and desire. Nevertheless, if we consider the account of the emergence of the white man, it is possible to see how Walker's particular experimentation with 'reincarnated' memory leads to some very significant problems. Most importantly, the myth of originary separation between black and white, described in the 'Eden' myth above, is dangerously close to the imaginaries of 'natural' segregation promoted by nineteenth-century racial theorists such as Joseph-Arthur de Gobineau, which were popular amongst Southern white supremacists from the 1850s onwards. Elsewhere in the novel, the notion of the cyclical return of the individual through reincarnation proves similarly problematic.

Above all, I would argue, the major political difficulty with the project of *The Temple of My Familiar* is the way it relies on a notion of the individual as an unchanging essence. For Lissie's unnamed friend, multiple reincarnations have simply refined her essential wisdom and gentleness. No problem there. But for other characters, one oppressive life as a slave-handler proceeds equally naturally into another as a drug-pusher and thief. So what we seem to have ultimately is the opposite of redemption: an eternal reaffirmation of the division between benign and malignant, elect and reprobate:

> A few days before we left the coast they made us kneel in the sand outside the fort and proceeded to cut great clumps of our hair out, and then to shave our heads . . . Hidden in this hair were all manner of precious small items, tokens of home: gold beads, silver pins, bits of gris-gris. In my brother's and sister's hair and in my own the silver coins were discovered. These items were pocketed by the brutes who held us, and they grunted in satisfaction upon discovering each one. You sometimes see these same faces on the streets of our larger cities; these are the young men selling the dope, or terrorising the young ones while they take the little money that was pinned in the smaller children's pockets for them to buy lunch. They haven't left us, those faces; they are never hard to find.
>
> (pp. 80–1)

The Temple of My Familiar undoubtedly goes far further in its attempts to move away from canonical Western forms of historicising, even than texts like Morrison's *Beloved* or Achebe's *Things Fall Apart*. It radically revisions the African past in terms of the birth and suppression of originary, matriarchal religions. In so doing, the novel does involve a substantial investment in essentialism, most importantly in the twin notions of spirituality and reincarnation. But as we can see above, what this leads to is an essentially static notion of the 'individual', which is not necessarily transformative or emancipatory. Certainly, the text makes full use of what we might call a postmodernist scepticism towards the established grand narratives of history, of religion and of humanist rationality. But as we can see in its summary treatment of Islam, the mythological narratives it seeks to establish in their place are potentially as exclusionary as they are redemptive.

In this sense it is useful to think of *The Temple of My Familiar* not as a settled ideological manifesto, as many critics seem to have done (with distaste), but instead as an experiment in radical revisionism. It provides neither a modest 'appendix' to white history, nor a simple return to African or South American 'roots'.

The Temple of My Familiar is, on many levels, a vast text which requires far more detailed discussion than is possible here. Certainly, from a feminist point of view, the novel offers much food for thought in terms of the deconstruction of patriarchal discourse. Like *The Color Purple* it begins with a model of female passivity. The love affairs between the musician Arveyda and Carlotta and Zedé are almost reminiscent of Lawrence in their description of his masculine potency and the overawed sexual passivity of the two women. As the novel progresses, however, there is a gradual and inexorable breakdown of that whole economy of desire. Not a reversal of power relations, but rather a paradigmatic reorientation towards a womanist ideal of holistic reciprocity. From the point of view of anti-racism, on the other hand, the text's effects are, as we have seen, rather more problematic. On this level it is with mixed expectations that we turn to the sharp political focus of *Possessing the Secret of Joy*.

Possessing the Secret of Joy

Published in 1992, *Possessing the Secret of Joy* marks the final volume of the trio of novels that began with *The Color Purple*, picking up on the character of Tashi, a young African woman and friend to Olivia, who disappears to undergo the rite of 'initiation'. In many ways, this novel stands out amongst the canon of Walker's fiction as the one that comes closest to activism in its familiar sense.

Though certainly an important political/publishing event, *Possessing the Secret of Joy* did not initiate the global movement of resistance to female genital mutilation. At the latest, efforts to mitigate the tradition can be traced from the seventeenth century onwards, and female genital mutilation has been a part of the human rights agenda of the United Nations since 1958. In 1979 the World Health Organisation's dedicated seminar in Sudan led to a series of African governmental initiatives, a decade before Walker's own intervention. In Western countries including the USA and the UK, legislation outlawing female genital mutilation has also been enacted in recent years, but as in Africa, Asia and the Middle East, with limited and unquantifiable effect.

In addressing the issue of female circumcision through the form of a novel, then, it is immediately clear that Walker's text is at least as much focused on the political problem of consciousness-raising as it is on the humanist ideal of literary 'originality'. As I suggested earlier, it is significant that Walker devoted a hundred and fifty thousand dollars of her royalties from sales of this novel to fund the production of *Warrior Marks* (1993), a film specifically intended for the viewing of African women whose daughters (or who themselves) remain at risk from traditional initiation practices. The film and accompanying book document exchanges with an impressive range of interviewees, ranging from lawyers, gynaecologists and campaigners against circumcision to recently circumcised girls, circumcision refugees and the traditional circumcisers themselves. It undoubtedly makes a contribution to the understanding of the practice and its effects.

Striking quite a different note from the ideological vastness of *The Temple of My Familiar*, the novel foregrounds its political and pedagogic agenda in a much more focused way. Lest we be confused, Walker dedicates the text 'with tenderness and respect to the blameless vulva', and in the narrative we are constantly reminded that the protagonist Tashi's soul has been 'dealt a mortal blow' (p. 63) by circumcision. Similarly, the text is at pains to set down comparisons between the fate of the circumcised and uncircumcised. Amongst the most explicit of these is the opposition between the white French woman Lisette's orgasmic experience of childbirth, and Tashi's profoundly painful and traumatic one. On another level, as we will see, the novel explores Tashi's own vacillation between the roles of victim and activist.

Two of the major foci of the text are Tashi's experiences in relation to circumcision in Olinka, and her attempts to be psychically healed in Europe and the United States. Clearly, one of the problems that arises out of this narrative strategy is that it can easily become a schematic comparison between 'oppressive/traditional' Africa versus some notion of Western 'advance'. Africa is liable to become the site of a pathological sexuality and morality, whilst the West becomes the site of intellectual – medical, psychoanalytic, political – enlightenment. Both the novel and the film make strenuous efforts to avoid this potentially racist scenario.

One of the tools Walker uses to this end in *Warrior Marks* is that of autobiography. The film's subtitle, *Female Genital Mutilation and the Sexual Blinding of Women*, refers to the wound inflicted on the eight-year-old Walker herself by her brother. Briefly, her brothers (not sisters) were bought air guns by their parents, and one of them experimented with his, by aiming a shot at her face. The shot blinded her in one eye and caused a facial disfigurement which devastated her confidence and led to her social withdrawal as a child. Walker's analysis of this incident is primarily a sexual-political one. She focuses not on the wounding itself but on the conspiracy of silence that followed within her family, reflecting an instantaneous and unanimous agreement to deny the son's role in 'Alice's accident'. From here, she seeks to build a set of analogies between different forms of social collusion in relation to violence against women, in Africa and the West alike.

In the example of her own case, it is the sacrifice of the daughter in the face of the brother's violence that constitutes her blinding as a 'patriarchal wound' analogous to circumcision. Widening the scope of her analysis, both the film and the novel also strive to make the connection between 'abusive' genital mutilation and the 'cosmetic' modification of breasts, faces, penises and (increasingly) vaginas in the USA and the West. Through each of these strategies, the texts attempt to offset the potential for their feminist/ womanist critique of female circumcision to be read along neo-colonialist lines.

This clear political self-reflexivity is evident throughout the novel. But it by no means precludes the text from attacking crucial aspects of African culture and politics through the fictive model of Olinka. In the text's treatment of AIDS, for example, we can clearly see an attack on the history of non-engagement with the implications of HIV and AIDS, in countries like South Africa. In Tashi's Olinkan prison, the AIDS floor is uncompromisingly painted against a backdrop of popular ignorance and governmental denial. From a question that starts at the back of Tashi's mind, 'why are there more little girls dying than boys?' (p. 234), we proceed with the momentum of inevitability towards the realisation of circumcision's complicity in spreading the virus:

> Tashi is convinced that the little girls who are dying, and the women too, are infected by the unwashed, unsterilized sharp stones, tin tops, bits of glass, rusty razors and grungy knives used by the *tsunga*. Who might mutilate twenty children without cleaning her instrument. There is also the fact that almost every act of intercourse involves tearing and bleeding, especially in a woman's early years.
>
> (p. 235)

By contrast to the traditional protagonist-centred, developmental dynamics of earlier texts like *Meridian* and *The Color Purple*, the free development of character is, at least in part, clearly subordinated to these core thematic concerns in *Possessing the Secret of Joy*. That said, however, it would be wrong to conclude that the novel is not centrally interested in questions of subjectivity. In fact to a great extent, the text formalises its psychoanalytic interests, especially in relation to repression, through the analysis of Tashi conducted by Carl Jung ('Mzee') and later by Raye. From the beginning of Walker's career as a writer, the thematics of depression and of suicide – especially as a form of self-sacrifice – are a central feature. Her first published collection of poems, *Once*, was written (by her account) precisely as an alternative to taking her own life, after an abortion that followed her first visit to Africa. In that sense *Possessing the Secret of Joy* represents a focusing and politicisation of the notion of trauma, rather than a fundamentally new departure. As much as *The Color Purple*, which begins with child sexual abuse, it is an exploration of the cultural complexity of black women's oppression, through the lens of one of its most unpalatable manifestations.

Again, as in *The Color Purple* and *The Temple of My Familiar*, Walker's emancipatory project in the novel is framed in post-Christian terms. That is, in critical relation to the discourse of patriarchal Christianity. For Tashi the circumcised woman is envisaged as a Christ figure who is not once, but repeatedly and continually crucified, 'not in some age no one even remembers, but right now, daily, in many lands on earth' (p. 259). One of the aims of Tashi's submission to trial and execution is to break the fabric of taboo that surrounds the tradition of genital mutilation. And this clearly is also a key motivation for Walker's own text. Both the novel and film are relentless in their publication of the facts. In the face of institutionalised silence, they anatomise the differences between clitoridectomy, excision and infibulation, together with their medical, social and psychic effects.

One of the consequences of this commitment within the novel is that it necessitates a revision of the anti-intellectual position explored through Fanny, Lissie and other characters in *The Temple of My Familiar*. In *Possessing the Secret of Joy* it is interesting that Walker has the Harvard-educated Frenchman, Pierre, articulate the most developed analysis of circumcision. For him, circumcision of both sexes can be seen as a violent bodily intervention designed to reinforce the social division of gender. In the novel as a whole, we see graphically how excision and infibulation ensure a position of struggling victimhood for women in relation to intercourse (which remains permanently painful and dangerous), at the same time as rendering non-penetrative sexual practices such as cunnilingus virtually redundant in relation to sexual pleasure. By the same token, the violence necessary to achieve first and subsequent penetration (made more difficult by the lack of a foreskin) clearly functions to constitute male heterosexuality as a process of aggressive, even perhaps sadistic domination.

In Pierre's social analysis of gender relations, circumcision works to reinforce patriarchal femininity as normative. It is an extremely graphic instance of the 'writing' of a certain idea of femininity on the body. Over the course of the text, this analysis develops in tension with Tashi's own conception of what has been taken from her. For Tashi, it is as if the genital parts she has lost 'contained' an essential femininity that cannot be recovered. Thus in this way the novel uses the two characters to recapitulate the established opposition between the ideas of 'constructed' and 'essential' femininity that were explored in chapter 3. Tashi's identification of the excised vulva as the 'missing contents' of her female identity seems to fit into the latter (essentialist) position. Arguably, this is an ideological tension that the novel cannot finally resolve. Rather, the text sets it up in the form of a question, in order to explore some of the cultural complexity surrounding the practices of female circumcision.

Clearly, the fact that circumcision is almost universally a procedure carried out on girls by older women rather than by men is one particular aspect that Walker's text needs to address from the point of view of resistance. At the beginning of the novel, M'Lissa, Tashi's circumciser, is constituted as the murderer of her sister Dura and the mutilator of other girls. As the novel progresses, however, the victim/aggressor relation between the two women shifts in interesting ways. Not only does M'Lissa herself emerge as the victim of a violent and botched infibulation, she is also ultimately revealed as a worshipper of women's sexual pleasure, for whom religious faith consists only in the belief that 'the God of woman is autonomy' (p. 207). Unlike M'Lissa, on the other hand, Tashi's own infibulation is voluntary. And in a crucial reversal, at the end of the text she finds herself fulfilling and glorifying the traditional destiny of the *tsunga*, who the tradition dictates must be killed and burned by a woman she has herself circumcised. In M'Lissa's final monologue, the 'I' who speaks is first the circumciser, but then shades subtly into that of Tashi herself. Consistently, then, the narrative as a whole works to entangle their initially separated roles and to uncover their mutual entrapment within a cycle of self-sustaining abuse.

The construction of Olinka as the matrix of their patriarchal oppression, as I have suggested, brings the novel into a (potentially) extremely uncomfortable confrontation with the notions of indigenous tradition and colonialism. At the beginning of the novel, where Walker picks up her theme from *The Color Purple*, Tashi undergoes circumcision quite clearly as an anti-colonial gesture. She refers to it 'not as a wound but as a healing' (p. 60), an autonomous response to the cultural and economic rape of the Olinkan people. It is only later that she begins – through a dream – to understand circumcision's role within a different layer of (patriarchal) oppression. Her dream of the enormous cockerel, puffed up by 'his diet of submission' (p. 76), represents a key turning point in this process of ideological realignment.

By the time of the trial in Olinka, the shift away from her initial colonial analysis is explicit:

> White is not the culprit this time. Bring me out paper of the colors of our flag.
>
> There was a sort of collective gasp in the courtroom . . . I felt even more eyes boring holes in the back of my neck. The judges surreptitiously scratched the natural kinky hair at the edges of their straight brush wigs.

(p. 100)

At the end of the text, we come full circle to a moment in which the condemned Tashi is confronted, on the one hand, by the liberatory recognition that 'resistance is the secret of joy' (p. 264) and on the other hand, by the ultimate oppression of being denied her life. The work of activism is ongoing – and, as if to reinforce this point, Walker provides us with an exhortatory afterword and list of further reading.

From her first published collection, *Once*, onwards, there is a consistent refusal in Walker's writing to equate liberation for the black American with a romanticised vision of Africa. What is particularly significant about *Possessing the Secret of Joy* in this respect, perhaps, is that by taking such a specific political focus and by grounding itself so clearly in existing conditions, it forces the reader to acknowledge that white racism is by no means the black woman's only source of oppression. Of course, this is not out of keeping with the politics of *Meridian*, *The Color Purple* and *The Temple of My Familiar*, in each of which, arguably, liberation seems only to be achievable 'within'. And it does re-establish Walker as a writer whose work has the capacity to disrupt complacent notions of struggle, and to force a confrontation with the most unwelcome of political contradictions.

Alice Walker's writing is, as I have argued, symbiotic with activism. Rather than repeating orthodox agendas, it is marked by a concern to confront the uncomfortable contradictions and stumbling blocks that lie in the path of self-emancipation for black women. In the 1976 novel, *Meridian*, what this might mean is a reappraisal of the political and sexual-political legacy of the 1960s. In *The Color Purple*, it might involve challenging the ethical centrality of feminine self-sacrifice, and a rejection of the African American Christian tradition. In *The Temple of My Familiar*, it might imply the attempt to forge a union between feminist politics and pre-colonial African notions of identity. In *Possessing the Secret of Joy*, it might mean the willingness to confront oppressive traditional practices, in the face of black America's romanticisation of the old continent, even at the risk of complicity with racist assumptions about African 'barbarity' and Western 'advancement'. Like those of Zora Neale Hurston, Alice Walker's texts are most compelling where they operate outside the frame of acceptability. Their task is to cross political and cultural lines, not to toe them.

Students' guide to further reading

The purpose of this section is to help orientate readers who may be less familiar with the field of contemporary fiction criticism. Like the book as a whole, it focuses on anglophone writing. Where possible, authoritative but accessible studies are picked out. Because of the volume and range of good work in this area, this guide is necessarily partial, providing ways into a few aspects of the field, and by no means a survey of all significant work. Many of the books mentioned do, however, provide their own bibliographies, which can be used to navigate further through the jungle of critical reading.

General studies

Amongst **older criticism** on post-war fiction, the downbeat emphasis on the 'death of the novel' is often a feature. In the United States, Leslie Fiedler is a notable figure, with his 1965 study *Waiting for the End: The American Literary Scene from Hemingway to Baldwin* (London: Cape) following on from a very influential earlier (1960) study, *Love and Death in the American Novel* (New York: Criterion). Raymond Federman's (1975) collection, *Surfiction: Fiction Now . . . and Tomorrow* (Chicago: Swallow), includes a number of influential essays of the time by Jerome Klinkowitz, Donald Barthelme and others, addressing the perceived malaise in fiction. In this collection, John Barth's (1967) essay 'The Literature of Exhaustion', originally published in the periodical *The Atlantic*, is a canonical critical statement. As a text of its time, Jacques Ehrmann's polemical (1971) 'The Death of Literature' in *New Literary History* 3: pp. 31–47, voicing irritated dissatisfaction with the 'banality' and lack of meaningful innovation amongst contemporary fiction writers, is also worth a look.

In Britain in the 1970s, Bernard Bergonzi's (1970) *The Situation of the Novel* (London: Macmillan), Malcolm Bradbury's (1973) *Essays on the State of the Novel* (Oxford: Oxford University Press) and David Lodge's (1971) *The Novelist at the Crossroads* (London: Routledge) review the field of British fiction in an authoritative if angst-ridden way. A further well-read and extremely accessible text is Anthony Burgess' (1967) *The Novel Now* (London: Faber), which, whilst idiosyncratic in tone, is nevertheless admirably wide-ranging in its sense of contemporary world literature in English. The *Granta* volume on *The End of the English Novel* (vol. 3, 1980), including several significant critical essays and the draft opening of Rushdie's *Midnight's Children*, marks an interesting pivotal moment in fiction criticism in Britain.

Recent general studies

By 'recent studies', here, I am including texts from the 1980s onwards, because of the change to a more fully theorised approach that we can see in studies of this period. In this group, Linda Hutcheon is a major figure, with a series of texts beginning in 1984 with *Narcissistic Narrative: The Metafictional Paradox* (London: Methuen), and progressing to the very widely read pair of volumes *A Poetics of Postmodernism: History, Theory, Fiction* (London: Routledge, 1988) and *The Politics of Postmodernism* (London: Routledge, 1989), which were important early influences in the analysis of postmodern fiction. At the same time, Patricia Waugh's (1984) *Metafiction* (London: Methuen) provides another important study of the strategies of contemporary fiction, tracing the techniques of self-referentiality and parody which are so characteristic of postmodernist writing. Brian McHale's (1987) *Postmodernist Fiction* (London: Methuen) and *Constructing Postmodernism* (London: Routledge, 1987) complement this project, developing the notion of postmodernism as a constructed sensibility rather than as a definable historical 'period'. Whilst each of these critics includes important discussions of selected texts, Marguerite Alexander's (1990) *Flights from Realism: Themes and Strategies in Postmodernist British and American Fiction* (London: Routledge) concentrates its energies on sustained readings of individual writers, from Jorge Luis Borges to Salman Rushdie. More recently amongst general studies, Rod Mengham's (1999) collection, *An Introduction to Contemporary Fiction: International Writing in English Since 1970* (Cambridge: Polity), picks out a number of common themes and includes essays on several world writers.

General studies: British and Irish emphasis

In a British context, until his death in 2000 Malcolm Bradbury continued to stand as a kind of godfather figure in the field, producing a series of popular and traditionally framed overviews of the state of British fiction, from *The Novel Today: Contemporary Writers on Modern Fiction* (Manchester:

Manchester University Press, 1977) and *The Contemporary English Novel*, edited with David Palmer (London: Edward Arnold, 1979) to the second, revised (2001) edition of *The Modern British Novel 1878–2001* (Harmondsworth: Penguin), published posthumously. In a similar vein, Alan Massie's (1990) *The Novel Today* (London: Longman) is a very accessible introduction to the British contemporary fiction scene. Although Randall Stevenson's (1986) study *The British Novel Since the Thirties* (London: Batsford) covers considerably more than just contemporary fiction, it is also well worth looking at as an authoritative survey of developments.

In the 1990s, a new group of critical studies emerged, focusing and redefining work on recent British fiction in significant ways. These continue to form the major landmarks in this area. Amongst these, Alison Lee's (1990) *Realism and Power: Postmodern British Fiction* (London: Routledge) complements Marguerite Alexander's *Flights from Realism* (cited above) of the same year, focusing on post-realist and postmodernist techniques in the novel. In 1995, however, the project of Patricia Waugh's *Harvest of the Sixties: English Literature and Its Background 1960–1990* (Oxford: Oxford University Press) is considerably more ambitious. Moving away from her earlier emphasis on the ideas and techniques of postmodernism (see *Metafiction* above), Waugh returns to a more historical approach in this book, providing an authoritative literary history for the period. Published in the same year, Andrzej Gasiorek's (1995) *Post-War British Fiction: Realism and After* (London: Edward Arnold), on the other hand, is orientated around specific author studies and close textual analysis, focusing on the continuing schism between realism and experimentalism in key fictions of the period. In Steven Connor's (1996) book *The English Novel in History 1950–1995* (London: Routledge), meanwhile, we see a different approach again. Whilst Connor deals with the relations between contemporary fiction and history, he opens this whole question out as a theoretical and critical problem. Thus for Connor, the novel is seen not simply as a reflection of existing social and political conditions, but beyond that as 'one of the ways in which history is made, and remade' (p. 1). Gender, sexuality, ethnicity and national identity are all important thematic concerns.

Focusing on the literary influence of **black and Asian British writers**, Robert Lee's (1995) collection, *Other Britain, Other British* (London: Pluto), looks at the changing face of British literature in the postcolonial era, with contributions on Salman Rushdie, V. S. Naipaul, Caryl Phillips, Hanif Kureishi and others. Other studies of postcolonial fiction which include Britain and Ireland in a wider focus will be mentioned in the section on postcolonial criticism, below. In the Frankfurt publisher Peter Lang's *Scottish Studies* series, Susanne Hagemann's (1996) collection, *Studies in Scottish Fiction: 1945 to the Present*, gives a flavour of the variety of current fictional writing in **Scotland**, with a recurring focus on questions of nationhood. In an **Irish** context, Gerry Smyth's (1997) *The Novel and the Nation: Studies in the New Irish Fiction* (London: Pluto) is a useful study, including sections on theoretical approaches and readings of a range of novels. Liam Harte and Michael Parker's (2000) collection, *Contemporary Irish Fiction: Themes, Tropes, Theories* (Basingstoke: Macmillan), meanwhile, looks at writing from both north and south of the border, including essays from a diversity of critical perspectives. Christine St. Peter's (2000) study, *Changing Ireland: Strategies in Contemporary Women's Fiction* (Basingstoke: Macmillan), focuses on questions of gender, war, exile and romance in novels by Irish women.

General studies: North American emphasis

In criticism which focuses on **American writing**, Malcolm Bradbury and Sigmund Ro's (1987) collection, *Contemporary American Fiction* (London: Edward Arnold), does a characteristic job of surveying the literary scene up until the mid-1980s, providing coverage more than in-depth engagement. Jerome Klinkowitz's (1980), *Literary Disruptions: The Making of a Post-Contemporary American Fiction* (second edition, Urbana, IL: University of Illinois Press), is, for its time, a comparatively upbeat examination of the radical new fictions of Kurt Vonnegut Jr, Donald Barthelme, Jerzy Kosinski and others in the late 1960s and 1970s. His later (1992) study, *Structuring the Void: The Struggle for Subject in Contemporary American Fiction*, (Durham, NC: Duke University Press), is a continuation of that project, examining the capacities of radical contemporary fiction writers to restructure our sense of the real.

In more recent criticism, an accessible and wide-ranging analysis of American fiction since 1960 is provided by Kathryn Hume's (2000) study, *American Dream, American Nightmare* (Urbana, IL: University of Illinois Press), reading fiction in terms of what Hume continues to see as a 'slough of despond'. Kenneth Millard's (2000) *Contemporary American Fiction* (Oxford: Oxford University Press) is another useful study, examining developments in the American novel since 1970, looking at individual texts as well as focusing the reader on key contexts and issues. For an orientation in the so-called 'multi-ethnic' literature of the United States, meanwhile, a good place to begin is Gilbert Muller's (1999) wide-ranging *New Strangers in Paradise: The Immigrant Experience and Contemporary American Fiction* (Lexington, KY: University Press of Kentucky), which gives a sense of the complexity of the cultural traditions which have produced the current scene in American writing. In the field of **Asian American** writing, Elaine Kim's (1982) *Asian American Literature: An Introduction to the Writings and their*

Social Context (Philadelphia: Temple University Press) is a classic text, whilst Sau-Ling Cynthia Wong's (1993) *Reading Asian American Literature: From Necessity to Extravagance* (Princeton: Princeton University Press) deals accessibly with a range of important contemporary figures, including Maxine Hong Kingston and Amy Tan. More recently, Helena Grice's (2002) *Negotiating Identities: An Introduction to Asian American Women's Writing* (Manchester: Manchester University Press) is wide ranging in its coverage of Kingston and other leading writers, locating them carefully within the traditions of feminist and ethnic American writing in the United States.

Amongst the enormous amount of recent work in **African American** studies, Henry Louis Gates Jr's (1987) *Figures in Black: Words, Signs and the 'Racial' Self*, and (1988) *The Signifying Monkey: A Theory of African-American Literary Criticism* (both Oxford: Oxford University Press) have been particularly influential. Focusing on questions of gender, the 1997 essay collection by the leading African American scholar Barbara Christian, *Black Feminist Criticism: Perspectives on Black Women Writers* (New York: Teachers College), is also an important text, drawing together a number of critical pieces, written in Christian's characteristically authoritative but engaging style. The book follows on from Christian's more wide ranging earlier (1980) study, *Black Women Novelists: The Development of a Tradition, 1892–1976* (Westport, CT: Greenwood Press). Amongst other leading critics, Houston A. Baker Jr's (1991) *Workings of the Spirit: The Poetics of Afro-American Women's Writing* (Chicago: University of Chicago Press) focuses on women's writing, whilst his more recent (2001) *Critical Memory: Public Spheres, African American Writing and Black Fathers and Sons in America* (Athens, GA: University of Georgia Press) focuses on black masculinity. All of these studies draw variously on contemporary African American fiction. Keith Clark's 2001 collection, *Contemporary Black Men's Fiction and Drama* (Urbana, IL: University of Illinois Press), meanwhile, is an accessible and wide-ranging survey of recent writing by African American men.

Focusing on **Canadian fiction** in English, Margaret Atwood's *Survival: A Thematic Guide to Canadian Fiction* (Toronto: McClelland & Stewart), published in 1972 and 1996, is an influential and well-read study of Canadian writing, which includes discussions of many individual novels and novelists. Amongst other influential works, *The Canadian Postmodern* (Oxford: Oxford University Press, 1988), by the leading Canadian critic Linda Hutcheon, provides authoritative discussion of a range of important contemporary literary figures, including Margaret Atwood herself and Michael Ondaatje. Amongst more recent critical works, Glenn Deer's (1994) *Postmodern Canadian Fiction and the Rhetoric of Authority* and Marie Vautier's (1998) *New World Myth: Postmodernism and Postcolonialism in Canadian Fiction* (both Montreal: McGill-Queen's University Press) approach recent Canadian fiction from the direction of contemporary theory.

In the area of **Indian** English-language fiction, Meenakshi Mukerjee's (1971) *The Twice Born Fiction* (New Delhi: Heinemann) is a pioneering text of its day, now perhaps a little outdated. Gobinda Prasad Sarma's (1978) *Nationalism in Indo-Anglian Fiction* (New Delhi: Sterling) is another early and popular study with a strongly historical focus, whilst N. Radhakrishnan's more recent (1984) *Indo-Anglian Fiction: Major Trends and Themes* (Madras: Emerald) focuses on nationalism, partition, asceticism and alienation. Working in a more theoretical idiom, meanwhile, Monika Fludernik's 1998 collection, *Hybridity and Postcolonialism: Twentieth Century Indian Literature* (Tubingen: Stauffenburg Verlag), reads writings in English by Indians at home and abroad in relation to the ideas of the postcolonial thinker Homi Bhabha.

History, memory, time

For a focus on questions of time, memory and historical representation, Peter Middleton and Tim Woods' (2000) *Literatures of Memory: History, Time and Space in Postwar Writing* (Manchester: Manchester University Press) is a useful recent text, with strong and accessible discussions of key theoretical and thematic concerns. In this book, as well as discussions of aspects of contemporary fiction, there are also sustained treatments of radical theatre and autobiographical lyric poetry. Specifically on the problem of time, Elizabeth Deeds Ermarth's (1992) *Sequel to History: Postmodernism and the Crisis of Representational Time* (Princeton: Princeton University Press) is an excellent, theoretically informed study. In terms of authors and texts, Ermarth's main foci are on Alain Robbe-Grillet, Julio Cortazar and Vladimir Nabokov, all important figures in the formation of postmodernist fiction. For a different emphasis, Bonnie J. Barthold's (1981) *Black Time: Fiction of Africa, the Caribbean and the United States* (New Haven, CT: Yale University Press) offers a way into thinking about the representation of time in black writing. Seven writers are studied in detail, including Chinua Achebe, Toni Morrison and Wole Soyinka.

On the question of history and representation, Lois Parkinson Zamora's (1989) *Writing the Apocalypse: Historical Vision in Contemporary US and Latin American Fiction*, and her (1997) *The Usable Past: The Imagination of History in Recent Fiction of the Americas* (both Cambridge: Cambridge University Press) look at fiction of the Americas in an authoritative and distinctive way, usefully comparing postmodernist Latin American writing with major figures from the USA. Nancy J. Peterson's (2001) *Against Amnesia:*

Contemporary Women Writers and the Crisis of Amnesia (Philadelphia: University of Pennsylvania Press) focuses on questions of historical silence and collective amnesia in the writing of Toni Morrison, Louise Erdich and others. On Bakhtin's notion of the chronotope, two notable studies are Lynne Pearce (1994) *Reading Dialogics* (London: Edward Arnold) and Paul Smethurst (2000) *The Postmodern Chronotope: Reading Space and Time in Contemporary Fiction* (Amsterdam: Rodopi).

In criticism which deals with **Holocaust fiction**, a connected set of themes frequently arise. Here Sara Horowitz's (1997) *Voicing the Void: Muteness and Memory in Holocaust Fiction* (Albany, NY: State University of New York Press) is a good place to start. Sue Vice's (2000) *Holocaust Fiction* (London: Routledge) discusses major Holocaust novels, providing a way into key concerns in this difficult field by examining the controversies which have often accompanied them. Amongst other studies, Berel Lang's (1988) collection, *Writing and the Holocaust* (New York: Holmes and Meier), includes essays by several major figures, exploring the problems of representing the Holocaust across a number of genres of writing.

Gender and contemporary women's fiction

Especially in the area of women's writing, a huge amount of work has been produced examining gender, sexuality and the body in contemporary fiction. Amongst these, Patricia Waugh's (1989) *Feminine Fictions: Revisiting the Postmodern* (London: Routledge) is an influential study, seeking a rapprochement between feminism and the emergent themes of postmodernism. Published within a few years of each other, three other critical texts are especially useful for the way they map the radical strategies of contemporary women's writing in this period. These are Ellen Friedman and Miriam Fuch's (1989) collection, *Breaking the Sequence: Women's Experimental Fiction* (Princeton: Princeton University Press), Linda Anderson's (1990) collection, *Plotting Change: Contemporary Women's Fiction* (London: Arnold), and Patricia Duncker's (1992) *Sisters and Strangers: An Introduction to Contemporary Feminist Fiction* (Oxford: Blackwell). All of them challenge the androcentric tendencies of the critical establishment in the 1970s and 1980s. Paulina Palmer's (1989) study, *Contemporary Women's Fiction: Narrative Practice and Feminist Theory* (New York: Harvester Wheatsheaf), explores the theory/practice relationship in feminist writing in a sophisticated but accessible way, whilst Palmer's later (1999) *Lesbian Gothic: Transgressive Fictions* (London: Cassell) is more generically focused, exploring the development of lesbian Gothic in writing from the mid-1970s. Patricia Smith's (1997) *Lesbian Panic: Homoeroticism in Modern British Women's Fiction* (New York: Columbia University Press) examines same-sex desire as a point of crisis in a range of writings, including those of Jeanette Winterson, Emma Tennant and Fay Weldon. Amongst other recent studies, Lucy Armitt's (2000) study, *Contemporary Women's Fiction and the Fantastic* (Basingstoke: Macmillan), looks at leading women writers from 1965 onwards, focusing variously on the grotesque, vampirism, ghosting, and other manifestations in magic realist fiction.

With a focus geared more clearly towards issues of **gender and ethnicity**, Susheila Nasta's (1991) collection, *Motherlands: Black Women's Writing from Africa, the Caribbean and South Asia* (London: Women's Press), seeks to expand the critical horizon of anglophone fiction criticism beyond Britain and the United States, whilst Florence Stratton's (1994) study, *Contemporary African Literature and the Politics of Gender* (London: Routledge), is an example of feminist criticism devoted to anglophone African writing. Amongst the wide range of other high-quality work, Gina Wisker's (2000) *Postcolonial and African American Women's Writing: A Critical Introduction* follows on from her earlier (1993) collection, *Black Women's Writing* (both Basingstoke: Macmillan), critically surveying a wide variety of writing from Africa, the Caribbean, Australia and New Zealand, North America and black communities in Europe.

Race, ethnicity, postcoloniality

For texts which deal with the question of '**race**', it is likely that readers will find themselves moving in the direction of sociology, on the one hand, and postcolonial studies on the other. For a general introduction to approaches and ideas, Tim Youngs' (1997) *Writing and Race* (London: Longman) is a possible place to start. Whilst it does not focus specifically on contemporary fiction, Henry Louis Gates Jr's (1985) collection, *'Race,' Writing and Difference* (Chicago: University of Chicago Press), contains statements by many key figures, and is an important port of call. Gates' other related studies, *Figures in Black* (1987) and *The Signifying Monkey* (1988), were cited above. More recently, C. K. Doreski's (1998) study, *Writing America Black: Race Rhetoric in the Public Sphere* (Cambridge: Cambridge University Press), puts contemporary literature by black authors in the context of journalism and other forms of public writing, examining the ways in which each has worked to rewrite the narrative of American national identity. Patricia McKee's (1999) *Producing American Races: Henry James, William Faulkner, Toni Morrison* (Durham, NC: Duke University Press), meanwhile, examines the production of whiteness and blackness as discourses of American-ness in the work of three major twentieth-century writers.

Over the past three decades, **postcolonial literary studies** have expanded to become one of the fastest-moving and most important areas. Again, only a small selection of texts can be mentioned here. Amongst these, Bill Ashcroft, Gareth Griffiths and Helen Tiffin's (1989) study, *The Empire Writes Back: Theory and Practice in Postcolonial Literatures* (London: Routledge), is an important landmark signalling, more than any other critical text, the movement of postcolonial criticism into the mainstream of the literary curriculum. The book provides a very accessible and engaging introduction to terms, issues and debates, as well as demonstrative studies of a number of literary texts. A useful readers' guide is included.

For those less familiar with the range of global anglophone writing, John Thieme's (1996) anthology, *Postcolonial Literatures in English* (London: Edward Arnold), navigates the field of postcolonial writing with extracts from the work of two hundred writers. In terms of more recent criticism, Elleke Boehmer's (1995) *Colonial and Postcolonial Literature: Migrant Metaphors* (Oxford: Oxford University Press) gives a sense of how debates have moved on in subsequent years. Boehmer's book provides focused analysis of anti-colonial resistance in literature, and spends time looking in detail at postcolonial writings by women, by indigenous peoples and by migrant writers – all increasingly important areas of study within the field. Amongst the large number of other useful studies, Deborah Madsen's (1999) collection, *Postcolonial Literatures* (London: Pluto), is a wide-ranging text which seeks to expand the horizon of postcolonial literary studies beyond the earlier 'Commonwealth Studies' framework. Madsen's book is notable for its inclusion of criticism on the 'ethnic literatures' of the United States, Canada and Australia. Another accessible and wide-ranging study is provided by John Skinner's (1998) *The Stepmother Tongue: An Introduction to New Anglophone Fiction* (New York: St Martins Press), which, besides some insightful discussions of literary texts, also helps less expert readers by spending time in defining potentially confusing terms such as 'Commonwealth Literature', 'New Literatures' and 'Postcolonial Literature'.

Individual authors

In recent years **Ian McEwan** has become an increasingly important figure in contemporary British fiction. In terms of book-length criticism, Kiernan Ryan's (1994) *Ian McEwan* (Plymouth: Northcote House) and Jack Slay Jr's (1996) *Ian McEwan* (New York: Twayne) are both accessible introductions to his work. David Malcolm's (2002) *Understanding Ian McEwan* (Columbia, SC: University of South Carolina Press) represents a useful addition to the press's *Understanding Contemporary British Literature Series*, which has released titles on a number of significant writers. Criticism of individual novels can also be found in the journals *Critique: Studies in Contemporary*

Fiction, Modern Fiction Studies and ARIEL, each of which is an important resource for contemporary fiction scholarship.

In recent years **Maxine Hong Kingston**'s work has generated an increasing amount of critical discussion, most notably in the specialist journal MELUS. Amongst book studies, Diane Simmons's (1999) Maxine Hong Kingston (New York: Twayne) is an accessible and reliable volume from Twayne's wide-ranging United States Authors Series, complementing Laura Skandera-Trombley's (1998) collection, Critical Essays on Maxine Hong Kingston, by the same publisher. E. D. Huntley's (1999) Maxine Hong Kingston: A Critical Companion (Westport, CT: Greenwood Press) is geared more towards the general reader, whilst the Paul Skenazy and Tera Martin (1998) edited Conversations with Maxine Hong Kingston (Jackson, MS: University Press of Mississippi) is a useful and often provocative collection of interviews.

Whilst discussions of **Jeanette Winterson** have appeared in the journals Critique, Mosaic, Feminist Review and the Journal of Gender Studies, only recently have book-length studies begun to emerge. In the Writers and Their Work series, M. Reynolds' (1998) Jeanette Winterson (Plymouth: Northcote House) is an introductory study, whilst Helena Grice and Tim Woods' (1998) collection, I'm Telling You Stories: Jeanette Winterson and the Politics of Reading (Amsterdam: Rodopi), in the Postmodern Studies series, is much more theoretically orientated, with contributions from major feminist critics. Christopher Pressler's (2000) So Far So Linear: Responses to the Work of Jeanette Winterson (Nottingham: Paupers Press) is an expanded second edition, including essays on six of Winterson's major works. Helene Bengtson, Marianne Borch and Cindie Maagaard's (2002) collection, Sponsored by Demons: The Art of Jeanette Winterson (Agedrup: Scholars Press), is written in an inviting, teacher-friendly style and covers the major works. Jeanette Winterson herself maintains a substantial web presence at http://www.jeanettewinterson.com, which may be worth exploring.

Amongst all contemporary writers, few can have sustained so much critical interest as **Toni Morrison**. Articles on her work have appeared in African American Review, College Literature, Critique, Journal of Gender Studies, MELUS, Twentieth Century Literature and elsewhere. The following represents just a selection of the range of high-quality book-length studies: Harold Bloom, ed. (1990) Toni Morrison (New York: Chelsea House); Barbara Hill Rigney (1991) The Voices of Toni Morrison (Columbus, OH: Ohio State University Press); Jan Furman (1996) Toni Morrison's Fiction (Columbia, SC: University of South Carolina Press); Nancy Peterson (1998) Toni Morrison (Baltimore, MD: The Johns Hopkins University Press); Jill Matus (1998) Toni Morrison (Manchester: Manchester University Press); Linden Peach (2000) Toni Morrison: Historical Perspectives and Literary

Contexts (revised edition, Basingstoke: Palgrave). Danille Tayor Guthrie's (1994) collection, *Conversations with Toni Morrison* (Jackson: University Press of Mississippi), is a useful volume of interviews in the *Literary Conversations* series.

Salman Rushdie has also been a major focus of critics' and publishers' attention, especially in the wake of the Rushdie affair. Explorations of the 'Rushdie phenomenon' can be found in a vast variety of publications, whilst *Contemporary Literature, Critique, Journal of Commonwealth Literature, Modern Fiction Studies, Studies in the Novel,* and *Twentieth Century Literature* have all published serious critical discussions of the novels. Amongst the range of book studies, the following are amongst the most useful: Timothy Brennan (1989) *Salman Rushdie and the Third World: Myths of the Nation* (Basingstoke: Macmillan); M. D. Fletcher (1994) *Reading Rushdie: Perspectives on the Fiction of Salman Rushdie* (Amsterdam: Rodopi); James Harrison (1992) *Salman Rushdie* (New York: Twayne); Catherine Cundy (1996) *Salman Rushdie* (Manchester: Manchester University Press); D. C. R. A. Goonetilleke (1998) *Salman Rushdie* (Basingstoke: Macmillan); and Damian Grant (1999) *Salman Rushdie* (Plymouth: Northcote House). On the Rushdie affair, a good place to start is the wide-ranging 1989 volume edited by Lisa Appignanesi and Sara Maitland, *The Rushdie File* (London: ICA/Fourth Estate).

Discussion of **Angela Carter**'s writing can again be found in a range of scholarly journals, including *Critical Survey, Critique, Journal of Gender Studies, Review of Contemporary Fiction, Studies in Short Fiction* and *Women's Studies.* Several well-written book studies are also available, of which the following are particularly significant: Lorna Sage (1994) *Angela Carter* (Plymouth: Northcote House), and in the same year, Sage's collection, *Flesh and the Mirror: Essays on the Art of Angela Carter* (London: Virago); Sara Gamble (1997) *Angela Carter: Writing From the Front Line* (Edinburgh: Edinburgh University Press), followed up by Gamble's 2001 collection, *The Fiction of Angela Carter* (Basingstoke: Palgrave); Joseph Bristow and Trev Lynn Broughton, eds (1997) *The Infernal Desires of Angela Carter: Fiction, Femininity, Feminism* (London: Longman); Linden Peach (1998) *Angela Carter* (Basingstoke: Palgrave); and Aiden Day (1998) *Angela Carter: The Rational Glass* (Manchester: Manchester University Press).

On **Hanif Kureishi**, much less critical work is available, despite Kureishi's prominence on the British stage and screen. Articles have appeared in *ARIEL: A Review of International English Literature, Critical Survey* and *Screen.* There are also three book-length studies. Kenneth Kaleta's (1998) *Hanif Kureishi: Postcolonial Storyteller* (Austin, TX: University of Texas Press) provides a critical biography of Kureishi, focusing on his work from a media-orientated perspective. Ruvani Ranasinha's (2001) *Hanif Kureishi* (Plymouth: Northcote House) provides an introductory guide in the *Writers and Their*

Works series. Bart Moore-Gilbert's (2001) *Hanif Kureishi* (Manchester: Manchester University Press), on the other hand, is a more substantial critical assessment, putting the writer's entire *œuvre* in the context of contemporary British culture and postcoloniality.

Buchi Emecheta has been the subject of critical analysis in a number of academic journals, including *ARIEL, Critique, Research in African Literatures* and *Women's Studies*. Marie Umeh's (1996) collection, *Emerging Perspectives on Buchi Emecheta* (Trenton, NJ: Africa World Press), is a wide-ranging volume, putting Emecheta's work in the context of her Nigerian and British backgrounds, and focusing on her exploration of sexuality and gender relations. In Tuzyline Jita Allan's (1995) *Womanist and Feminist Aesthetics: A Comparative Review* (Athens, OH: Ohio University Press), *The Joys of Motherhood* is read through the lens of Alice Walker's black feminist notion of womanism, where it is usefully set alongside Walker's own novel *The Color Purple*. However, at present the only single-authored study of Emecheta is offered by Katherine Fishburn's (1995) *Reading Buchi Emecheta: Cross-Cultural Conversations* (Westport, CT: Greenwood Press). The strategy of Fishburn's study runs interestingly counter to much previous feminist criticism of Emecheta's work, reading her texts' sexual politics through the prism of their hybridity and cross-cultural concerns.

As one of the most popular of current US writers, **Alice Walker** is the subject of much critical comment and analysis. In critical journals, articles can be found in *African American Review, Comparative Literature, MELUS, Studies in Short Fiction, Women's Studies* and elsewhere. There are also a number of strong book studies of Walker's work, of which Donna Haisty Winchell's (1992) *Alice Walker* (New York: Twayne), Ikenna Dieke's (1999) collection, *Critical Essays on Alice Walker* (Westport, CT: Greenwood Press), and Maria Lauret's (1999) *Alice Walker* (Basingstoke: Palgrave) are all excellent examples. Harold Bloom's collection (revised 1999), *Alice Walker* (New York: Chelsea House), Caroline Evensen Lazo's (2000) *Alice Walker* (Minneapolis, MN: Lerner), and Henry Louis Gates Jr's collection (1993), *Alice Walker: Critical Perspectives Past and Present* (New York: Amistad), are the most useful examples from the range of studies on Walker aimed specifically at the student market.

Bibliography

Achebe, Chinua (1972) *Girls at War*, Ibadan: Heinemann.
—— (1975, 1988) 'Racism in *Heart of Darkness*' in *Hopes and Impediments: Selected Essays 1965–1987*, London: Heinemann.
Adorno, Theodor W. (1966, 1973) *Negative Dialectics*, trans. E. B. Ashton, London: Routledge.
Alexander, Marguerite (1990) *Flights from Realism: Themes and Strategies in Post-modernist British and American Fiction*, London: Routledge.
Allan, Tuzyline Jita (1995) *Womanist and Feminist Aesthetics: A Comparative Review*, Athens, OH: Ohio University Press.
Anderson, Benedict (1983) *Imagined Communities: Reflections on the Origin and Spread of Nationalism*, London: Verso.
Anderson, Linda, ed. (1990) *Plotting Change: Contemporary Women's Fiction*, London: Arnold.
Angelo, Bonnie (1994) 'The Pain of Being Black: An Interview with Toni Morrison' in Guthrie (1994), pp. 256–71.
Appiah, Anthony (1985) 'The Uncompleted Argument: Du Bois and the Illusion of Race' in Gates, ed. (1986), pp. 21–37.
Appignanesi, Lisa and Maitland, Sara, eds (1989) *The Rushdie File*, London: ICA/ Fourth Estate.
Armitt, Lucy (2000) *Contemporary Women's Fiction and the Fantastic*, Basingstoke: Macmillan.
Ashcroft, Bill, Griffiths, Gareth and Tiffin, Helen (1989) *The Empire Writes Back: Theory and Practice in Postcolonial Literatures*, London: Routledge.
Asian Women United of California, eds (1989) *Making Waves: An Anthology of Writing by and about Asian American Women*, Boston: Beacon Press.
Atwood, Margaret (1972, 1996) *Survival: A Thematic Guide to Canadian Fiction*, Toronto: McClelland & Stewart.
Azam, Umar Elahi (1990) *Rushdie's Satanic Verses: An Islamic Response*, Manchester: Private Publication.
Baker, Houston A. Jr (1991) *Workings of the Spirit: The Poetics of Afro-American Women's Writing*, Chicago: University of Chicago Press,.
—— (2001) *Critical Memory: Public Spheres, African American Writing and Black Fathers and Sons in America*, Athens, GA: University of Georgia Press.

Baker, Houston A. Jr and Redmond, Patricia (1989) *African American Scholarship: Afro-American Literary Study in the 1990s*, Chicago: University of Chicago Press.

Bakhtin, Mikhail (1965, 1984) *Rabelais and His World*, trans. Helene Iswolsky, Bloomington, IN: Indiana University Press.

—— (1934–41, 1981) *The Dialogic Imagination: Four Essays*, ed. and trans. Caryl Emerson and Michael Holquist, Austin, TX: University of Texas Press.

Banerjee, Ashutosh (1990) 'A Critical Study of Shame', *The Commonwealth Review* 1, 2: 71–2.

Barth, John (1967) 'The Literature of Exhaustion' in Federman, ed. (1975), pp. 19–33.

Barthes, Roland (1957, 1972) *Mythologies*, trans. Annette Lavers, London: Jonathan Cape.

Barthold, Bonnie J. (1981) *Black Time: Fiction of Africa, the Caribbean and the United States*, New Haven, CT: Yale University Press.

Beauvoir, Simone de (1949, 1953) *The Second Sex*, ed. and trans. H. M. Parshley, London: Jonathan Cape.

Bengtson, Helene, Borch, Marianne and Maagaard, Cindie, eds (2002) *Sponsored by Demons: The Art of Jeanette Winterson*, Agedrup: Scholars Press.

Bergonzi, Bernard (1970) *The Situation of the Novel*, London: Macmillan.

Bergson, Henri (1889, 1910) *Time and Free Will: Essay on the Immediate Data of Consciousness*, trans. F. L. Pogson, London: George Allen & Unwin.

Bhabha, Homi ed. (1990) *Nation and Narration*, London: Routledge.

—— (1994) *The Location of Culture*, London: Routledge.

Bigsby, Chris (1980) 'The Uneasy Middleground of British Fiction', *Granta* 3: 137–49.

Birke, Lynda (1999) *Feminism and the Biological Body*, Edinburgh: Edinburgh University Press.

Bloom, Harold, ed. (1989) *Alice Walker*, New York: Chelsea House.

—— (1990) *Toni Morrison*, New York: Chelsea House.

Boehmer, Elleke (1995) *Colonial and Postcolonial Literature: Migrant Metaphors*, Oxford: Oxford University Press.

Bonetti, Kay/Maxine Hong Kingston (1998) 'Conversation with Kay Bonetti' in Skenazy and Martin (1998).

Borges, Jorge Luis (1970) *Labyrinths*, trans. Donald A. Yates, James Irby, John M. Fein, Harriet de Olis, Julian Palley, Dudley Fitts and Anthony Kerrigan, Harmondsworth: Penguin.

Bowers, Frederick (1980) 'An Irrelevant Parochialism', *Granta* 3: 150–4.

Boyarin, Jonathan, ed. (1994) *Remapping Memory: The Politics of Timespace*, Minneapolis, MN: University of Minnesota Press.

Bradbury, Malcolm (1973) *Essays on the State of the Novel*, Oxford: Oxford University Press.

—— (1977) *The Novel Today: Contemporary Writers on Modern Fiction*, Manchester: Manchester University Press.

—— (2001) *The Modern British Novel 1878–2001*, 2nd edition, Harmondsworth: Penguin.

Bradbury, Malcolm and Palmer, David, eds (1979) *The Contemporary English Novel*, London: Edward Arnold.

Bradbury, Malcolm and Ro, Sigmund, eds (1987) *Contemporary American Fiction*, London: Edward Arnold.

Brennan, Timothy (1989) *Salman Rushdie and the Third World: Myths of the Nation*, Basingstoke: Macmillan.

Bristow, Joseph and Broughton, Trev Lynn, eds (1997) *The Infernal Desires of Angela Carter: Fiction, Femininity, Feminism*, London: Longman.

Burgess, Anthony (1967) *The Novel Now*, London: Faber.

Butler, Judith (1990) *Gender Trouble: Feminism and the Subversion of Identity*, London: Routledge.

Carlyle, Thomas (1853) 'Occasional Discourse on the Nigger Question', reprinted in Chauncey Burr, ed. (1866) *The Old Guard*, vol. IV, 4–6, pp. 239–45, 308–11, 372–77.

Carter, Angela (1979) *The Sadeian Women*, London: Virago.

—— (1998) *Shaking a Leg: Collected Journalism and Writing*, London: Vintage.

Chaudhuri, Una (1990) 'Imaginative Maps: Excerpts from a Conversation with Salman Rushdie', *Turnstile* 2, 1: 36–47.

Chin, Frank, Chan, Jeffery, Inada, Lawson, and Wong, Shaun, eds (1974) *Aiiieeeee! An Anthology of Asian-American Writers*, Washington, DC: Howard University Press.

—— (1991) *The Big Aiiieeeee! An Anthology of Chinese American and Japanese American Literature*, New York: Meridian.

Christian, Barbara (1980) *Black Women Novelists: The Development of a Tradition, 1892–1976*, Westport, CT: Greenwood Press.

—— (1997a) 'Beloved, She's Ours', *Narrative* 5, 1 (January): 36–49.

—— (1997b) *Black Feminist Criticism: Perspectives on Black Women Writers*, New York: Teachers College.

Clark, Keith, ed. (2001) *Contemporary Black Men's Fiction and Drama*, Urbana, IL: University of Illinois Press.

Cleaver, Eldridge (1968) *Soul on Ice*, New York: McGraw-Hill.

Coffin, Levi (1876) *Reminiscences*, Cincinnati, OH: Western Tract Society.

Comfort, Alex (1963) *Sex in Society*, London: Duckworth.

Conboy, Katie, Medina, Nadia and Stanbury, Sarah, eds (1997) *Writing on the Body: Female Embodiment and Feminist Theory*, New York: Columbia University Press.

Condon, Sir Paul, letter to the Lawrence Inquiry dated 2 October 1998, published in Macpherson et al. (1999), para 6.25.

Connor, Steven (1996) *The English Novel in History 1950–1995*, London: Routledge.

Cottrell, W. F. (1939) 'Of Time and the Railworker', *American Sociological Review* 4: 190–8.

Cronenberg, David (1995) 'David Cronenberg meets Salman Rushdie', *Shift* 3, 4 (June–July).

Cundy, Catherine (1996) *Salman Rushdie*, Manchester: Manchester University Press.

Darwin, Charles (1871, 1882) *The Descent of Man*, London: John Murray.

Day, Aiden (1998) *Angela Carter: The Rational Glass*, Manchester: Manchester University Press.

Deer, Glenn (1994) *Postmodern Canadian Fiction and the Rhetoric of Authority*, Montreal: McGill-Queen's University Press.

Denard, Caroline (1993) 'Toni Morrison' in Darlene Clark Hine, ed., *Black Women in America*, New York: Carlson.

Derrida, Jacques (1993, 1994) *Specters of Marx: The State of the Debt, the Work of Mourning, and the New International*, trans. Peggy Kamuf, London: Routledge.

Diamond, Arlyn and Edwards, Lee R., eds (1977) *The Authority of Experience: Essays in Feminist Criticism*, Amherst, MA: University of Massachusetts Press.

Dickerson, Vanessa and Bennett, Michael, eds (2000) *Recovering the Black Female Body: Self-Representations by African American Women*, New Brunswick, NJ: Rutgers University Press.

Dieke, Ikenna, ed. (1999) *Critical Essays on Alice Walker*, Westport, CT: Greenwood Press.

Doan, Laura (1994) *The Lesbian Postmodern*, New York: Columbia University Press.

Donahue, Patricia, Powell, David, and Lee, Mary (1991) 'Clinical Management of Intersex Abnormalities', *Current Problems in Surgery* 28, 8 (August): 513–79.

Doreski, C. K. (1998) *Writing America Black: Race Rhetoric in the Public Sphere*, Cambridge: Cambridge University Press.

Du Bois, W. E. B. (1897, 1970) 'The Conversation of Black Races' in *W. E. B. Du Bois Speaks: Speeches and Addresses, 1890–1919*, ed. Philip Foner, New York: Pathfinder.

—— (1903, 1999) *The Souls of Black Folk*, New York: Norton.

Duncker, Patricia (1992) *Sisters and Strangers: An Introduction to Contemporary Feminist Fiction*, Oxford: Blackwell.

Ehrmann, Jacques (1971) 'The Death of Literature', trans. A. James Arnold, *New Literary History* 3: 31–47.

Emecheta, Buchi (1986) *Head Above Water*, London: Ogwugwu Afo.

—— (1988) 'Buchi Emecheta with Susheila Nasta', dir. Fenella Greenfield, ICA Guardian Conversations, London: ICA Video/Trilion.

Ermarth, Elizabeth Deeds (1992) *Sequel to History: Postmodernism and the Crisis of Representational Time*, Princeton, NJ: Princeton University Press.

Fausto-Sterling, Anne (1995) 'How to Build a Man', reprinted in Anna Tripp (2000) *Gender*, Basingstoke: Palgrave, pp. 109–14.

Federman, Raymond, ed. (1975) *Surfiction: Fiction Now . . . and Tomorrow*, Chicago: Swallow.

Fiedler, Leslie (1960) *Love and Death in the American Novel*, New York: Criterion.

—— (1965) *Waiting for the End: The American Literary Scene from Hemingway to Baldwin*, London: Cape.

Fishburn, Katherine (1995) *Reading Buchi Emecheta: Cross-Cultural Conversations*, Westport, CT: Greenwood Press.

Fletcher, M. D. (1994) *Reading Rushdie: Perspectives on the Fiction of Salman Rushdie*, Amsterdam: Rodopi.

Fludernik, Monika, ed. (1998) *Hybridity and Postcolonialism: Twentieth Century Indian Literature*, Tubingen: Stauffenburg Verlag.

Foucault, Michel (1966, 1970) *The Order of Things*, London: Tavistock.

—— (1971) 'Nietzsche, Genealogy, History' in Paul Rabinow, ed. (1984) *The Foucault Reader*, London: Penguin, pp. 76–100.

—— (1975, 1991) *Discipline and Punish*, trans. Alan Sheridan, London: Penguin.

—— (1976, 1990) *The History of Sexuality, vol. I*, trans. Robert Hurley, London: Penguin.

—— (1984, 1990) *The History of Sexuality, vols II and III*, trans Robert Hurley, London: Penguin.

—— (1980) *Power/Knowledge: Selected Interviews and Other Writings 1972–77*, ed. Colin Gordon, London: Harvester.

Friedan, Betty (1963) *The Feminine Mystique*, London: Penguin.

Friedman, Ellen and Fuch, Miriam, eds (1989) *Breaking the Sequence: Women's Experimental Fiction*, Princeton, NJ: Princeton University Press.

Fukuyama, Francis (1989) 'The End of History', *The National Interest*, Summer: 3–19.

Furman, Jan (1996) *Toni Morrison's Fiction*, Columbia, SC: University of South Carolina Press.

Gamble, Sara (1997) *Angela Carter: Writing From the Front Line*, Edinburgh: Edinburgh University Press.

—— ed. (2001) *The Fiction of Angela Carter*, Basingstoke: Palgrave.

Garvey, Marcus (1920) *Declaration of Rights of the Negro Peoples of the World*, New York: Universal Negro Improvement Association.

Gasiorek, Andrzej (1995) *Post-War British Fiction: Realism and After*, London: Edward Arnold.

Gates, Henry Louis Jr, ed. (1986) *'Race,' Writing and Difference*, Chicago: University of Chicago Press.

—— (1987, 1989) *Figures in Black: Words, Signs and the 'Racial' Self*, Oxford: Oxford University Press.

—— (1988) *The Signifying Monkey: A Theory of African-American Literary Criticism*, Oxford: Oxford University Press.

—— ed. (1993) *Alice Walker: Critical Perspectives Past and Present*, New York: Amistad.

Gilroy, Paul (2000) *Between Camps: Nations, Cultures and the Allure of Race*, London: Penguin.

Glover, David and Kaplan, Cora (2000) *Genders*, London: Routledge.

Gobineau, Joseph-Arthur de (1853–5, 1915) 'Essay on the Inequality of the Human Races', trans. Adrian Collins, London: Heinemann.

Goonetilleke, D. C. R. A. (1998) *Salman Rushdie*, Basingstoke: Macmillan.

Grant, Damian (1999) *Salman Rushdie*, Plymouth: Northcote House.

Granta (1980) *The End of the English Novel* 3.

Grice, Helena (2002) *Negotiating Identities: An Introduction to Asian American Women's Writing*, Manchester: Manchester University Press.

Grice, Helena and Woods, Tim, eds (1998) *I'm Telling You Stories: Jeanette Winterson and the Politics of Reading*, Amsterdam: Rodopi.

Guthrie, Danille Tayor, ed. (1994) *Conversations with Toni Morrison*, Jackson, MS: University Press of Mississippi.

Haffenden, John (1985) *Novelists in Interview*, London: Methuen.

Hagemann, Susanne, ed. (1996) *Studies in Scottish Fiction: 1945 to the Present*, Frankfurt: Peter Lang.

Haraway, Donna (1991) *Simians, Cyborgs and Women: The Reinvention of Nature*, New York: Routledge.

Harrison, James (1992) *Salman Rushdie*, New York: Twayne.

Harte, Liam and Parker, Michael, eds (2000) *Contemporary Irish Fiction: Themes, Tropes, Theories*, Basingstoke: Macmillan.

Heidegger, Martin (1927, 1962) *Being and Time*, trans. John Macquarrie and Edward Robinson, Oxford: Blackwell.

Hitchens, Christopher (1997) 'The Progressive Interview: Salman Rushdie', *The Progressive*, October.

hooks, bel (1989) 'Writing the Subject: Reading *The Color Purple*' in Bloom (1989), pp. 215–28.

—— (1992) 'Selling Hot Pussy: Representations of Black Female Sexuality in the Cultural Marketplace' reprinted in Conboy et al. (1997), pp. 113–28.

Horowitz, Sara (1997) *Voicing the Void: Muteness and Memory in Holocaust Fiction*, Albany, NY: State University of New York Press.

Hotze, Henry (1856) *Analytical Introduction to Count Gobineau's Moral and Intellectual Diversity of Races*, Mobile: n.p., cited by Young (1995).

Howard, Lillie P. (1993) *Alice Walker and Zora Neale Hurston: The Common Bond*, Westport, CT: Greenwood Press.

Hughes, Langston (1926) 'The Negro Artist and the Racial Mountain' in Van Deburg (1997) p. 52.

Hume, Kathryn (2000) *American Dream, American Nightmare*, Urbana, IL: University of Illinois Press.

Huntley, E. D. (1999) *Maxine Hong Kingston: A Critical Companion*, Westport, CT: Greenwood Press.

Hurston, Zora Neale (1942, 1982) *Dust Tracks on a Road: An Autobiography*, London: Virago.

Husserl, Edmund (1905) *The Phenomenology of Internal Time Consciousness*, ed. Martin Heidegger, trans. James Churchill, The Hague: Martinus Nijhoff.

Hutcheon, Linda (1984) *Narcissistic Narrative: The Metafictional Paradox*, London: Methuen.

—— (1988a) *The Canadian Postmodern*, Oxford: Oxford University Press.

—— (1988b) *A Poetics of Postmodernism: History, Theory, Fiction*, London: Routledge.

—— (1989) *The Politics of Postmodernism*, London: Routledge.

Huyssen, Andreas (1995) *Twilight Memories: Marking Time in a Culture of Amnesia*, London: Routledge.

Ingold, Tim (1995) 'Work, Time and Industry', *Time and Society* 4, 1: 5–28.

Irigaray, Luce (1977, 1985) *This Sex Which Is Not One*, New York: Cornell University Press.

Iyayi, Festus (1986) *Heroes*, Harlow: Longman.

James, William (1902, 1936) *The Varieties of Religious Experience*, New York: The Modern Library.

Jameson, Fredric (1991) *Postmodernism, Or, The Cultural Logic of Late Capitalism*, London: Verso.

Jones, Gayl (1991) *Liberating Voices: Oral Tradition in African American Literature*, Cambridge, MA: Harvard University Press.

Kaleta, Kenneth (1998) *Hanif Kureishi: Postcolonial Storyteller*, Austin, TX: University of Texas Press.

Kant, Immanuel (1781, 1890) *Critique of Pure Reason*, trans. J. M. D. Meiklejohn, London: George Bell.

Kim, Elaine (1982) *Asian American Literature: An Introduction to the Writings and their Social Context*, Philadelphia, PA: Temple University Press.

Klinkowitz, Jerome (1980) *Literary Disruptions: The Making of a Post-Contemporary American Fiction*, 2nd edition, Urbana, IL: University of Illinois Press.

—— (1992) *Structuring the Void: The Struggle for Subject in Contemporary American Fiction*, Durham, NC: Duke University Press.

Kristeva, Julia (1991) 'Women's Time' in Robyn Warhal and Diane Hernde, eds (1991) *Feminisms*, Brunswick, NJ: Rutgers University Press, pp. 443–62.

Kubota, Gary/Maxine Hong Kingston (1998) 'Interview with Gary Kubota' in Skenazy and Martin, eds (1998), pp. 1–4.

Kureishi, Hanif (1986) 'The Rainbow Sign' in Kureishi (1996), pp. 71–102.

—— (1992) *Outskirts and Other Plays*, London: Faber.

—— (1996) *My Beautiful Laundrette and Other Writings*, London: Faber.

—— (1997) 'The Flesh Made Word', BBC Radio 3, 18 August.

Kuznetsov, Anatoly (1970) *Babi Yar*, trans. David Floyd, London: Sphere.

Lang, Berel, ed. (1988) *Writing and the Holocaust*, New York: Holmes & Meier.

Langland, Elizabeth (1997) 'Sexing the Text: Narrative Drag as Feminist Poetics and Politics in Jeanette Winterson's *Sexing the Cherry*', *Narrative* 5, 1 (January): 99–107.

Lauret, Maria (1999) *Alice Walker*, Basingstoke: Palgrave.

Lazo, Caroline Evensen (2000) *Alice Walker*, Minneapolis, MN: Lerner.

Lee, Alison (1990) *Realism and Power: Postmodern British Fiction*, London: Routledge.

Lee, Robert (1995) *Other Britain, Other British*, London: Pluto.

Locke, Alain, ed. (1925) *The New Negro*, New York: A. & C. Boni.

Lodge, David (1971) *The Novelist at the Crossroads*, London: Routledge.

Long, Edward (1774) *History of Jamaica*, London: Lowndes.

Lubiano, Wahneema, ed. (1997, 1998) *The House That Race Built*, New York: Vintage.

Lukács, Georg (1938) 'Realism in the Balance' in Theodor Adorno, Walter Benjamin, Ernst Bloch, Bertolt Brecht and Georg Lukacs (1977, 1980) *Aesthetics and Politics*, London: Verso, pp. 28–59.

Lyotard, Jean-François (1979, 1984) *The Postmodern Condition: A Report on Knowledge*, trans. Geoff Bennington and Brian Massumi, Manchester: Manchester University Press.

—— (1988, 1991) *The Inhuman: Reflections on Time*, trans. Geoffrey Bennington and Rachel Bowlby, Cambridge: Polity.

McEwan, Ian (1988) 'Ian McEwan with Martin Amis', *Guardian Conversations*, London: ICA Video/Trilion.

McGowan, John (1991) *Postmodernism and Its Critics*, London: Cornell University Press.

McHale, Brian (1987a) *Constructing Postmodernism*, London: Routledge.

—— (1987b) *Postmodernist Fiction*, London: Methuen.

McKee, Patricia (1999) *Producing American Races: Henry James, William Faulkner, Toni Morrison*, Durham, NC: Duke University Press.

McLuhan, Marshall (1962) *The Gutenberg Galaxy*, London: Routledge.

Macpherson, William et. al. (1999) *The Stephen Lawrence Inquiry* [Cm 4262-I], London: HMSO.

Madsen, Deborah, ed. (1999) *Postcolonial Literatures*, London: Pluto.

Maechler, Stefan (2000, 2001) *The Wilkomirski Affair: A Study in Biographical Truth*, trans. John E. Woods, London: Picador.

Malcolm, David (2002) *Understanding Ian McEwan*, Columbia, SC: University of South Carolina Press.

Marvel, Mark (1990) 'Winterson: Trust Me, I'm Telling You Stories', *Interview* 20: 165–8.

Marvell, Andrew (1681) 'The Mower Against Gardens' in Mary Marvell, ed., *Miscellaneous Poems*, London: Robert Boulter.

Marx, Karl (1852, 1954) *The Eighteenth Brumaire of Louis Bonaparte*, Moscow: Progress.

Massie, Alan (1990) *The Novel Today*, London: Longman.

Matus, Jill (1998) *Toni Morrison*, Manchester: Manchester University Press.

Mengham, Rod (1999) *An Introduction to Contemporary Fiction: International Writing in English Since 1970*, Cambridge: Polity.

Middleton, Peter and Woods, Tim (2000) *Literatures of Memory: History, Time and Space in Postwar Writing*, Manchester: Manchester University Press.

Millard, Kenneth (2000) *Contemporary American Fiction*, Oxford: Oxford University Press.

Mills, Sara, ed. (1989) *Feminist Readings, Feminists Reading*, London: Harvester Wheatsheaf.

Montagu, Ashley (1972) *Statement on Race: An Annotated Elaboration and Exposition of the Four Statements on Race issued by the United Nations Educational, Scientific, and Cultural Organisation*, New York: Oxford University Press.

Moore-Gilbert, Bart (2001) *Hanif Kureishi*, Manchester: Manchester University Press.

Morrison, Toni (1990) 'The Site of Memory' in Russell Fergusen, Martha Gever, Trinh Minha and Cornel West, eds (1990) *Out There*, Cambridge, MA: MIT Press, pp. 299–305.

—— (1992) *Playing in the Dark: Whiteness and the Literary Imagination*, Cambridge, MA: Harvard University Press.

—— (1997) 'Home' in Lubiano, ed. (1997, 1998), pp. 3–12.

Mukerjee, Meenakshi (1971) *The Twice Born Fiction*, New Delhi: Heinemann.

Muller, Gilbert (1999) *New Strangers in Paradise: The Immigrant Experience and Contemporary American Fiction*, Lexington, KY: University Press of Kentucky.

Nasta, Susheila, ed. (1991) *Motherlands: Black Women's Writing from Africa, the Caribbean and South Asia*, London: Women's Press.

Nasta, Susheila and Emecheta, Buchi (1988) 'Buchi Emecheta with Susheila Nasta', Guardian Conversations, London: ICA Video/Trilion.

Ngugi wa Thiong'o (1981) *Decolonising the Mind: The Politics of Language in African Literature*, London: James Currey.

—— (1993) *Moving the Centre: The Struggle for Cultural Freedoms*, London: James Currey.

Nguyen, Dan Thu (1992) 'The Spatialization of Metric Time: The Conquest of Land and Labour in Europe and the United States', *Time and Society* 1, 1, pp. 29–50.

Nietzsche, Friedrich (1887, 1969) *On the Genealogy of Morals*, trans. Walter Kaufmann, New York: Vintage.

Nowotny, Helga (1984) *Time: The Modern and Postmodern Experience*, Oxford: Polity.

Obasanjo, Olusegun (1980) *My Command*, Ibadan: Heinemann.

Ogilvie, John, ed. (1848) *Imperial Dictionary, English, Technological, & Scientific*, Glasgow: Blackie.

Palmer, Paulina (1989) *Contemporary Women's Fiction: Narrative Practice and Feminist Theory*, New York: Harvester Wheatsheaf.

—— (1999) *Lesbian Gothic: Transgressive Fictions*, London: Cassell.

Parmar, Pratibha (dir.) and Walker, Alice (1993) *Warrior Marks* (Channel 4) accompanied by the book Parmar and Walker, *Warrior Marks: Female Genital Mutilation and the Sexual Blinding of Women*, New York: Harcourt Brace.

Peach, Linden (1998) *Angela Carter*, Basingstoke: Macmillan.

—— (2000) *Toni Morrison: Historical Perspectives and Literary Contexts*, revised edition, Basingstoke: Palgrave.

Pearce, Lynne (1994) *Reading Dialogics*, London: Edward Arnold.

Peterson, Alan and Bunton, Robin, eds (1997) *Foucault, Health and Medicine*, London: Routledge.

Peterson, Carla (2000) 'Foreword' in Dickerson and Bennet (2000).

Peterson, Nancy, ed. (1997) *Toni Morrison: Critical and Theoretical Approaches*, Baltimore, MD: The Johns Hopkins University Press.

—— (1998) *Toni Morrison*, Baltimore, MD: The Johns Hopkins University Press.

—— (2001) *Against Amnesia: Contemporary Women Writers and the Crisis of Amnesia*, Philadelphia, PA: University of Pennsylvania Press.

Porter, Abioseh (1996) 'They Were There Too: Women and the Civil War' in Umeh, ed. (1996), pp. 313–32.

Pressler, Christopher (2000) *So Far So Linear: Responses to the Work of Jeanette Winterson*, Nottingham: Paupers Press.

Pritchett, V. S. (1946) 'The Future of Fiction', *New Writing and Daylight* 7: 75–81.

Radhakrishnan, N. (1984) *Indo-Anglian Fiction: Major Trends and Themes*, Madras: Emerald.

Ranasinha, Ruvani (2001) *Hanif Kureishi*, Plymouth: Northcote House.

Reyes, Angelita (1990) 'Rereading a Nineteenth-Century Fugitive Slave Incident: From Toni Morrison's *Beloved* to Margaret Garner's Dearly Beloved', *Annals of Scholarship* 7, 4: 465–86.

Reynolds, M. (1998) *Jeanette Winterson*, Plymouth: Northcote House.

Ricoeur, Paul (1984–8) *Time and Narrative*, 3 vols, trans. Kathleen McLaughlin and David Pellauer, Chicago: University of Chicago Press.

Rigney, Barbara Hill (1991) *The Voices of Toni Morrison*, Columbus, OH: Ohio State University Press.

Riviere, Joan (1929, 1986) 'Womanliness as a Masquerade' in Victor Burgin, James Donald and Cora Kaplan, eds, *Formations of Fantasy*, London: Methuen.

Rodrigues, Eusebio (1997) 'Experiencing *Jazz*' in Peterson, ed. (1997), pp. 245–66.

Rose, Steven (1992) *The Making of Memory: From Molecules to Mind*, Toronto: Bantam.

Rushdie, Salman (1991) *Imaginary Homelands*, London: Granta.

—— (1999) [interview] 'When Life Becomes a Bad Novel', *Salon* 6.

Rushdie, Salman and West, Elizabeth, eds (1997) *The Vintage Book of Indian Writing 1947–1997*, London: Vintage.

Ryan, Kiernan (1994) *Ian McEwan*, Plymouth: Northcote House.

Sage, Lorna (1994a) *Angela Carter*, Plymouth: Northcote House.

—— ed. (1994b) *Flesh and the Mirror: Essays on the Art of Angela Carter*, London: Virago.

Said, Edward (1993) *Culture and Imperialism*, London: Chatto & Windus.

Sarma, Gobinda Prasad (1978) *Nationalism in Indo-Anglian Fiction*, New Delhi: Sterling.

Seaboyer, Judith (1997) 'Second Death in Venice: Romanticism and the Compulsion to Repeat in Jeanette Winterson, *The Passion*', *Contemporary Literature* 38, 3 (Fall): 483–509.

Sebestyen, Amanda (1987) 'The Mannerist Marketplace', *New Socialist* 47 (March): 38.

Shanks, Michael and Tilley, Christopher (1987) *Social Theory and Archaeology*, Cambridge: Polity.

Simmons, Diane (1999) *Maxine Hong Kingston*, New York: Twayne.

Skandera-Trombley, Laura, ed. (1998) *Critical Essays on Maxine Hong Kingston*, New York: Twayne.

Skenazy, Paul and Martin, Tera, eds (1998) *Conversations with Maxine Hong Kingston*, Jackson, MS: University Press of Mississippi.

Skinner, John (1998) *The Stepmother Tongue: An Introduction to New Anglophone Fiction*, New York: St Martins Press.

Slay, Jack Jr (1996) *Ian McEwan*, New York: Twayne.

Smethurst, Paul (2000) *The Postmodern Chronotope: Reading Space and Time in Contemporary Fiction*, Amsterdam: Rodopi.

Smith, Patricia (1997) *Lesbian Panic: Homoeroticism in Modern British Women's Fiction*, New York: Columbia University Press.

Smyth, Gerry (1997) *The Novel and the Nation: Studies in the New Irish Fiction*, London: Pluto.

Spivak, Gayatri (1990) 'Reading the Satanic Verses', *Third Text* 11 (Summer): pp. 41–69.

Springhall, John (2001) *Decolonisation Since 1945: The Collapse of European Overseas Empires*, Basingstoke: Palgrave.

St. Peter, Christine (2000) *Changing Ireland: Strategies in Contemporary Women's Fiction*, Basingstoke: Macmillan.

Stevenson, Randall (1986) *The British Novel Since the Thirties*, London: Batsford.

—— (2000) 'Greenwich Meanings: Clocks and Things in Modernist and Postmodernist Fiction', *Yearbook of English Studies* 30: 124–36.

Stoller, Robert (1968) *Sex and Gender: On the Development of Masculinity and Femininity*, London: Hogarth.

Stowers, Cath (1998) 'The Erupting Lesbian Body: Reading *Written on the Body* as a Lesbian Text' in Grice and Woods, eds (1988), pp. 89–101.

Stratton, Florence (1994) *Contemporary African Literature and the Politics of Gender*, London: Routledge.

Thieme, John, ed. (1996) *Postcolonial Literatures in English*, London: Edward Arnold.

Todd, Richard (1996) *Consuming Fictions: The Booker Prize and Fiction in Britain Today*, London: Bloomsbury.

Todorov, Tzvetan (1986) '"Race," Writing, and Culture' in Gates (1986), pp. 370–80.

Tripp, Anna, ed. (2000) *Gender*, Basingstoke: Palgrave.

Turner, Bryan (1997) 'Foreword' in Peterson and Bunton (1997).

Twagilimana, Aimable (1997) *Race and Gender in the Making of an African American Literary Tradition*, New York: Garland.

Umeh, Marie, ed. (1996) *Emerging Perspectives on Buchi Emecheta*, Trenton, NJ: Africa World Press.

UNESCO (1950, 1967) *Statement on Race*, see Montagu (1972).

Van Deburg, William, ed. (1997) *Modern Black Nationalism: From Marcus Garvey to Louis Farrakhan*, New York: New York University Press.

Vattimo, Gianni (1991) 'The End of (Hi)story' in Ingebourg Hoesterey, ed. (1991) *Zeitgeist in Babel: The Postmodernist Controversy*, Bloomington, IN: Indiana University Press, pp. 132–41.

Vautier, Marie (1998) *New World Myth: Postmodernism and Postcolonialism in Canadian Fiction*, Montreal: McGill-Queen's University Press.

Vice, Sue (2000) *Holocaust Fiction*, London: Routledge

Walker, Alice (1984) *In Search of Our Mother's Gardens: Womanist Prose*, London: Women's Press.

Watkins, Susan (2001) *Twentieth Century Women Novelists: Feminist Theory into Practice*, Basingstoke: Palgrave.

Waugh, Patricia (1984) *Metafiction*, London: Methuen.

—— (1989) *Feminine Fictions: Revisiting the Postmodern*, London: Routledge.

—— (1995) *Harvest of the Sixties: English Literature and Its Background 1960–1990*, Oxford: Oxford University Press.

Weber, Max (1922, 1968) *Economy and Society*, trans. Guenther Roth and Claus Wittich, Berkeley, CA: University of California Press.

White, Hayden (1978, 1985) *Tropics of Discourse: Essays on Cultural Criticism*, Baltimore, MD: The Johns Hopkins University Press.

Williams, Linda (2001) *Playing the Race Card: Melodramas of Black and White from Uncle Tom to O. J. Simpson*, Princeton, NJ: Princeton University Press.

Winant, Howard (1998) 'Racial Dualism at Century's End' in Lubiano (1997, 1998), pp. 87–115.

Winchell, Donna Haisty (1992) *Alice Walker*, New York: Twayne.

Winterson, Jeanette (1997) Interview on *West Coast Live*, 5 April.

Wisker, Gina, ed. (1993) *Black Women's Writing*, Basingstoke: Macmillan.

—— (2000) *Postcolonial and African American Women's Writing: A Critical Introduction*, Basingstoke: Macmillan.

Wittig, Monique (1992) *The Straight Mind*, New York: Harvester Wheatsheaf.

Wong, Sau-Ling Cynthia (1992) 'Autobiography as Guided Chinatown Tour? Maxine Hong Kingston's *The Woman Warrior* and the Chinese-American Autobiographical Controversy' in James Robert Payne, ed., *Multicultural Autobiography: American Lives*, Knoxville, TN: University of Tennessee Press, pp. 248–75.

—— (1993) *Reading Asian American Literature: From Necessity to Extravagance*, Princeton, NJ: Princeton University Press.

Woolf, Virginia (1929) *A Room of One's Own*, London: Hogarth.

Wyatt, David (1993) *Out of the Sixties: Storytelling and the Vietnam Generation*, Cambridge: Cambridge University Press.

Yalom, Marilyn/Maxine Hong Kingston (1998) 'Conversation with Marilyn Yalom' in Skenazy and Martin (1998).

Young, Robert (1995) *Colonial Desire*, London: Routledge.

Youngs, Tim (1997) *Writing and Race*, London: Longman.

Zamora, Lois Parkinson (1989) *Writing the Apocalypse: Historical Vision in Contemporary US and Latin American Fiction*, Cambridge: Cambridge University Press.

—— (1997) *The Usable Past: The Imagination of History in Recent Fiction of the Americas*, Cambridge: Cambridge University Press.

Index